The Sync

Myths, Magic, Media, and Mindscapes

Featuring writers from:

The Sync Whole, Reality Sandwich, Etemenanki, The Mask of God, Labyrinth of the Psychonaut, Radio8Ball, The Stygian Port, Live from the Logosphere, Star Theory, The Patternist, Gosporn, All the Happy Creatures, Kosmos Idikos, Constellation Contemplation, Accidental Alchemist, Libyan Sibyl, Mercury's Messenger, Smoky Mirrors, A Few Shots to Shaman, Kozmikon, PrismReptileRobot, Synchromysticism Forum

Alan Abbadessa-Green + Goro Adachi + Jason Barrera
Douglas Bolles + Peg Carter + Tommy Fulks + Kevin Halcott
Kyle Hunt + Sibyl Hunter + Stefan Jablonski + Jeremy
Andras Jones + Crystal Kanarr + Jon Kidd + Jake Kotze
Neil Kramer + Rammer Martínez Sánchez + Justin Gray Morgan
Will Morgan + Christopher Myers + Eunus Noe
Jennifer Palmer + Jim Sanders + Michael Schacht
Toure + Steve Willner

EDITED BY ALAN ABBADESSA-GREEN

The Sync Book

Published 9/11/2011

All works remain the property of their respective authors
In art, as in life, all rights reserved

TheSyncBook.com

Cover design and chapter icons by Justin Gray Morgan

Interior layout by Alan Abbadessa-Green

For my mom

When I tried to tell her about conspiracies,
she looked at me like I was crazy.
When I tried to tell her about synchronicity,
she looked at me like I was crazy for not seeing it sooner.

"Nothing in existence is fundamentally divisible or separate. All things and events, even the observer of things and events, are part of an inseparable union. **Synchronicity** happens when we notice the bleed-through from one seemingly separate thing into another—or when we for a brief moment move beyond the mind's divisions of the world.

Synchromysticism explores this phenomenon—**the interpenetration of all things**—and seeks to increase the ability to recognize relationships by relaxing the rigid conceptualization of the world. This inevitably leads to a more joyful and whole everyday experience, as the environment and person experiencing that environment become part of a conscious interactive process of **Self-Realization**."

—Jake Kotze

Foreword

Over the last few years, synchronicity has become more and more important in my life. I found myself drawn to the many blogs that delve into synchronicity and the various topics that we have come to see as part of the same study. In February of 2010 I started my own blog and began interacting with others who had opened themselves to this quest. In a relatively short amount of time, I had come to think of many of these souls as my extended family and a part of myself.

Fast forward to February of 2011 when, after a year of blogging, I had the idea to put together a collection of writing on sync. I reached out to my extended online family and asked them if they would be interested in such a project. The response (and result) was enthusiastic, fast and beautiful.

Perhaps due to the very nature of the subject at hand, and the familiarity each author has with the act of synchronizing, this was a fairly easy book to put together. In many ways, this collection has come together naturally. While I *certainly* wouldn't call my task effortless, it did run smoothly. For that, I must thank the contributors. The people who put their time and effort into this book are some of the most amazing talents and thinkers I have come across. I feel blessed to know them and honored to appear alongside them.

I must also thank synchronicity for providing such a lovingly gentle guiding hand in the process. By each of us acknowledging that we, and our consciousnesses, originate from the same source, I believe we have opened ourselves up to creating the wonderful book you now hold.

Because of the way in which we seem to share a sort of brainspace, synchronicity has been compared to "cloud computing" with human consciousness. As the essays came in, I found another correlation between our organic minds and their electronic counterparts. Almost every text file I received had some sort of formatting hardwired into it that I had to fight with to get to the goods. This was one of the most difficult aspects of putting this book together. Essentially, to extract the raw text with its meaning and message, I had to strip the file of the preconceived notions of whatever computer it was typed on.

Here we have a perfect analogy for what each of you readers (and all of us on this incredible journey) must do to proceed. I know it is not easy, in fact, it can be very *very* difficult—but, for an honest exploration of sync, it is necessary to leave your preconceived notions and your hardwired programming at the door.

We decided we would present this as a sort of primer, an introduction to sync. It dawned on me a few weeks later that asking twenty-something people to introduce the same topic could very easily lead itself to a lot of repetition. Then the submissions started to come in and, amazingly, the repetition was minimal. Still, having taken on the role of editor, I was tempted to create a more streamlined reading experience by taking those commonalities out. What ultimately kept me from doing so was *an incredible difference in the similarities*. In the few places where repetition occurred, it was fascinating to see the different authors present the same material from vastly different perspectives and to draw vastly different conclusions from what they observed.

I have kept this book uncensored and as all-inclusive as possible, letting the difference of opinion stand for you the reader to assess. I have included pieces from authors whose work or opinions I myself disagree with (some more strongly than others) because there is no single approach—and no single answer. The essays that follow cover synchronicity from many different angles. There are pieces analyzing movies and aspects of pop-culture, ancient grimoires, mathematics and language, philosophy and spiritualism, religion and science. The world we live in is looked at through the many eyes of our authors and, in that place where all things overlap, we find synchronicity waiting for us.

None of us are trying to sell you on a new religion (or any old ones for that matter). We have no uniforms or insignia. We have no flag to wave. There are no membership fees or rules to follow.

We are merely a group of individuals exploring the strange and beautiful universe we have found ourselves in. If you're interested in joining us on this adventure, please do. There's still so much to discover.

Alan Abbadessa-Green

Sibyl Hunter:
The Individual Journey of Sync   1

Toure:
Message is Medium, Media is Message   15

Jeremy:
Reflections on the Cinematic Underworld   23

Stefan Jablonski:
Synchronous Reading   35

Alan Abbadessa-Green:
Cosmic Folk Art   47

Tommy Fulks:
Synchromystic Tome Utterance   61

Eunus Noe:
The Now   71

Andras Jones:
The Pop Oracle   77

Jim Sanders:
Mayahuasca   85

Jon Kidd:
Robin Hood and Little Jon   107

Jennifer Palmer:
The Feeling of Sync   115

Christopher "C" Myers:
The Magick of Synchronicity   125

Kyle Hunt:
The Rainbow Alphabet   137

Crystal Kanarr: *Twists of Fate*		157
Kevin Halcott: *The Synchromystic Aura*		171
Douglas Bolles: *Winter's Labyrinth*		189
Peg Carter: *Sweet Earth or Chthonic Underworld*		199
Will Morgan: *Confessions of a Sync Head*		215
Rammer Martínez Sánchez: *Poetry and Artwork*		223
Michael Schacht: *Porn Star Jesus*		237
Jake Kotze: *Sync*		245
Justin Gray Morgan: *Awakening at the Center of the Mandala*		261
Steve Willner: *Hacking Source Code Ciphers*		273
Goro Adachi: *Future Knowledge*		287
Neil Kramer: *Go Your Own Way*		299
Jason Barrera: *A Child's Treasury of the Tarot*		307
Suggested Reading		344

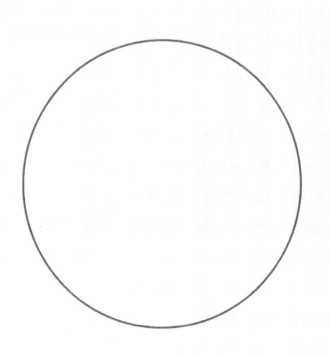

SIBYL HUNTER
THE LIBYAN SIBYL

Sibyl Hunter is the author of the blog The Libyan Sibyl. *Her interests are an eclectic mix of creative writing, ancient history, Jungian analysis, mythology, religious studies, extraterrestrial and conspiracy theories, science fiction, and all things Michael Jackson. She is also an avid player of the online virtual reality game,* Second Life. *A corporate executive by day and a sync investigator by night, Sibyl began her blog in 2010 after being inspired by Jake Kotze's Synchromysticism theory of archetypal resonance in pop culture. In early 2011, she also became a contributor to the esoteric blog* The Mask of God. *Today, she continues to share her insights into the phenomena of Sync while seeking a PhD in Jungian Archetypal Studies. One of Sibyl's favorite quotes is, "If you can understand it, it isn't God."*

libyansibyl44.blogspot.com
themaskofgod.blogspot.com

The Individual Journey of Sync

If we see a God outside of ourselves, he tears us loose from the self, since the God is more powerful than we are. Our self falls into privation. But if the God moves into the self, he snatches us from what is outside us. We arrive at singleness in ourselves.
—Carl Gustav Jung

In the Beginning

Make no mistake . . . if you are reading this book, you did not stumble upon it by accident. You have been guided here by a combination of your own curiosity and an unquenchable thirst caused by some unseen force. More than likely you *have been* or *will soon be* faced with a difficult, unfamiliar choice and you are fervently seeking out answers in an attempt to make some sense of it.

This is how the personal journey into the realm of Synchronicity begins—with a choice. For religious observers, the choice may be presented in many different ways—such as the narrow path versus the wide path, indulgence in extremism versus the Middle Way, Yin versus Yang. In the movie *The Matrix*, it was exemplified by the hero Neo's initiatory decision between the red pill or the blue pill. In any case, initiates must make a decision to view themselves and the world around them in an entirely new way.

To be clear, Synchronicity is a concept first popularized by Swiss psychologist Carl Jung in the 1920s. He succinctly defined it as "temporally coincident occurrences of acausal events." In recent years, the idea of seemingly unrelated events intersecting to produce meaningful patterns has spawned new trains of thought from Synchrony, a scientific study of spontaneous order in the universe, to Synchromysticism, the discovery of convergent archetypal symbols in pop culture (i.e. books, television, music, and films). Here, we will generally use the term Sync to encompass all aspects of Synchronicity, both scientific and esoteric.

THE INDIVIDUAL JOURNEY OF SYNC

Sync operates as an undercurrent of divine awareness personified through the myriad processes and symbols that make up the building blocks of our reality. Within that current, we spin our modern-day myths into books, fairy tales and movies, subconsciously retelling ourselves the same story over and over again in hopes we will be prepared when the time comes to see reality for what it actually is. Unfortunately, we are rarely prepared for it: the tearing loose of our *selves*, our virulent egos. The tidal wave of Sync overcomes us and we barely notice until we are already deep in it, swimming for our lives.

A Personal Struggle

Although writing is my first love, I was formally trained as an engineer. As such, mathematics became my second language. Anchored in the cool, calm logic of numbers, in my world two plus two would always equal four. It was this knowledge that allowed me to breathe, to move through each day with any measure of surety. Even my faith and spirituality boiled down to a basic equation: I believed that if I lived my life a certain way I would attain my goals. A plus B equaled C. Period.

All in all it was a very narrow existence, but it would take a life-altering jolt to alert me to that fact. At the age of 30 I experienced the gradual onset of a period of depression and disenchantment that poets, religious scholars, psychologists, and alchemists alike have termed the 'Dark Night of the Soul.' On the one hand, worldly things no longer brought me pleasure. Career, house, car, money . . . all of these were suddenly unfulfilling. On the other hand, there arose within me what I can only describe as an impassioned yearning to search for answers to philosophical and religious questions. From childhood, I was always a spiritual person with some awareness of certain unseen forces working in my life, but never before had I thought to pinpoint exactly what those forces were or what the existence of such things implied for my life on a deeper level.

I pored over ancient myths, religious writings, and New Age books, spending many sleepless nights trolling the Internet to quench my thirst for information until, eventually, something incredible started happening. Answers began coming to me in my mind, in waking dreams, as if I were receiving a direct download from an outside source. When you experience Sync for the first time you are literally "synched" up to a flow of collective consciousness that has always existed. All answers and all possibilities exist within an eternal cloud of knowingness accessible to each of us. Think of it as a cosmic radio station, but in order to hear it we must tune our internal dial (the heart) to the correct frequency.

My dark night and subsequent roller coaster of awakening would continue until it peaked out three years later. Its onset age range, the early thirties, was a fact not lost on me. This was the same age of Buddha during his quest for enlightenment and Jesus Christ at the time of his earthly ministry. It was also the onset age for Prophet Muhammad's season of discontent with life in general (which eventually led him to retreat into a cave to find spiritual revelation). Of course, this in no way indicates that everyone will have an awakening in their thirties. Windows of awareness can open at any junction in your life. But perhaps that period can be a jumping off point of sorts, a time when, if there is even a sliver of question in your soul that something more than this mortal coil exists, the whole egg cracks open. Humpty Dumpty falls and breaks, never to be put together again.

An essay by F. Scott Fitzgerald, fittingly entitled *The Crackup*, begins with the line: *"Of course all life is a process of breaking down."* Indeed we must come to understand that this great work, this chaotic inner ordeal of cracking apart and becoming empty *is* the human process. It is the next step in our spiritual evolution. And when you are finally empty, when you are devoid of any ingrained notions of what you ought to be, only then are you truly ready to become what you already are. Only an empty vessel can be completely filled. In ancient Egyptian mythology, the hearts of the dead in the underworld were said to be weighed against a feather in the divine court of Osiris. To pass the test, the heart had to be lighter than the feather, empty of all earthly cares and the weight of the world.

> *Are you willing to be sponged out, erased, canceled,*
> *made nothing? Are you willing to be made nothing?*
> *dipped into oblivion? If not, you will never really change.*
> —Excerpt from the poem "Phoenix" by D.H. Lawerence

After four years my personal grail quest ended when I discovered that the vessel I had been searching for all along was my own heart. Through a realization of the mechanisms of Sync I was finally able to see how I was interconnected to everything in the universe. My life morphed into an ecstatic blossoming of consciousness. Darkness turned to light. Life became an indescribable state of joy within which I now choose to exist.

However, this process of tuning oneself to the frequency of Sync is a lifelong inside job, a serious personal work that is different for everybody. It requires a constant vigilance to remain anchored and balanced in the present moment. No two people's journey will be exactly the same because we all have differing earthly cares—viewpoints, attitudes, belief systems, and hang-ups—to overcome along the way. These disjointed fragments of your Self (the "Other") must be gathered up, contemplated, some discarded, and others re-integrated into a whole new you.

Yet, even after taking into account individual idiosyncrasies, interviews with various people who have undergone the process of discovering Sync reveal a general theme of inner struggle culminating in multidimensional growth. One woman (who for anonymity's sake I will call Carla) candidly described her experience to me:

> **Q:** *What, if any, difficulties did you experience along the way?*
>
> **Carla:** I think you have to break down or fall down to see things from another angle. Literally. That's what happened to me. No struggle, no progress. I also think it always happens in a way that was specifically synchronized for you. Yes, mentally it was challenging accepting that school, a career was not going to bring me all the wisdom and prosperity. Emotionally that was a heavy one. Also, I realized some friendships had reached their final destination. Afterward I was freer to be myself at all times, to be authentic. I'm sure of the things I believe in because I opened my eyes to new dimensions.
>
> **Q:** *What advice would you give to someone who is just beginning their own journey of awareness of Synchronicity?*
>
> **Carla:** Stay open minded. The next thing you lay your eyes

on, or person around the corner, might tell you the answer to something you've been struggling with or help you in the right direction. Nothing happens randomly. Embrace that thought.

As you embrace your place in the flow of the Sync stream your interests may change—causing old friendship, family, and relationship dynamics to end and new ones to replace them, including job relationships. Ultimately, you may feel as if you are losing your mind (note: it is advisable to visit a doctor and/or therapist if this is the case). But at some point, after discovering that your mental and physical health are fine, you will then be left with only one conclusion: That things truly are not as they seem. As the 13th century Persian mystic poet Rumi wrote: *"On truth's path, wise is mad, insane is wise. In love's way, self and other are the same."*

Reality is Not Real

From an early age we are taught to believe in an objective reality. The stove is hot. The sky is up. Beneath our feet lies the cold, hard ground. But in truth reality is not objective at all. Everything is relative. Life is a subjective experience, a mere projection based upon a malleable set of universal definitions. Rather than being set in stone, reality is actually a very elastic process in which our individual choices play an active role.

This information can come as quite a shock to the average person and many would choose to close their eyes to it, to remain in their comfort zones, rather than be forced to challenge their perceptions of what is. Therefore, it is critical to note that in order to understand Synchronicity you must suspend your belief in those learned notions of reality and open your mind to other ideas.

Here are four main concepts, without an acceptance of which, you may find it nearly impossible to proceed along your journey:

#1: There exists a pervasively loving, all-encompassing Entity from which everything in existence flows. It is the Universe as All That Is. It is known by many names.

#2: Although we exist as separate individuals, we all emerged from that One source. Thus, on a higher dimensional level, we are all inexorably linked as one *Collective Consciousness*.

#3: The phenomena of Sync is a natural expression of that Collective Consciousness. It is proof of Universal cause and effect—that our every choice or action changes some aspect of reality somewhere.

#4: There is no such thing as coincidence.

This is certainly not an exhaustive list, but simply an attempt to boil down a few key components I found to be necessary elements on my own journey. Note that you can find these ideas steeped in the foundations of virtually every religion, woven into myths and fairy tales, sung about in our favorite songs, and acted out on the big screen in television and movies. Recently, even mainstream scientists have quietly proven that we live in a holographic universe. This is the great beauty of Sync—you can find it everywhere, if only you're willing to look.

Spontaneous Transcendence and a Warning

Once you have come to accept that Sync is real, that it is a part of you and you are a part of it, you will become open to experiencing more intense manifestations of it. At this point it is not unusual to have spontaneous, transcendent experiences, particularly in your interactions with Nature. You may feel a heightened ability to interact on an empathic level with plants and animals. Daily life can become quite wondrous as your thoughts seem to almost effortlessly reflect back to you in everything from the people you meet to the books you read.

However, anything that distracts your mind from remaining in a constant state of present being can be detrimental. For this reason, it is of the utmost importance to keep the concept of Sync in its proper perspective. As you delve deeper into the realms of Sync you will have increasingly numerous and exciting experiences, but always remember that in reality nothing exists outside of yourself. The occurrences themselves hold no power other than that which you ascribe them. They are simply projections of your consciousness interacting with Sync to inject meaningful experiences into your reality as guideposts to help along your journey.

By Any Means Necessary

Sync has a distinct personality. It does not conform to human standards of logic and reason. Yet, when observed from the perspective of a higher plane of understanding it does behave in ways that exhibit as patterns across all space and time.

An example of this patterned behavior can be found in the power of words. A word can contain the information for an entire concrete concept in an audio-visual and emotive format. This is why the Bible states that the world was created by the *Logos*, or Word, of God and also why visual representations of a company's brand are called "logos." Once a word has been imbued with a particular meaning, it can become a powerful symbol in itself. That word-symbol is then transmittable as a compactly formatted idea, or meme, across all time. It bypasses communication barriers by overriding our limited verbal and written abilities and directly activates the brain's naturally-encoded symbolic language structure.

> *'When I use a word,' Humpty Dumpty said in rather a scornful tone, 'it means just what I choose it to mean —neither more nor less.'*
>
> *'The question is,' said Alice, 'whether you can make words mean so many different things.'*
>
> *'The question is,' said Humpty Dumpty, 'which is to be master—that's all.'*
>
> —Lewis Carroll, Through the Looking Glass

As an example, we will examine the word "sun." Over 5,000 years ago ancient Sumerians worshiped sun gods. The Egyptians would similarly incorporate this idea into their sun god Ra. Following suit, the Persians wove these traditions into their heroic mythological sun god Mithras. In the Christian era, the "Sun" became the "Son", Christ the savior. Clearly the idea of a sun symbol fused with the archetype of a figure who is a hero, leader, and savior has traveled down to us from ancient times.

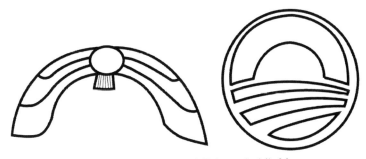

Sumerian solar winged disk symbol (left)
compared to elements of Obama's 2008 campaign logo (right).
Both portray the concept of a "Rising Sun."

It seems no coincidence then that a sun symbol was used in President Barack Obama's campaign logo during his 2008 U.S. presidential election bid. No doubt Obama is an inspiring speaker, but consider the fact that before he ever uttered a word to the masses, his logo was already being transmitted through Internet, television, and print media all around the globe. In subconscious minds worldwide he was automatically associated with one of our most ancient and revered cultural archetypes—the hero/redeemer. Was this the purposeful doing of a crafty campaign marketing strategist with foreknowledge of mystic symbolism, or did the elements of Synchronicity conspire to point out the next leader of the free world to us, or both? You decide.

Sync also interacts with us through numbers. As humans we are obsessed with numbers. We relegate ourselves to the imaginary construct of Time, constantly counting and measuring each second of our existence. The ability to quantify brings a sense of control and meaning to our lives. Our singular focus on quantification makes numbers a perfect medium for Sync to catch our attention.

An example of the way Sync communicates through numbers can be found in the symbol of the planet Jupiter. As the largest planet in the solar system it was worshiped in ancient Vedic Sanskrit texts and Roman mythology alike as the loving father or king of the gods. Jupiter also achieved modern pop culture fame as the planet where we make first contact in the movie *2001: A*

Space Odyssey. In astrology, Jupiter's influence is a catalyst for limitless inner growth. Its symbol is formed by combining the numbers 1, 2, and 4; often called the "Jupiter numbers."

The Jupiter symbol is a stylized combination
of the numbers 1, 2, and 4.

There is an alchemical precept, known as the *Axiom of Maria*, which states: "*One becomes two, two becomes three, and out of the third comes the one as the fourth.*" Jung used this as an analogy for the psychological process of moving from unconscious to conscious wholeness.

Similarly, the Jupiter numbers 1, 2, and 4 are symbolic of the progression from conscious states 1 to 2 to 3 to 4 (and back to 1). The 3rd state is understood to be transitory and transcendent, the invisible vehicle of movement from one state to another, and is therefore not included in the symbol. In the 1st state we are unconscious, meaning we do not know ourselves as separate from All That Is.

Adam and Eve were both naked, and they felt no shame.
—Genesis 2:25

As exemplified in the illustration above, the serpent (symbolic of the kundalini or seven chakras culminating in the head chakra) is the process of individuation that produces the *idea* of separation. This brings us to the 4th state where we consciously perceive ourselves in the illusory form of a separate, individualized entity.

Then the eyes of both of them were opened, and they realized they were naked. —Genesis 3:6

But the idea of separateness is only a negative thing when we forget the original state of wholeness from which we both emanated and are still a part of, simultaneously. Thus, it becomes necessary to transcend ourselves (the self being the Ego that is utterly convinced it is omniscient, omni-powerful, and alone) in order to recover and reintegrate the memory of wholeness—"... *out of the third comes the one as the fourth.*" Ego death commences and fear of death ends. Ultimately, this may be the greatest embedded meaning in the Jupiter symbol.

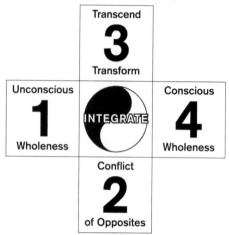

Another famous quote from F. Scott Fitzgerald's essay *The Crackup* reads, "*In a real dark night of the soul it is always* **three o'clock** *in the morning.*" The significance of three o'clock is further underscored by the fact that the Bible gives it as the time Christ's spirit left his body on the cross (Matt. 27:45, 50). If you look at the face of a clock at three o'clock, the minute hand is pointing to the number 12 and the hour hand is pointing to the number 3. Here we can see that three o'clock is symbolically synonymous with the numbers 1-2-3. Further, it is apparent that the 1-2-3 pattern in the language of Sync describes a process leading up to a shift or transition out of darkness and into a 4th state of light, or out of form and into spirit.

Did Fitzgerald, as he was penning his intimate dark night experience, understand that he was also reverberating an ancient theme of regeneration, rebirth, and transcendence through words and numbers? Did the Bible scribes? On a personal level, maybe not. On a soul level, definitely. Through Synchronicity, a language of the Universe that our brains innately understand, such transcendental nuggets of wisdom have been passed down and preserved to the modern day to help us make sense of the inevitable phase of awakening that we must all undergo.

THE INDIVIDUAL JOURNEY OF SYNC

In the book *Synchronicity: An Acausal Connecting Principle*, Jung wrote that the numbers one through four occur most frequently and are an archetype of "the most primitive element of order" within the human mind. Remarkably, this may even be an explanation for the well-documented 11:11 phenomenon, where people's attention is spontaneously drawn to digital clocks displaying that sequence of four numbers. Both the clock and the numbers are a symbolically alerting us to the spontaneous creation of order out of chaos through the awakening of individual and collective consciousness.

Synchronicity teaches us that every event on the spiritual plane is accompanied by an event on the physical plane. As above, so below. These are translational events because what we experience is but our mind's best attempt to translate higher dimensional spiritual concepts into the lower dimensional reality here on Earth. This concept was exemplified nicely in the movie *Inception* when Cobb reveals to Fischer that the quaking and gravity shifts in the hotel bar are caused by the careening van (in which they are really sleeping) one dream-level up.

In this sense Sync is a tool to help bring you into a greater state of awareness. The Universe, as All That Is, is literally doing whatever it takes to force you to be present in this moment so you can first realize that you have the power to choose, and then go on to make a conscious decision for yourself. What type of person do you want to be? In what kind of world do you want to exist? In this pursuit it will use everything possible—scrambled words, magical numbers, symbols hidden in movies and logos, or any other synchronous manifestations at its disposal to get your attention. Whatever it takes to snatch your consciousness awake.

"In the end, there can be only One."

The line above is my favorite quote from the *Highlander* television series and it encapsulates the underlying principle of life in general. Everything is, literally, a projection from out of the One. Sync, in its incredible, quirky, sometimes humorous way, constantly reminds us of this fact. It is the tirelessly persistent finger of the Divine forever prodding us to wake up. It is a manifestation of Love in its highest form.

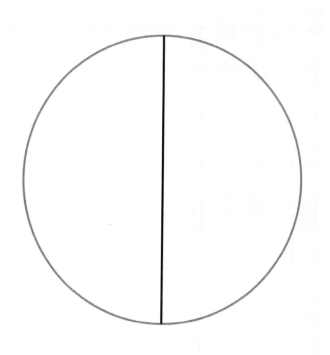

Toure

The Patternist

Since 2009, Toure has authored The Patternist, *a research blog on synchronicities in popular culture media, history and mythology. Toure is a classically-trained practicing freelance web designer with a schizophrenic educational history— including collegiate training in computer, mechanical and aerospace engineering, classical illustration, film editing, marketing psychology and graphic design. Toure's unique perspective on the concept of sync comes from a reconciliation of the right-brain creative spiritual and the left-brained analytical practical. Toure is a dedicated amateur film critic, a skilled* Magic: The Gathering *deckbuilder, and a performing poet in his current hometown of Atlanta, Georgia.*

thepatternist.blogspot.com
g8ors.blogspot.com

Message is Medium, Media is Message

At this very moment, as you read this, your brain is processing a complex stream of mixed-media information; the subtle sounds around you, peripheral vision, awareness of biorhythms, blood flow, heart-rate, breathing.... You get the picture. Rhythms.... Repeated messages that form patterns, patterns that form, inform and reaffirm life. This information, these messages, like all messages, come in the form of media; sound, image, scent, flavor, texture and "feeling." **Media is the envelope through which messages reach us.** Media is context.

The Pattern began with a commercial, but after a little research, the connections transcended pop music, or video games, or film, or even wide-scale globalist agenda. The pattern transcended the research itself, and began to poke its head out in the goings-on of my daily life. The pattern transcended the time in which the actual research occurred, reaching backwards into previous patterns I'd written about and to films of the 1920's, while simultaneously reaching forward into connections that I hadn't even realized were there under my nose, into patterns that I had yet to see.
—*From* The Patternist

We define our reality, quite simply, through patterns we process and accept. Collectively. If you drop an object, it falls, so we all agree, based on a pattern, that gravity is real (whatever that may be). But this is more than just Newtonian math.... There is a feeling. Something *understood*.... An empathy for the experience of humanity that allows us to relate to one another via our connections. Our synchronicities. This is the pattern. Shared experience understood, reinforcing the idea that we are actually all connected in very real, very practical ways.

You see, Dad, Professor McLuhan says that the environment that man creates becomes his medium for defining his role in it. The invention of type created linear, or sequential thought, separating

thought from action. Now, with TV and folk singing, thought and action are closer and social involvement is greater. We again live in a village. Get it?
—The New Yorker *1966,*
"The Medium is the Massage"

Medium, or *media* in plural, shapes and defines the message it delivers. Your experience of hearing a song, for example, is dramatically transformed when you hear it recorded, rather than live. Words that are spoken have different meanings than words that are written. It's not something easily quantifiable, but a very real *feeling*, and part of the common experience we share as human creatures.

This experience, the understanding and perception of context, is a very clear, yet indescribable, commonality; unspoken, but shared. This perception-sharing has been sent into immersion overload now that we have ubiquitous access to the most transformative technology of our age: the Internet. **We are a global village.** We live nearly every waking moment immersed in an (almost) all-connected age of digital information sharing. User-created information sharing, no less. Ubiquitous shared creation expression. What are you thinking, world . . . ? The 2009 superfilm *Avatar* portrayed a world that could think; constructed—and literally described—as a giant brain. We are the world.

As we should've expected, this set-up gives rise to the expression of some eerily strong patterns (when you decide to take a look). The patterns present in the human experience; the journey, the ego, the hero, the villain, etc., are all seen interpreted in our modern mythology media; allegory telling the story of our view of the world. Once it was played out in drum circles by bonfire and behind masks on coliseum stages—now, we see it in our films, music, television, advertising. . . . Media mythology expression repurposed precisely to speak to our base motivators (albeit, to sell beer and iPads). Now that thought and action are closer than ever, our mythology is more immersive than ever. Our mythology now transports us to new worlds, escapism via 3D glasses and pocket-size movie screens, avatars plugging into a dreamworld of cultural expression. Online. Together.

These connections are not arbitrary, and therefore cannot be simply dismissed as coincidence. A coincidence is a connection that occurs by chance, without any deeper meaning. The creative or technical choices leading to the pattern (in expressed media) had specific meaning. The pattern's significance doesn't come from the acknowledgment of the repetition, it comes from the shared meaning.
—From The Patternist

Togetherness affirms our reality and gives the pattern meaning.

The meaning, of course, is the real meat of the matter. The pattern's meaning is hidden in that difficult-to-describe shared context: information, indicators of our psycho-cultural development and our collective evolution. Once the patterns of our myth-stories and their meanings are revealed—via something some of us call *sync*—the watcher suddenly becomes compelled to share these discoveries and the strange joy they bring. Once the revelation—the feeling—is shared, a feedback loop is created by the simultaneous confirmation:

You see that? Wow. I see it too. Maybe it's real.

Now take that reality-affirming nigh-indescribable joy-information media-context-communication feedback loop, and multiply it by a billion, spread out over a network that—collectively—operates aptly enough just like the brain of the individual. The high school-level scientific concepts paralleling cell-organisms with body-organisms with eco-system organisms has become literal, thanks in no small part to the ubiquitous instantaneous global interconnection of our *thoughts*. Poured out over electrons. Electrons jumping synapses and bandwidth. We see one another in the pattern through our shared experience and this recognition gives meaning, context, to our very existence. Together. Connection. Sync.

Connections alone don't validate a thesis unless those connections prove relevant. What if the pattern itself is the thesis? The connections are the point. Perhaps one can always find meaning in the pattern because meaning is the pattern.
And pattern is the meaning.
—From The Patternist

Recognition of connection gives meaning, context, to our very existence by reaffirming our inherent oneness. Our synchronicity. To make matters worse, for lack of a better phrase, the patterns, once recognized, become ingrained as a larger part of our *general awareness*. The same way that something the brain focuses on begins to appear prevalent in the environment (i.e.: If you get a blue car, you start seeing blue cars everywhere), something a community recognizes begins to appear prevalent in the consciousness of the community. A group of people who study synchronicities will see their lives become synchronized, as their experience of the world becomes synchronized, as the media information they process becomes synchronized. Furthermore, the same way an electron snaps into place when you observe it, someone immersed in—and synchronized with—their media will begin to realize their ability to affect the patterns around them, and their meaning.

Power, purpose and responsibility. Collectively.

In the dramatic finale of *The Matrix* film series, the main character Neo (anagrammed as "o-n-e") realizes that the digital shared dreamworld he believed was imprisoning him was essentially no different than the reality he considered freedom. Despite the expressed potential of any dreamer to simply "wake up" from the Matrix, mentally deny the shared programmed dream, people remained "asleep" because they believed they were *powerless* to affect their reality. Powerlessness affirmed by the hardships hardwired into the dream programming by its creators. As the first *Matrix*'s villain, Agent Smith, explained to Morpheus (the Greek god of dreams—transl. "shaper"), without such programmed dysfunction, "entire crops were lost." People simply, subconsciously, rejected their realities. . . . Trying to wake up, in disbelief.

The potential to reject a reality denotes the potential to choose. At the metaphysical level, our ability to push and pull our patterns denotes the ability to change things in our existence/experience—even, rather notably, without our "consciousness"—even in our sleep.

. . . films, we concluded, are stories, and stories are just plain ineffective when they're bogged down by too much accurate fact. In

> *most cases, in order to better communicate the message/moral/truth of a story/myth/history, one must re-write the real to fit the rhetoric. On one hand, this seems wrong . . . manipulative, dishonest, and at worst, a betrayal of history—and reality—itself. On the other hand, this is precisely the way our subconscious sends us messages in our dreams.*
> —*From* The Patternist

Speaking of choice: what does that say about **intention**? If we push and pull unconsciously, our choice is being made by something we may not be aware of, something bigger than ourselves. Something many of us define as fate, as nature, as the very hand of god. That is, if you believe in that sort of thing.

> *The need to revisit the concept of The Pattern came while watching "I Am Sylar," episode 24 of the third season of* Heroes. *Overlooking the recent significance of 3's in my research on the triple-goddess connection to former three-woman pop-group member Beyonce, I noticed that episode 24 aired on April 20th (024 on 420), and that the episode was titled "I AM," reflecting the self-affirming naming device seen in the title of Beyonce's latest album,* I Am . . . Sasha Fierce, *Madonna's new 'humanitarian' documentary,* I Am Because We Are, *(which premiered in New York on April 24th), Will Smith's uniquely-titled* I Am Legend *(William or Will I Am), and the translation of the Hebrew name for God, Yahweh [I am that I am].*
> —*From* The Patternist

You see that? Wow. I see it too. Maybe it's real.

Maybe I'm real. Maybe you're real.

Maybe you see me. Maybe it sees me.

Maybe it is me. Maybe you're me.

Maybe.

Again: Once the patterns of our myth-stories and their meanings are revealed—via something some of us call *sync*—the watcher suddenly becomes compelled to share these discoveries and the strange joy they bring. Once the revelation—the feeling—is shared, a feedback loop is created.

Whether it's between a lone paranoid theorist and his/her inner ego voice, or two people who think they alone are crazy, or openly discussed in a community, or a Tweet across a global digital information super-highway—that feedback loop expresses itself through reflective, reflexive information. Media. The media itself becomes the message. The medium becomes the message, and the meaning of it all. Spiritual context to our existence through the patterns of information-media we share.

Obvious, ubiquitous, constant, and real—nearly impossible to describe or deny. . . . The media connects us and shows us we are, ultimately, all in sync. All of us. What would you do differently in your life if you truly believed this? Literal spiritual oneness?

Not so fast. The first step, shared-dreamer, is seeing our connection. Perhaps then we can decide for ourselves, together, if the sight of our collective organism has meaning, if seeing is believing, and if we can choose, consciously, to wake our collective one-self up. Sync.

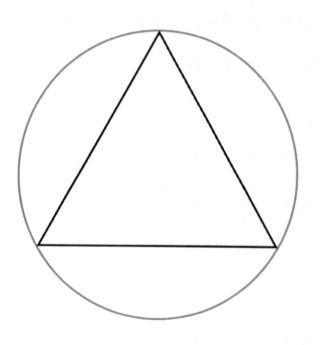

Jeremy
The Stygian Port

Better known as ViølatoR, Jeremy is the author of The Stygian Port. *His interests tend to hover around science fiction, cyberpunk, post-apocalyptic, and dystopian books and movies as well as "non-fiction" arenas of interest such as ancient history, theology, alchemy, general occult subjects and conspiracy and alternate history research. Jeremy started sharing his ideas online in 2006-2007, finally being persuaded to start his own blog in late 2007. He began making videos in mid-2009, and has a recent, as of this publication, feature-length video called* Here Is Wisdom, *which can be found on his Vimeo account. "I am a well known sloth, a procrastinator, and, contrary to what you may think with all my quotes and movie references, have a notoriously bad memory." He is an infrequent guest of* The Rebel Path *radio show on the online* Oracle Broadcasting Network *as well as the* Star Theory *podcast by Kyle Hunt. He can also sometimes be found online playing* Worms: Armageddon.

thestygianport.wordpress.com
thestygianport.blogspot.com
vimeo.com/violator
youtube.com/user/thestygianport
violator.atspace.com/worms

Reflections on the Cinematic Underworld

In the beginning God created the heavens and the earth. Now the earth was formless and empty, darkness was over the surface of the deep, and the Spirit of God was hovering over the waters. And God said, 'Let there be light,' and there was light.
—Genesis 1:1-3

What God saw in those waters which would later become the material world was his own reflection. Jay Weidner's *Alchemical Kubrick 2001: The Great Work on Film* puts forward the interpretation that the black rectangular monolith from the film *2001: A Space Odyssey* is in fact the movie screen in the theater, and that the dimensions of the monolith were identical to those of movie screens of the day.[1] Rob Ager's analysis of the same film goes one step further in suggesting that not only is the monolith the movie screen, but that the characters on the screen become self-aware that they are 2-dimensional projections upon it.[2] The loud "signal" apparently emitted from the monolith on the moon when the astronauts take a group photo in front of it can be likened to acoustic feedback, similar to that which results from speakers too close to a microphone, looping the sound back around again. In this case, the feedback-loop is due to the characters within the movie taking a picture of themselves in front of the monolith-movie-screen.

All things are in the universe, and the universe in all things.
—Giordano Bruno

Motion picture film stock contains a silver halide emulsion, creating a connection between projected cinema and the element silver. Silver is the metal commonly associated with the moon, earth's extremely reflective satellite, and to this day silver is still used to create glass mirrors. You may recall that Jim Carrey's entire life as Truman Burbank in *The Truman Show* is filmed and televised from a stationary moon-base hung in the sky of his artificial world. As a godly *Bruce Almighty* he pulls the moon closer to the earth. As Lloyd Christmas in *Dumb and Dumber*, Carrey expresses amazement at an old moon landing newspaper clipping, exclaiming: "We've landed on the moon!" He has also played the *Man on the Moon*, Andy Kaufman. Another Andy becomes a werewolf, ruled by the moon, in *An American Werewolf in Paris*. And, after the character Andy is introduced in the remake of *The Dawn of the Dead*, one of the survivors on the mall's rooftop quietly states that Andy "might as well be on the moon." Well, maybe not *on* the moon, but certainly reflected upon it. Like the sun's light reaching the earth at night by way of the moon, the light-body of Divine Man (or God) comes into the dark material world in a similar fashion: a fall into matter very much like in the story of Narcissus who fell into a body of water after becoming enamored with his own reflection. The word "water" with a flipped "w" becomes *mater,* Latin for mother, the maternal energy associated with water, matter, and the world we call Mother Earth. *Matar* in Spanish means "to kill," and is fitting because a person's material incarnation is equated to a spiritual death or dormitory state. The Egyptian deity Maat created order from chaos in the beginning of the universe, which we might see as the formation of "Maatter." Thus, the entire universe of material creation is the same reflective substance from before time which continues to serve as a mirror for our individual psyches.

> *I saw people coming toward me, but all were the same man. All were myself. I had never known this world before. I had believed that I was created, but now I must change my mind. I was never created; I was the cosmos: no individual existed.*
> —The World's Religions *by Huston Smith*

Ian McKellen, as Number 2 in the 2009 remake of *The Prisoner*, explains that The Village (the entire universe as far as its villagers are concerned) exists entirely within the mind. He continues to explain that the mind is capable of anything because everything is within it. There is not one aspect of reality that a person experiences which is not first filtered through the brain and mind. One's vision of the world around them is completely unique to them, though a large amount of consensus reality still exists. Alan Watts, in *The B∞k: On the Taboo Against Knowing Who You Are,* demonstrates this with an example of the ephemeral rainbow. A group of people could all be watching what appears to be the same rainbow, but if one person started walking towards it, the rainbow would appear to be moving away from him, yet remain stationary for the others. The rainbow exists only in the mind of each unique observer. The observer is as integral to the existence of the rainbow as are sunlight and moisture in the atmosphere. Take away any one part of this equation and the rainbow ceases to exist. Which is to say, it ceases to exist when you close your eyes; in the same way it would cease to exist if the sunlight was temporarily obscured, or if the water vapor dissipated and the sunlight and observer remained.

Reality is inconceivable without an experiencing subject, without an ego. It is the product of the exterior world, of the sender and of a receiver, an ego in whose deepest self the emanations of the exterior world, registered by the antennae of the sense organs, become conscious. If one of the two is lacking, no reality happens, no radio music plays, the picture screen remains blank.
—Albert Hoffman

I love watching movies, even bad ones (even more than I love (over)using parentheses and quotes!). As a result of my continued dedication, I've formed the hypothesis that the monolithic movie screen and reflective silver film present each viewer with a reflection of their own internal psyche. This has probably been put forward by others, or could be a well known industry secret. (I really don't have any idea what one learns in a screen-writing class or by schmoozing with writers and directors.) It could be proposed that the reflective waters of pre-creation which formed the material world continue to serve as a mirror for the unconsciously divine creature called Man. Everything Man is, in his mind, is reflected/projected out before him as the apparent universe. Everyone will see a slightly different film because different parts will resonate with them and touch on areas of knowledge they personally have. Besides this basic psychological idea that we all see what we want to see, there are also parts of film which are intended to represent our psyche and present us with a model ego to adopt.

Battle not with monsters lest ye become a monster; and if you gaze into the abyss, the abyss gazes into you.
—Friedrich Nietzsche

Luke Skywalker's battle with an illusory Darth Vader in the cave on Dagobah may represent a battle within himself, with his ego. In fact, the planet itself may represent the unconscious realm. Luke's internal battle is revealed when the mask covering Vader's decapitated head explodes to reveal Luke's own face. Viewers may not have caught it, but Yoda later refers to this as Luke's failure at the cave. The knight enters the cave of the dragon at the base of the mountain, home to the greedy ego representing our base instinctual nature. The dragon is hoarding gold (knowledge) yet lacking the ability to utilize it (wisdom). The knight is not supposed to eradicate the dragon and be done with it. Instead, he must drink its blood, or take a scale for a shield, or in some way overcome and incorporate this part of himself. Darth Vader later removes his own mask after killing the emperor and re-joining Luke and the light side of the force. In the third *Austin Powers* film it is revealed that Dr. Evil, Austin's arch enemy, is actually Austin's brother. Remember, Dr. Evil told Austin that, "We're not so different, you and I." Dr. Evil turns good and rejoins the family. An additional hint is that both Austin Powers and Dr. Evil, two sides of the same coin, are played by the same actor. Not only are you meant to associate yourself with the hero in any myth, you are also meant to see your darker egoic nature as the villain. A villain only until he is defeated, and preferably redeemed.

If you bring forth what is within you, what you bring forth will save you. If you do not bring forth what is within you, what you do not bring forth will destroy you.
—Jesus, in the Gospel of Thomas

Because everyone is unique, what they experience is unique, and their interpretations of the world around them, including movies, is obviously going to be unique as well. At times they might see what appears to be political-commentary, like the "Red Menace from Mars" of McCarthy-era science fiction films, or George A. Romero's depiction of "brain-dead zombies" converging on the local mall. Detractors of symbol-heavy film interpretation will put forward the basically correct assumption that pretty much everything that makes it into the frame was intentional, and therefore it is not mystically significant if a connection is found between the movie's symbols and other symbols found elsewhere. For instance, in *Transformers*, Shia LaBeouf's character has an eBay account with the username "Ladiesman217." 217 happens to be the numeric value of the Hebrew name Deborah which means "bee," and Shia's character is protected by the Transformer named Bumble**bee**. Is it simply a happy coincidence? Maybe, but given the 'Jewish' nature of Hollyweird, I wouldn't rule out the possibility that the symbolic connection was a conscious choice made by a filmmaker with a knowledge of Hebrew gematria (the numeric value of each letter and word correspondences). That being said, I believe there is room for an unlimited number of interpretations of anything, especially of movies, and that no one interpretation is more correct than another, at least not in the cosmic sense of things. It can only resonate with the reader or not resonate with the reader. The situation might be compared to a complex piece of abstract art where everyone sees something different in it, all unaware that the artist simply let his kids splash paint on the canvas because he needed something new for his art show.

It isn't up to the painter to define the symbols. Otherwise it would be better if he wrote them out in so many words!
The public who look at the picture must interpret the symbols as they understand them.
—Pablo Picasso

Synchromysticism, a portmanteau of the words "synchronicity" and "mysticism," is what most of the fellow authors of this book and I call our brand of symbolic investigation. It's almost holographic in nature, in that by focusing on one small part of reality, many other connections, which are usually not immediately apparent, will come into view.

Imagine a multidimensional spider's web in the early morning covered with dew drops. And every dew drop contains the reflection of all the other dew drops. And, in each reflected dew drop, the reflections of all the other dew drops in that reflection. And so ad infinitum. That is the Buddhist conception of the universe in an image.
—Alan Watts

Those who practice synchromysticism tend to follow the same basic assumption that no source of information is off-limits. One blog article might connect a news headline from the Internet to:

tarot cards, the zodiac, events in history, word etymology, the meaning behind a person's name, music videos, and areas of conspiracy theory research. Synchromysticism can be used to find meaning in situations where that meaning may not have been implied or even originally intended. I would say that there are similarities to the art of divination because it is the observer who finds the meaning in the randomness. It probably takes people who are a bit more in touch with their right brain to see something of significance in the patterns found by the left brain. Whether or not some ideas hit or miss really depends on how well the information resonates with the reader. I believe it takes an observer to bridge the subjective and objective, symbol and meaning, heaven and earth, and bring synchromysticism into existence. That is to say, maybe contrary to other opinions on the matter, that synchromysticism doesn't exist 'out there' in a mishmash of random information all too available these days via the Internet, waiting for us to find it. I think only the potential is there, like the void before creation, and that by discriminating amongst an overabundance of information, an individual perspective will cause part of the abyss to coalesce into solid creation unique to its observer-creator.

> *It's not what you look at that matters. It's what you see.*
> —Henry David Thoreau

One area of film investigation I enjoy is that of noticing the use of movie props in multiple movies. For instance, the same painting of a beach coastline found in the waiting room of the afterlife in *Beetle Juice* is also found above the bed in the motel room where Butch is hiding out in the movie *Pulp Fiction*. Is Butch in the waiting room of the afterlife, or is he symbolically or actually dead? Or, did the person in charge of set design simply pull a painting at random out of a storage shed on the studio lot? I can't tell you, but that doesn't mean there can't be an interesting story there. Later, outside this motel room, Butch exclaims that "Zed's dead." The letter "z" in "the Queen's English" is called "zed." The character Zed, played by Sean Connery in *Zardoz*, was bred solely for the purpose of penetrating the artificial world of a future society of immortals in order to bring death to them. In *Shaun of the Dead*, the word "zombie" is referred to as "the zed word." Zed's dead alright, but he's up and walking around! (Like Butch, perhaps?) Another interesting use of a movie prop which comes to mind is Egon's PKE-meter from *Ghost Busters* (it's a handheld box with two light-up arms which rise in the presence of psychokinetic energy), which appears four years later in *They Live* as a communication device for the "aliens" who run the world. Only, these "aliens" who operate from the underworld (oops, I mean: "underground") are actually called Ghouls. Is there a reason that decayed looking ghouls, who are found six-feet under, communicate with each-other using a device intended to find ghosts? The use may or may not be intentional, but either way, an interesting story can be created using this information. In the end, whether a consensus can be formed about the interpretation or not, it really comes down to the unique story that one can tell using the numbers, names, symbols, and themes which they find. It's more important that the audience of this material feels the same sense of revelation, the epiphany that I feel, while researching their own story.

All phenomena are real in some sense, unreal in some sense, meaningless in some sense, real and meaningless in some sense, unreal and meaningless in some sense, and real and unreal and meaningless in some sense.
—Robert Anton Wilson

Because of a recent video project, my particular area of interest of late is that of an unintentionally Gnostic inspired world-view which has us living in a literal Hell or underworld alongside or *as* the dead. The ideas which shaped this viewpoint came from my interests in religious mythology and philosophy, having recently read Philip K. Dick's *VALIS*, as well as too much movie watching. As a result of this focus, much of what I see in certain types of films ends up fitting perfectly into this perspective. I'm working under the assumption that a lot of film makers are intentionally putting out this theme, and that only part of the information which I'm gleaning is a reflection of my own psyche. I can't know for sure, of course, but I do recognize the fact that the film makers have their own agendas separate from what I'd like to see in their movies.

Going back to *The Truman Show*, Truman, played by Jim Carrey, and his wife live in house number 36. Adding every number from 1 to 36 equals 666, the number which represents the material part of the universe, the Beast, and Man. The actress who plays Truman's wife also stars in the film *The Mothman Prophecies* where she is marked as number 37 (an important Biblical number in its own right), and takes great interest in hearing that 36 people have died in the collapse of the Silver Bridge (there's that reflective lunar element). The house facing her and Truman's house in *The Truman Show* is numbered 32. In *The Number 23*, Jim Carrey plays a 36 year-old who met his wife when he was 23. He gets a personal lesson on the 23 enigma ($2/3 = 0.66\bar{6}$) from his wife's professor friend, ending with: "There are only 22 chapters in the Book of Revelations. We all know how that ends." The actress who plays Carrey's wife in that movie also stars in *The Prophecy* where the Book of Revelation actually does have 23 chapters. She also stars in *The Haunting in Connecticut* where her son wears a shirt with the number 23 on it. Her son sleeps in an old morgue in the basement where bodies had been mutilated in order to keep the souls trapped in the house. Her husband has, in his recreation room (re-creation/resurrection room?), a framed picture of the Egyptian underworld.

Nobody, I think, ought to read poetry, or look at pictures or statues, who cannot find a great deal more in them than the poet or artist has actually expressed. Their highest merit is suggestiveness.
—Nathaniel Hawthorne

There are, of course, many more symbols running through these movies and others, but it's almost as if you could draw a line straight through many films showing one continuous theme of the material universe representing the underworld. Truman's world is, as I've mentioned previously, watched over by its "creator" operating from a moon base set into a stationary spot in the sky. Every morning as Truman leaves for work he is attacked by his neighbor's dog named Pluto. Pluto is the Greek god of the underworld. The largest moon of the *planet* Pluto, Charon, is both in a synchronous orbit and is gravitationally-locked with Pluto. This means that not only does the same side of Charon always face Pluto (as our moon does earth), but from the surface of the planet, Charon would appear motionless in the sky, always stuck in the exact same place; very much like the moon-observatory of the *Truman Show* dome. We are left with the underworld and "The

True-Man Show" as symbols representing the (fictional) material world and our position within it.

Whether your enlightenment comes in the microcosm through battling your ego, or in the macrocosm by achieving liberation from physical incarnations, I hope you have as much fun utilizing synchromysticism as I have, as an aid to you on your quest.

If you dream and see several men, and then wake up and recall your dream, do you try to ascertain if the persons of your dream creation are also awake?
—Sage Ramana Maharshi

---

1) http://www.jayweidner.com/kubrick4.htm
2) http://collativelearning.com/2001%20chapter%205.html

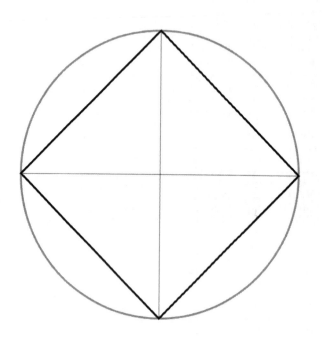

Stefan Jablonski
PrismReptileRobot

Born in Tasmania on Guy Fawkes Night in the year of the Dragon, 1976, Stefan grew to experience a spontaneous 'awakening' at the age of 12 that gave him an insight into the fractal-like nature of his own being. During the 90's he became interested in conspiracy theories and UFOlogy, which led to discovering synchromysticism. Commencing blogging about sync at PrismReptileRobot.net in early 2009, Stefan now contributes to the sync blog, The Sync Whole. *Sync has grown to compliment Stefan's insights gained from his 'awakening,' various forms of meditation and entheogen practice. Stefan's sync writing stems from his interest in plant consciousness, love of music and his heart. Stefan is a father who works in IT at Monash University in Australia.*

prismreptilerobot.net
g8ors.blogspot.com

Synchronous Reading

When I started out sync-blogging, I did intend on creating an introduction for those interested in sync. I haven't quite realized this with my blogging yet—a byproduct of both my laziness and simply going with the flow of whatever is syncing with me at any given time. Hopefully this piece will assist in filling that void in some way. I have always felt the mutual benefits of sharing—be it music, literature, ideas, food, whatever. I share online with others who like to share sync too. I feel that the value of the medium is proportionate to the positive relationships that are formed within it. Sync, realized and expressed in the plethora of formats that it is, would not be possible if it weren't for the Internet. That being said, sync can appear to be a bit of a black-box. Let's see if we can have a look inside.

I'll be referring to synchromysticism and synchronicity as "sync" in the following pages. Sync is such a free medium that it allows one to refer to it as one feels appropriate. This piece will attempt to highlight this flexibility. In order to be receptive to this type of thinking, it's a good idea to do away with convention. Sure, this is a pretty conventional medium, however *it's ezy 2 br34k the r00ls.*

Not binding oneself to convention can be seen as a convention in and of itself. However, I feel that once one enters the stream that is sync, and a comfortable flow becomes apparent, the richness of each moment can override all convention and all form. Sync shows us what we are seeing in a different light. We see every atom within the cosmos—no matter what form it may take at any given point in time—as a manifestation of our true nature. Sync has been described as "an observance of meaningful coincidences that are perceived within the seemingly mundane." This can be likened to viewing the divine within in a piece of trash. This ability can be handy in a world which, at some times, can appear as if it is the galaxy's symbol-junkyard. Trash transforms into a blooming flower which has sprung forth from the singularity that is the source of all things.

SYNCHRONOUS READING

Syn can be defined as "united or acting together." *Khronos* is the personification of time in Greek mythology. The convention of synchronicity is demonstrated in movies when members of a team "synchronize their watches." These team members, once in the same place at the same time, split up. They are now in separate places at the same time, their watches being a link to their synchronized unity. All of us, living in our apparently separate time zones, are living within an underlying Coordinated Universal Time (UTC). The syncing of watches shows that the modern form of measuring time and dividing the planet into time zones defies this natural clock. Regardless of where the hands sit on our watches, we are all here now. Our natural watches are always synced. The implementation of UTC in 1884 is a nod to the now, which contains all of our unique perceptions of reality.

In utero we were connected to our mothers. In perfect sync, we were nourished by her. Both of us simultaneously experienced many events, perceived both internally and externally. On a genetic level we are paired with our mother's and father's DNA, making us living totems of their love. We read these words as super-cells. Synchronous masses, consisting of trillions of cells, laden with DNA that is acting in a manner that facilitates this physical existence. Were it not for this tight bond—that could only be achieved with nanosecond-precise synchronicity—our many constituents would never have bonded in the first place.

The more I work towards developing an awareness of my surroundings, the better I get at gauging those that are actually interested in sync. Occasionally I am a bit off the mark and I wax-sync to individuals that aren't ready to hear about it. The chances are that they thought I was a little cuckoo. However, chances are—just like you, dear reader—that they know how to read. If they are literate, then they could really be thought of to be just as bonkers as I, if we look at sync and compare it to reading.

Reading is a process of decoding symbols. As a pre-literate being, we're reading our environment as a Sync Head does. Symbols float in and out of our scope and these symbols begin to develop their own meaning. We don't have any other frame of reference within this space, so that's all we can do. Attaching meaning to any given symbol is a coding process. Once this initial code is written, a swift decoding process is possible when the symbol resurfaces.

As an infant, we meet mother from time-to-time, face-to-face. These meetings are often meetings of joy that further cultivate an archetypal symbol of our mother that represents sustenance and comfort. However the first symbol that we are met with, given ideal circumstances, is the circle-dot: ⊙. This symbol of life support is the mother's breast—and from an even more granular perspective could also be seen to represent the areola and nipple of the breast. Infant's eyes are fully developed before we are born, though our brain doesn't develop an ability to focus further than a couple of feet until we are around three months old. Until this time, we also can't see the full spectrum of colours, so the darkness of the areola and nipple stand out by sheer contrast. This perfect design allows us to code this symbol with its nourishing meaning within the first few minutes of life.

As our eyes develop, so too does our personal library of symbols, which no doubt will include the sun. Within the schools of astrology and astronomy the sun has been assigned a glyph. That glyph is the same breast/nipple circle-dot: ⊙. The bull's-eye/circle-dot is also used as the [al]chemical/elemental symbol for gold. The golden sun. The cosmic breast that delivers life-supporting energies to all that orbit it. Those life-supporting energies can easily be visualized as white packets of light. This imagery allows us to progress further with metaphors, the web broadens, yet closes up simultaneously, as we visualize those white packets as droplets of milk. Further linking the breast and the sun via language can be done via the areola of the breast and the aureola, or corona, of the sun.

With sync, one symbol can evolve to represent many things (those things all pointing back to the same symbol). It's the context which defines this representation. Sync as a form of reading differs from the reading you are now doing, as there is a great deal more flexibility with sync. And while we may appear to be determining symbolic relativity in accordance to external contexts, the ever-present context—whether reading conventionally or doing so while wearing sync-goggles—is always the reader.

SYNCHRONOUS READING

Progressing from the breast, the sun and other archetypes, we begin to develop conventional reading skills. And this is another skill that starts out with baby steps. We first learn the alphabet by rote. Eventually we develop what is a shared understanding of what individual letters and numbers are. It's at this stage that we return to a similar standpoint as when we were newborns searching for the circle-dot. The identification of individual letters is a crucial stage within the overall process of learning to read and write. As with sync, an initial meaning is attributed to any given symbol, such as the number 8 or a bolt of lightning.

With sync as a supplement to our initial mechanisms that we use to personally code and decode symbols, we can add additional elements of our own choosing to our initial coding. This adds richness and depth to what before may have seemed to be barely relevant detail. One cannot attribute meaning to a symbol that is not relevant to one's self, and because of that, when the task of relaying personal syncs is undertaken it may not make sense to another. So when sync is shared, symbols are often re-coded with the assistance of common code from other shared systems (such as religion, ancient civilizations or popular culture). Coding in this fashion allows us to swiftly move past the fixed meanings of the consensus and utilize an open-source coding system. We will use the 8 and the lightning bolt to explore this a little further.

The number 8 can be seen as the symbol for infinity/eternity: ∞. Sure, it has been rotated 90-degrees from its numerical orientation, but this does little to alter its infinite meaning. All you have to do to move from a relatively static symbol—a reference point—is tilt your head when looking at 8. Meditating on 8 as ∞ for a while may alleviate the requirement to tilt one's head at all—the two seemingly separate symbols become one. An eight-pointed star has been used for aeons as a representation of celestial balance and order. I see it as a representation of the star that resides at the centre of our galaxy—Sagittarius A. Fittingly, I often notice Queen Elizabeth II wearing this symbol in the form of The Queen's Garter Star. This gels for me as I also see the star at the centre of the galaxy as a royal mother. The Q at the centre of The Queen's Royal Garter Star is also central to the coat of arms of the United Kingdom. The flag of the United Kingdom, the Union Jack, is an eight-rayed star too.

The Union Jack

The Coat of Arms
of the United Kingdom

The Queen's Garter Star Brooch

Our local star has been referenced in the previous paragraphs as a life-giving energy source, and the galactic centre provides the same sustenance on a galactic scale. Scientists have stated that Sagittarius A is a super-massive black hole and that all other galaxies contain black holes at their centres. Black holes are commonly viewed as destructive entities that consume all that drift into their vicinity. As there are no galaxies without black holes, we can view black holes as governors of galactic order. We can now relate the circle-dot to Sagittarius A too—the dot representing the black star, the circle being all that orbits it. Sagittarius A can be seen as facilitating the union of the seemingly separate portions of our galactic kingdom.

Lightning is an interesting one. First, we all know of the phenomenon of lightning and its accompanying thunder. What is interesting is that, though we know what lightning is, we are not certain how it is formed. Science can't agree on its cause and mechanism.  This is fertile ground for imbuing one's own meaning, as lightning is such a prominent force of nature, yet still contains great mystery for the modern scientific mind. From a mythological standpoint, lighting belongs to the Greek god of gods, Zeus. And if the Greeks' Zeus is not the Romans' Jupiter, may God strike me down! Sync allows us to see lightning as Jupiter itself. Just as 8 & ∞ are one and the same—sync assists in making no separation between the two.

&

Let's—just for sync's sake—examine what happened in the previous sentence. Where did that "&" come from? I'm here trying to get this silliness down in some easy to digest form and I'm thrown into a distracting sync vein. I'll capture this one and we will see where we go.

The ampersand, &, looks a lot like an 8, which is ∞, and vice-versa. The ampersand is closely related to the mathematical plus sign, +, since one & one equals two. Now we also have electronic terminal-ology slipping in to further our bond, as + is used in electronic diagrams to indicate the origin of a conventional electrical current, the positive (in electronics, a conventional current flows from positive to negative). The ampersand, &, actually looks like an 8 that grows from an **x** (**x** being a 90° flip of +).

Let's break from drilling into the various components of the glyph and examine what has been gleaned from this brief exercise. The ampersand contains two elements that can be separated into:

1. 8 or infinity

    and

2. **x**, which is a slightly rotated + sign. The plus-sign carrying the electrical current that is the force wielded by Jupiter, the god of the gods.

Furthermore, the ampersand has similar features to Jupiter's logo, ♃. If we tilted the & clockwise, we'd see a symbol that somewhat resembles a 4. A prominent difference between & and ♃'s 4-like qualities is that ♃ is comprised of two strokes, the 2 and the 1. The & symbol is made up of one beautifully knotty line. ∞ is a symbol that not only refers to eternity but also a balance between two equal opposites in a similar fashion to yin and yang. Two make one. The union, via addition, is represented by the ampersand's own singularity.

Let's Read

We begin to string letters together and cultivate reading and writing skills only after coding each letter of the alphabet. Reading and writing are sync in action. Our memory contains countless amounts of code. When a symbol containing this code shows up we recognize it, and it's placed into its current context. That recognition is a synchronicity in and of itself. When reading fonts familiar to us we are receiving a transmission that we are in sync with. Attempting to read text penned in foreign character sets demonstrates how out of sync we are with symbols that have no previous meaning to us. Not being able to place symbols that are not 'conventional'—and by conventional I am referring to letters and numbers—into one's own context can be equated to being shown a book written in alien text. So we may now see how one may not be able to read the signs that another refers to as sync worthy.

Looking now at sync as a form of reading, we note the level-up gained by stringing letters together. When reading one's environment from a sync standpoint, multiple symbols may become apparent simultaneously. Patterns begin to form and composites are created. The humble stop-sign, seen at every other street corner is an octagonal red spot. The octagon, being an 8-sided polygon, harkens back to the infinity symbol. The red colour of the sign and bold STOP (which is an anagram of SPOT) reminds us that Jupiter sports an iconic *red spot*. A stop-sign vibrates simultaneously with the same two frequencies as the ampersand (those being the center of our galaxy and the largest planet in our solar system, Jupiter), melding the two into a new frequency altogether.

As I put these ideas down, I receive unsolicited feedback from the cosmos that relates directly to Jupiter and Sagittarius A's relationship. I perceive this feedback via my noticing symbols and themes that I encounter, which have meaning to me. While perusing my Twitter feed, a sync-buddy quotes Terrence McKenna's *True Hallucinations*. McKenna, after ingesting a mixture of Ayahuasca and Psilocybin mushrooms, perceives a connection with a conscious source of data and information. The connection to this all-knowing intelligence allowed McKenna to receive instant answers to questions he put to it. Once McKenna moved past the question and answer game, he asked this upper-mind what he should do next. After following the entity's instructions and resolving all the wrongs that McKenna had committed in his life, the voice imparted this on McKenna, and this is what I read in my feed, "You've found it. This is it. It's all over now. There is no more. Within a few hours, the superstructure of earthbound, human civilization is going to collapse and your species will depart. First you will go to Jupiter and then to Alpha in Sagittarius. A day of high adventure dawns at last for the human beings."

Sync has now evolved for me, from reading a glossary of symbols to having a conversation with its author. Sync reveals the universe's inherent synchronicity. There are periods where I don't feel as close to the pulse as I have at other times. I still flow during these dry spells. These are times to listen and watch intently, without judgment and with compassion. Before long though, my entire environment is teeming with sync. Sequences of composite symbols catch my attention. While writing this piece, I took a break and chaperoned my son as he rode his bike around the block. The first street number that I noticed was a brass 8 on a blue wooden plaque. At another point of the journey, I crossed the street towards a vacant block. It had a letter box at the front with the number 21—the numbers 2 and 1 being composite partners within the symbol for Jupiter, ♃.

The moment one realizes a profound sync can cause an influx of endorphins. Endorphins are endogenous morphine, or morphine made inside your body and used by your body. It's what your body pushes out when you are hurt so that you don't go into complete shock. β Endorphins have been found to have been produced by the outermost foetal component of the placenta. The cells that make up this layer are referred to as syncytiotrophoblasts or syncytium. These are cell-like structures that, unlike conventional cells, contain multiple nuclei. It has been hypothesized that unborn babies can control the amount of endorphin that is released by this layer, thus dosing their mothers when the situation favours the foetus. The hypothesis goes on to suggest that the mother can then be controlled by the foetus in order to increase nutrient allocation to the placenta.[1] This idea ties into the phenomenon known as "runner's high," which has produced generations of "fitness junkies."

Syncytium, by its name alone, syncs with the subject matter already explored here—cellular life has been mentioned above. We have referred to ⊙ as a symbol with multiple meanings—breasts, the sun and gold—and now we can add cells to the list of the circle-dot. The dot represents the cell's nucleus and the circle represents the cell's membrane. Cellular biology shows that all the daily survival processes that occur on a macro level—reproduction, respiration, consumption and survival—are mirrored at the cellular level. This highlights the ability of using sync as a tool that assists in demonstrating the fractal-like nature of all things.

Sync shows us that, like the old adage says, "the writing is on the wall." With sync though, the potential for reading each other's writing is relative to our own ability to integrate additional codes to the ones we already sync with. We are all connected to this reality by a consciousness that is aware of its perceived surroundings. The cosmos is talking to us via each element that our surroundings consist of. Though we may not receive transmission as a sync, we are each integral synchronous components of the universe.

---

1) Apari, Peter; Rozsa, Lajos (2006). "Deal in the womb: Fetal opiates, parent-offspring conflict, and the future of midwifery". *Medical Hypotheses* **67**: 1189–1194.

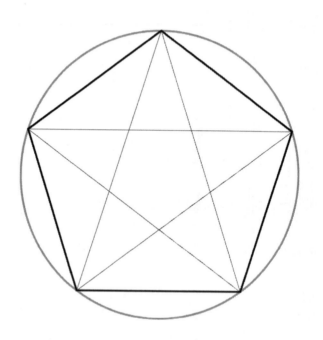

ALAN ABBADESSA-GREEN

LOOK AT ALL THE HAPPY CREATURES

I began the Happy Creatures *blog with the original intention of using it merely as a sync diary. However, it has proven to be an invaluable tool in my own personal development—allowing me to explore ideas, test hypotheses and document results, share experiences, and communicate with others doing the same.*

Prior to the blog, I had been published in comics and prose—getting an excellent review in Comic Buyers Guide *and having a self-published anthology on display at The Baltimore Museum of Art. My animation has been projected onstage, commissioned by a Bollywood director, used in boardrooms and music videos. Earlier this year, shortly before I began to edit this collection, I published my first novel,* Look at All the Happy Creatures, *from which the blog gets its name. I also host podcasts on my site and am a proud member of* The Mask of God *blog.*

I live with my wife in New York City.

In the following piece, I set out to prove that synchronicity is accessible to anyone and everyone, as well as attempting to disprove "predictive programming" as the main explanation for all the high weirdness we are observing.

allthehappycreatures.blogspot.com
themaskofgod.blogspot.com

Cosmic Folk Art

Something you will see very often within writings on the subject of synchronicity is the reduction or comparison of one subject to a universal archetype that it seems to be expressing. As an example, we can look at the world-famous comic book character of Superman. In the comics, he gains his god-like powers from the Sun. Therefore, we can say that Superman fits the archetype of a solar deity and, as such, we can safely compare him to other solar gods like Horus and Ra of Egyptian lore.

Many newcomers to this field have told me that they find the wealth of comparisons to be intimidating. Someone once told me they felt unable to express the synchronicities they were experiencing because they were not familiar with the various mythologies that are so often cited. As in any form of communication, there needs to be common ground for people to understand one another. In the search for this common language, we come back to synchronicity itself, for in many ways it is the universal language of our lives and perhaps even the language of the universe. In an effort to demonstrate this, a number of authors have chosen to point out the archetypes present in movies and books and other popular forms of entertainment because they are recognizable as our modern mythology (or modern interpretations of old mythology).

There is a good reason that so many choose to point to artwork as a way of demonstrating these patterns; art is the arrangement of symbols and stories, archetypes one and all—and these are *the* common language. Rather than thinking of synchronicity as something to be relegated to the halls of academia, I choose to think of it as cosmic folk art. It is something that anyone can do. No matter what method you use to try and describe it, or what aspect you choose to focus on, the truth is that you—no matter who you are—can experience synchronicity in your everyday life. In fact, it is something that we are always interacting with—both *creating* and *being created by*—more often than not, without even realizing it.

While many who study synchronicity are looking at the archetypes in media and trying to discern what hidden gems can be found in the author's subconscious, I come at this from a slightly different perspective simply because of my own personal experiences. I don't have to guess or debate what may or may not have been intentional on the part of any particular author. I've been writing fiction for many years now under the assumption that I was the only force in bringing my stories to life. What I've come to learn is that those of us in the creative arts might better be considered *conduits*. I can look at my own work and tell you that, without a doubt, the "unintentional" is by far the greater mystery. Let me share with you a few of the stunning things I found planted in my work—things I can assure you I did not intend—some of which I have only recently learned the meaning of.

When I was in my senior year of high school (1997-1998), I started writing a story called *The Saga*. It was inane, narcissistic, and very poorly written. Imagine the worst "buddy comedy" movie you've ever seen and make it about five times worse than that. Actually, considering the quality of most movies made nowadays, it was so bad that it would probably do very well. Regardless, you understand that I was a young kid, without a rich esoteric vocabulary, writing a silly story about me and my friends. It was not the sort of thing that I would expect to find deep meaning in nor phrases from ancient texts that I had never even heard of. But, over a decade later, as I became more acquainted with esoteric philosophy and alchemy, I found very exact plot points and phraseology from this terrible script I wrote. For example, the story ends with a character referred to as "Old Adam" having to sacrifice himself to create a new beginning for mankind—which directly parallels the Kabbalistic ideas of *Adam Kadmon* and the Christian study of 1 Corinthians 15:45-49.

It was not just elements of what some might consider an esoteric monomyth either, there were also powerful similarities between the story and real-life future events. There was the fictional plot point of characters traveling back in time, specifically from 2010 to 1998, to alter history. In the non-fiction flesh and bones timeline you and I live in, just such a claim was made when 2010 finally rolled around. Dr. David Lewis Anderson came out in 2010 to claim that they had succeeded in creating time travel technology—and went on to add that they had reason to believe someone using this technology traveled back in time to 1998 and altered history. I cannot verify the authenticity of this man's statements, and I do not include this example to imply confirmation of his claims, yet the synchronicity is too much for me to outright dismiss them, extraordinary though they may be. A similar synchronicity has led me to consider the research of Dr. Judy Wood with a bit more seriousness. In the world of *The Saga* (written 1998), there was a world-altering terrorist attack that hinged around the use of a very particular snack food, that being Cheetos. I would have never expected this to be anything more than the pure silliness it was meant to be. However, in our reality, Dr. Wood has raised some questions about the events of 9/11, and has pointed to the strange appearance of orange puffs at the scene of the crime as evidence of higher weirdness than crashing airplanes or even nano-thermite. She calls these anomalies "Cheetos."

After realizing that the secrets of the universe imprint themselves into even the most banal text, I became convinced of this "Cosmic Folk Art" concept. Since then, I've read some theories that these types of occurrences are actually more likely to occur within really immature writing, such as *The Saga* was. The theory is that silly and vulgar stories are written more from the Id, the part of your psyche that would be more in tune to the collective unconscious and the vast mysteries contained there. The argument would follow that authors of "more serious" works would end up placing too much of their Ego into the text and miss out on all the subtle cues being tossed out by the cosmos. Perhaps this is true to a degree, but I am inclined to disagree with that as a full answer. My conclusion stems from experiences I had over the last two years as I set out to write a more literary work with my novel, *Look at All the Happy Creatures*. That began as more of an Egoic, Rational, or Left-Brain endeavor. Yet it was only *after* I began learning about synchronicity—and noticed all the unintended extra material in what I had already written—that the story shifted to include many of these concepts.

COSMIC FOLK ART

And it is here, with the intentional integration of synchronicity, that a third variation enters the mix. Around 2007 I had the idea to write a graphic novel which was all about the interconnectivity of every action with every other action and every person's life with the lives of every other being. Though I was not yet familiar with the term synchronicity, I was essentially writing a story about just that. The concepts I wanted to explore are those at the very heart of Synchronicity and the more spiritually leaning Synchromysticism. They are also the very same concepts being explored at the cutting edge of Quantum Physics. It is within these realms that spirituality and science have found common ground after far too long of a separation. The evidence of interconnectivity that is so familiar to anyone observing synchronicity may very well be the same phenomenon that physicists call Quantum Entanglement.

Since I did not have a scientific term for the concepts I wanted to write about, I ended up with a title that was much simpler. I called the graphic novel *Squares That Touch*. For a number of reasons, I did not end up writing more than sixteen pages of that script back in 2007. However, last year I was asked by Peter Palmiotti, the artist I was developing the project with, if I wanted to restart the book. Since I had become even more interested in these concepts over that span of time, I was very excited to do so. With the addition of my wife, Melissa, as the interior artist, I was even more eager to get started. We decided to present the story as a series of issues instead of releasing the entire book in one chunk.

We kept the original sixteen pages of the script exactly as they were written in 2007, as well as keeping the original cover design that Peter and I had discussed around the same time. I then built upon the script, with the added idea that I would use synchronicity within the story. Let me clarify: the story was always about synchronicity, though I wasn't familiar with the term—but now I was going to use the naturally occurring patterns of interconnectivity that had been discovered and established by myself and other synchromystics as elements within the story. What I eventually started doing was methodically and Egoically placing pearls of wisdom discovered by the Id into the art and text. With the amount of planning I put into those pages, and my knowledge of what to be on the look-out for, I assumed there would be no unexpected surprises. I was very wrong. In fact, I may very well have unintentionally amplified the weirdness factor.

When Melissa and I were about half-way through the second issue, we had finished a scene that takes place under a waterfall and I had an unused photo that I really liked. So, I decided to play with turning that into a cover.

A few days later I saw the #2 and the waterfall together and made a connection to the second degree tracing board of Freemasonry which also features a waterfall.

This unintentional little sync made me look back at the cover to the first issue (which, again for the record, was designed by myself and Peter back in 2007 or so). Though I knew nothing of Masonic tracing boards, or really anything having to do with Masons at that time, the similarities between our first cover and the first degree tracing board are striking: Both feature beings descending from an astral staircase, onto the checkerboard pattern, beneath twin pillars.

COSMIC FOLK ART

It is here that the question must be raised: *Are symbols alive and/or speaking to us (or through us)?*

My current viewpoint of these particular similarities is that they are natural outcroppings that came from dealing with "squares" as subject matter. Considering the fact that Masons consider themselves "square men" or to be "on the square," I can only infer that *the square itself has a deep archetypical subset that reveals itself through common motifs, using the artist as medium.*

Though I am not affiliated with Masonry in any way, I also do not fear it, as many people do. I'll go deeper into all of this shortly, but suffice to say, I thought it would be fun to acknowledge the artistic similarities between the imagery I had extracted from the Square and the imagery that the Masons (and their predecessors) had extracted from it. So, what was at first unintentional became intentional and I integrated the third degree board into the comic itself. I did this without considering what page it went on, as it was merely the page that I was up to when I discovered the connection between the covers and the tracing boards.

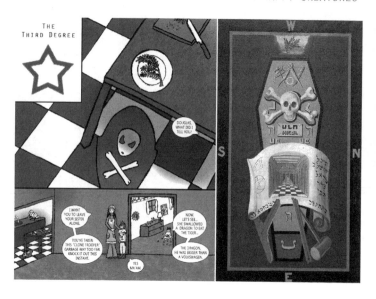

This turned out to be page 42, which spawned a slew of other unintentional treasures that I discovered a few weeks later. In the panel that mimics the third degree tracing board, there is a single word bubble, spoken by a mother to her son, Douglas. This was due to having already established the child and his toy shield earlier in the story. I simply thought his toy shield would substitute nicely for the coffin found on the third degree board. However, having the name "Douglas" appear on page 42 is notable because the idea of "42" being the "answer to life, the universe, and everything" was made famous by Douglas Adams in his book, *The Hitchhiker's Guide to the Galaxy*. The number 42 is something that has been the subject of intense study among synchromystics and is often connected to the planet Jupiter.

Now the name Douglas I picked essentially at random, trying to think of a name that sounded like it would belong to an annoying kid brother (no offense to those sporting the name). But, this gets even funnier, since I later realized that the only other time the name Douglas appears is on page 24, which is just an inverse of "42." Add to that, I (unconsciously or subconsciously) placed the 42-resonating (and therefore Jupiter-resonating) "Douglas" directly on top of his little sister's Lego tower. This again resonates with

Jupiter, since I had wanted that Lego tower to stand-in for the Black Monolith that sends a signal to and from Jupiter in the movies *2001: A Space Odyssey* and *2010: The Year We Make Contact*.

From page 24

From page 23

In this other panel from page 23, you will note that I intentionally placed the combination of Jupiter and the word "tiger" with this Monolith-resonating tower since 2010 is the Year of the Tiger in the Chinese Zodiac and the planet Jupiter has tiger-like stripes. While there are many such things that I encoded into each panel, much to my amazement, by trying to encode certain motifs into the art, I ended up with many more unintentional and very powerful synchronicities.

Shortly after I discovered some of these patterns within *Squares That Touch*, I was sent an audio conversation between Will Morgan and Jake Kotze, both of whom write at the *Sync Whole* blog. Within their conversation, the question was raised as to what would happen if a filmmaker decided to use synchronicities within the work. Jake theorized, "Okay, then you're consciously doing synchronicity, but then there's still the greater which will be doing ever more things. So it just adds to it, it doesn't take away. So, it doesn't bother me when people consciously put things in because I know that there's always new levels to it. Always. The hole just gets deeper."

And indeed it does always get deeper. Let us add to this examination the fact that the second issue of *Squares* features a flash-back story, taking place in Japan, that uses water as a metaphor for death. We finished this issue on April 4, 2011—just a week prior to the massive tsunami that devastated Japan. Then Melissa and I started working on the third issue. We finished a series of pages where two men, meant to represent the Military Industrial Complex, plot to kill an Arab man. These pages were finished on April 21, 2011—eleven days before Obama told the world that US forces had killed bin Laden. Certainly, synchronicities like these add fuel to the debate: Does art imitate life or does life imitate art?

Note: On the Happy Creatures *blog I have been studying the way in which our pattern watching often points to otherwise-unknowable future events. In a short amount of time we have collected a good number of correct projections, well in advance. I am attempting to refine this study and I welcome your participation in the process.*

There are entire communities on the internet devoted to finding synchronicities within movies or other artwork that predate, and seem to foreshadow, major world events. Very often within conspiracy circles, these are pointed to as proof of some sort of "great revealing" by Hollywood culture creators. The concept of "predictive programming" is that some cabal of evil intent has planted these cues into mainstream entertainment, and therefore into popular consciousness, as a way to make the events more digestible when they occur. The argument is sometimes made that we artists are the victims of brainwashing, and that we are helping this evil cabal without our realizing it.

Truth be told, I entertained this idea while working on my novel, *Look at All the Happy Creatures*. It is the story of an Orwellian police state that controls its populace with propaganda and manipulation. It is a fable and, like *Animal Farm*, it uses anthropomorphized animals to tell of political misdeeds. The original concept was that I wanted to show people how they were being controlled. I wanted to free people—I certainly didn't want to further anyone's enslavement. And, as I set out to tell this story, I was still within the mindset that Masonic influences were a big part of that control system. So, when I learned that Freemasons revere the Dog-Star of Sirius, which they call "The Blazing Star," I stopped writing for a few months. That's because one of my main characters, the philosophical hero of the story, is named "Zabu the Sun-Stroked Dog"—and the similarity to a "Blazing Dog Star" was too much for me to dismiss. I began to wonder if I was being manipulated and, in turn, manipulating others.

Luckily, this moment of self-reflection, though initiated by a paranoid fear, led me to fully examine the nature of that fear. I researched feverishly and meditated on my findings. I dissected the information with a rational mind and an open heart. I came out of my dark night of the soul with an understanding of synchronicity, or at least an understanding that the mystery is far greater than any human conspiracy. Yes, manipulation takes place daily. Yes, propaganda is very real, and there is plenty of evidence in the world around us that it is effective. But this line of thinking falls short and misses the bigger picture. Just as there were numerous outcroppings of unintentional symbolism in the fiction I wrote—so too would any fiction written by any propagandist also be subject to this phenomenon. A secret society attempting to manipulate and use symbols to their own end, may soon learn that they themselves are being manipulated and used *by the symbols*. Just as Ego cannot keep the unintentional syncs out of artwork, so too are the conspirators unable to keep out the self-organizing universe. Any conspiracy you can imagine, no matter how grand the scale, would still end up subject to what we might consider a higher conspiracy. As Jake would say, "the hole just gets deeper."

As to what this higher conspiracy truly is, we are still in the process of discovering. Ultimately, it comes down to how the viewer wishes to perceive it. Among those who choose to observe these events, there is a sect that chooses to see it only as something malevolent and another sect still that sees it only as something benevolent. There is this human tendency to reduce things down to good and evil, but if we are speaking of a force of nature—if, for example, what we are observing is something akin to gravity—then those concepts no longer apply. While I might suggest trying to avoid placing judgment or labels onto this force (or anything for that matter), if you insist on doing so, I would argue that the first place to start is with the person you see in the mirror. Because however much of a mystery the final answer may remain, we know enough to say that each of us is intimately involved in its working.

While there remain a million ideas as to where ideas originate—ranging from classical Muses to the great collective unconscious, from an Akashic record to transmissions broadcast out of Sirius, from Archonic manipulation to the Godhead itself—it would be foolish to trivialize the role of medium or the individual. After all, as Picasso said, "Inspiration exists, but it has to find you working." Once we realize it is a combined effort—that each of us plays a part in creating the world of ideas, that the universe responds to our actions and talks back to us—we begin to see our cosmic folk art for the beautifully intricate tapestry that it is.

I have come to a working model of the universe that is not unlike the game *Pictionary*. Whether it would hold up to academic scrutiny or not, I honestly do not care. It works very well as a metaphor. In *Pictionary*, one person has to draw a picture to communicate an idea or phrase to another player. They are arranging symbols and shapes, archetypes and hieroglyphs, to convey both simple and complex statements. In one sense, we can think of this as assisted telepathy. I have an idea in my mind that I want you to understand in your own. Currently, in this essay, I am using pages of arranged symbols to get that thought into your head. A painter will use arrangements of color and brush strokes to do the same. But, what if we take this idea to its most extreme? What if we are all higher dimensional creatures made of thought and energy using this three-dimensional space as our canvas? If I have a complex idea that I want to convey to you, I may have to shape all of reality down to its most subtle parts and long history in order to provide the full context. Carl Sagan made it clear: "If you wish to make an apple pie from scratch, you must first invent the universe."

What I'm describing is not solipsism, but a combined effort that we affect and which affects us. I believe we are the authors of our own Matrix. We are the ones painting with shadows on the wall of Plato's cave. Essentially, this is an ongoing conversation between each and every one of us, along with the universe itself speaking back, where the canvas never gets wiped clean. That would explain the added complexity found in Terence McKenna's models.

This complexity, while often intimidating, has its value in showing finer and finer detail. This same approach can be added to your further study of archetypes within synchronicity. When we add the context of ancient myths and various fields of study, we add shades of gray to our black and white world. Then, for example, we can learn to incorporate the differences between Horus and Ra (both solar gods, but each with their own unique history and personality) into our archetypical vocabulary. Steps like these eventually add brilliant colors to our canvas and our understanding of it.

However, it is also my belief that at some point we will need to, at least figuratively, toss the old stories away, like a Buddhist tosses away his teachings. For now we are still mapping the vast worlds of consciousness and dreamscapes—using sync as a form of fractal cartography. Yet I look forward to the day when we can toss the map away and forge new paths. We must let our imaginations grow—expand on the monomyth by adding new chapters and subplots. Eventually we may learn to imagine a world free of war and strife. And somewhere, in that uncharted territory, we may find our true selves or, at the very least, treasures and innovations that far exceed our wildest dreams.

I hope to see you there.

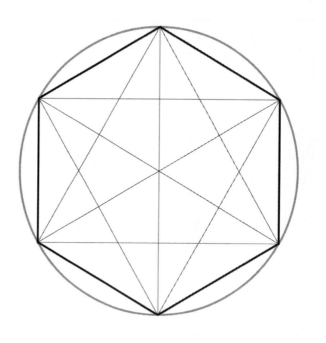

Tommy Fulks

Kozmikon

Tommy Fulks is the author of the Synchromysticism blog Kozmikon and a member of The Sync Whole. He lives in Georgia and works as a volunteer on an organic farm. He has been blogging since 2009, but has been interested in Synchromysticism since 2007 and has had a lifelong interest in déjà vu, dreams, cryptozoology and other unexplained phenomenon. When not working or tweeting syncs, he can be found playing music with local musicians and writing electronic music on his laptop. His biggest influences are Robert Anton Wilson and Terence McKenna.

kozmikon.blogspot.com
g8ors.blogspot.com

Synchromystic Tome Utterance

A frequency generated within—by a lack of disruptive thought patterns—has opened a door. Is the door an entrance or an exit? At this point, does it really matter? Going through this wavedoor, we exit "reality" and enter our own field of consciousness, like a torus passing through itself. The thing about the matter-pattern we usually wake into is that, whether or not we realize that we are consciousness experiencing itself, we return. So entering the wavedoor does not actually change anything, at least to our mind-based perception of the hologram which composes everything, including our bodies. But inside, intuitively, we know something has changed. We have chosen to be here. It is our choice entirely, as facets of one awareness, to be here and experience things at this frequency of space and time. Awakenings don't quite matter in the end, as we all awake each day into the world that we have chosen, and all that we experience is exactly what we wanted, whether we know it or not.

Synchronicity is an awareness of awareness, as is everything in existence. Synchromysticism is like surfing a nice wave instead of simply watching it crash to shore. Synchronicity involves a perceptual bending of space and time, in that patterns which occupy space form a pattern in time in a coherent event. We are all at once synchronized with everything in existence, whether we are aware of synchronicity or not, which is beautiful. The waves are affecting us, and we are affecting the waves, because we are one and the same experiencing itself. The fractal infinity of subdividing reality tunnels are all linked eternally to one source. Meaning that the symbols we see are ourselves, as is everything in existence.

Perhaps this is all a dream. As Neil Kramer says, a "very consistent dream." What most people consider reality is just what they're told it is, a sort of self-perpetuating mind virus seeded eons ago. Imagination and insight are no longer acceptable in the sphere of modern culture. Everything must be based on a previous model to be presented, even posited, without immediate ridicule and rejection. Synchromysticism, and all other types of open-source consciousness programs, are ways, not out, but IN to realms of knowing, of conscious real-time concepts becoming aware of themselves and self-replicating, spreading more like a seed than the virus of negative mass reality tunnels. To make everything shine with clarity, to have it all make perfect sense, is a sort of taboo these days. For anyone to find their own gnosis outside of a commonly accepted societal structure is heresy in the eyes of those who are unknowingly fully embedded into the Phoenix mold—that which finds its sustenance through the ashes of decay. In nature, this decay becomes new life to sustain the earth. Decomposition is the ultimate source of life. It reveals that our image of death as something to escape (usually through religion or science) and to fear is completely false. The mold which most human beings fit is not designed to empower themselves or the earth, but people who wish to act as gods over others in a conceptualized, imagined hierarchical structure. One that people bow down to, but it really does not hold any true power, once fear of death, fear of nature and avoidance of the real world is shed.

So, this is the essence of the dream we wake into each day. But what about outside of the dream? We can all remember the "real dreams" we've had where we are in bliss, completely unaware of fear or anxiety or living up to expectations. To me, this is actuality, the state of pure consciousness which our physical body is merely a specific density of. When the fear of the "outside world" penetrates the veil between densities, we have nightmares. Peaceful confrontation is the path inward, the bridge to that place we all know exists, yet consensus reality tells us is not so. It's funny how we have all grown to sort of avoid ourselves, in order to maintain a system in which we are merely cogs, tendons of a shadow being that we cannot immediately perceive, but just assume exists. We can do all the wishing we want, but until we face ourselves and ask what's really going on inside, why we put up this charade, why we have allowed ourselves to become desensitized to war and famine, nothing is going to change.

Consciousness flows and changes constantly, ever expanding, encompassing all and everything. Time is a filter which allows our physical density (including our brain functions) to change at a rate synchronized with the cycles of the stars, rather than exploding us into realizations at a rate far too intense for our minds to cope with. Stepping outside of this time cycle, we travel to infinite distances in the space of a nanosecond and take on the most alien yet familiar of forms, experiencing joyous life and painful death as one and the same a million times over, a strobe blurring into rainbow-tinted mist. Time itself will not change, but our perception of it is always changing.

Our experience, from beginning to finish, is a lesson. A lesson in loving, a chance to grow, to adapt and to simply "be." This form we take, the form in which you are reading this (if you've taken it upon yourself to sit through it) is a sight to behold. It is the vehicle by which our consciousness drives our will, and our consciousness, in its state of eternal peace and clarity, is none the happier to take on this form. Earth is comparable to a server in an online multiplayer game, new members joining, wondering what it's all about, wondering why there are so many other forms of consciousness here. I feel our consciousness is here to learn. In this game there are no tutorials, only experience through playing. Our connection to our "source," like a server list we can go back to at any time, is never lost. Not for one second. It exists beyond space and time. It is only through experience in the game that we can know this. Pain is a construct of time and the mind, a state which we exit through learning. In our current state, time is precious because we are convinced of linear properties to this construct, and the pain we feel is very much related to time, in that we feel we won't ever have a chance to heal, when truly there is all the time in the world to do so.

Synchromysticism itself lends to non-linearity, as has been stated many times by other Synchromystics. There is something very telling in how, as a group, we can entrain on a set of symbols and become aware through our observations of these symbols presenting themselves to us in "real time." It is space and time bending, like a curtain rising. Although the "easiest" symbols to interact with are visual, events in the lives of seemingly separate individuals (according to what we are taught) become connected and entangled in this "flow." It is our consciousness becoming aware of itself, our oneness showing its face. The sense of peace attained from this form of gnosis is unlike any other, since it is multi-dimensional. The only other way that I can feel I am truly in my most conscious state is during meditation, but that takes me out of the physical state. Synchromysticism joins truly inseparable states in a tangible way and makes it hard for us to avoid this multidimensional awareness, which is necessary if we are ever to find peace.

The evidence is around us all the time. We are like moviegoers or novel readers who don't want to have the ending spoiled for us. We want to find out for ourselves. And that is why we are here.

Let's consider the more popular notion of consciousness as a construct of nature. No one knows what happens after death. Except everyone who says they do. I think DMT production is accelerated in the pineal gland at death and acts as a higher dimensional gateway for consciousness to ascend, as it were. So, what is death? Death is the end, we assume. Yet in nature, it is a glorious beginning. To us conditioned humans, death indicates loss of a loved one, "Oh why couldn't they stay here with ME?" Paradoxically, to the generalized consensus mindset at least, this decomposing matter is the foundation of new life. Death is the breaking down of organic matter, and organic matter is cyclic. It's the circle of life. So, if looked at symbolically, temporal advancement of the evolution of life borne of death in nature indicates a helix. An upward spiral. If we are all entirely material-based, then our consciousness created by this material form is cyclic as well. The alpha is the omega. Order out of chaos and all that. The phoenix.

The plants are communicating with you on a level that you may or may not be aware of. All around you everything is constantly changing, constantly re-working itself/yourself among the parts that make the whole (a part containing the whole itself). I've often felt that, walking from point A to point B and back again like a robot, I am a sort of hyperdimensional entity traversing itself, a toroidal point of energy, non-static, ever-dynamic. The self as the metaprogrammer is the ultimate goal here—whether this selfhood is visualized as attainable or not, doesn't really matter.

Where Synchromysticism comes in is that, it is seemingly a more advanced sort of communication between your "self" (ego) and the outside world, with the communication itself seeming to indicate contact with a higher self to the observer. The experience of synchronicity usually (always?) has a chronological element, where one symbol will evolve into others with the same meaning before your eyes, as one stream of thought. My understanding of it as a phenomenon is that it must be directly experienced to truly be understood. In our current mass state we are like faux-anthropologists of the mind, inside of a realm generated within, and seeing ourselves as studying from the outside. Synchromysticism dissolves the illusory walls between observer and observed. What I find most interesting is that, while in contact with another Synchromystic, a sort of "sync chain" develops, as if our collective awareness of the phenomenon fuels its coming into being.

One of our biggest tools is Twitter. As I was writing this, I had tweeted some things relating consciousness to plants. I had a short conversation an hour or two later about farming stuff with another Synchromystic, and suddenly "Donald Duck" pops up on the "trending" list. This would sound like a ridiculous connection, except for the fact that the other Synchromystic was looking into the word "Donald" as meaning "Ruler of the World," and even had Donald Duck as his icon. So, while we were indirectly conversing about Donald Duck and consciousness, the character suddenly emerged in the consciousness of a large segment of the population. The mind has a capability of transmuting the random into a coherent stream of information. In our case, the information we are receiving is that of an infinite connectedness between everything, everyone, nothing, and no one. The experience is highly redeemable as one of wonder and joy.

I get the impression, during "Synchromystic states," that something is communicating with those of us who have chosen to pay attention to our own insight, and urging our perception towards one of a latticework involving the merging of reality tunnels. It speaks through an array of visual symbols in the normal context of sync, seemingly with Joy at the center, with all other symbols branching off from that. All symbols interpreted through sync can lead back to Joy, ultimately. It implies that this is an act of will, a sort of reverse spin, which brings our state of mind to that of solving a mystery, a willingness to investigate the phenomenon further. Our endeavor in researching sync is one of "no point," it places our consciousness at the center of a mandala from which all ideas and interpretations originate. What would, to one inexperienced with the phenomenon of synchronicity itself, come across as the mind's natural process of seeking patterns and therefore be reduced to a worthless "junk" thought process, is now something which encompasses all aspects of media through which ideas are communicated. Where one saw a funny coincidence, one now sees a joyous synchronicity. It is not a traditional mystery in the sense that it can have a temporal resolution, but a path through which a sort of "light" may be encountered. It is a natural process, sure, but the utilization of which can lead to ecstatic states of deep meaning. The neural pattern-seeking process is merely a tool which we are using to explore deeper states of mind consciously. It seems to work.

One may unconsciously follow negative patterns conditioned into their psyche as "normal" and find nothing but dismay and redundancy without meaning or constructive properties in the reality-model transforming occurrence of synchronicity, and therefore see it all as utter fluff. Becoming conscious of pattern in the realm of the exoteric has an adjacent effect in the internal realm—one becomes aware of previously unacknowledged patterns within and adjusts them to become more fruitful to their personal ends. The consensus state has us merely following patterns and not applying truly personal meaning to them, in that we are shown a pattern and in our minds we unconsciously attribute them to our own set of internal symbolic intelligence without thinking. This is normal. Association can only go so far as an individual's knowledge of a certain symbol. When one discovers several meanings to one symbol—same in the way as "SFR" is Hebrew for "sphere," "sapphire" and so on, and the word "can" means both a cylindrical storage object and the potential of doing—the synchronicities become much more clear, and can weave beautiful webs between seemingly unrelated concepts. In what I think of as "cinematic Synchromysticism," this is extremely apparent. The movies are simply a great medium for the symbols to communicate themselves and their interconnectedness, yet are a perfect example of how synchronicity and its mystical aspect can lead to long trails of meaning.

The amazing thing is that one can pluck just about anything out of their sphere of bio-consciousness and begin a string of thoughts which attribute several layers of meaning to one thing, and then apply these layers of meaning to another object, and then realize they are intimately connected through one's act of observation. It is an effect of the holographic aspect of reality. Let me give a quick run-through: In Terence and Dennis McKenna's *The Invisible Landscape*, they describe holographic reality thusly: A hologram is produced with three basic things, an array of lasers and mirrors (our sense organs), an object (immediately perceived three-dimensional reality), and a holographic plate (the brain). The object has a laser interference pattern projected onto it, and the mirrors reflect this image onto the holographic plate. The resulting image is a hologram (the mind). The image appears to have three-dimensional qualities, but it is only a representation of the object, and is not "real." A brain can be physically scrambled and yet maintain perfect memory. A hologram can be sliced and re-arranged and still produce the same three-dimensional image. Your true self is the one observing both the object and the image. In respect to Synchromysticism, it means that one master image or *Logos* is the root of all known aspects of being, and everything observable contains the whole of this symbol. It is the symbol of consciousness itself, consciousness observing itself, God beholding its Godhood. It also means that all symbols can relate to one another holographically. The potential of the mind to see this connection to "Godhood" is unlocked by will alone. No one can do it for you, as they say.

There is no limit to the potential unlocked through awareness of synchronicity. Objects in one's immediate surroundings take on celestial significance. We are artists of perception, charting the seas of consciousness.

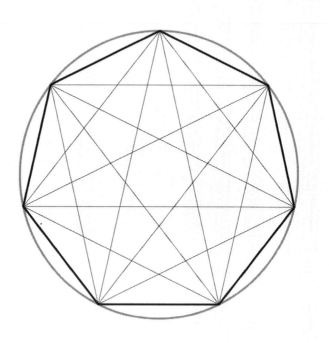

EUNUS NOE
THE MASK OF GOD

Eunus Noe is a Fool, Dilettante, and Joker who lives In Capital City. He was a deadman, but lives again and now participates in the sync collaboration, The Mask of God. *He has written* From the Belly of the Whale *and inside a* Sync Whole. *His sense of reality became less stable when he found himself as a character in a story on another sync blog: http://experiencebeingalive.blogspot.com/2009/04/aisle-13-can-i-help-you-i-had-been.html*

themaskofgod.blogspot.com
callmedjishmael.blogspot.com
thepurposeoflovers.blogspot.com

THE NOW
A brief introduction

Although the likely goal of this anthology is to describe the phenomenon of SYNC as clearly as possible from many different perspectives, I'd briefly like to touch upon the larger "age" on which the force of SYNC acts, **The Now**. (I've come to understand SYNC—the flowing, interconnectedness of all things—as the fundamental force of the universe. Thus, this anthology is an attempt to postulate *The Theory of Everything*.) And so I to give you, *The Now* (our Newly Ordered World).

Naturally there is a great difficulty in pinpointing one's historical moment due to lack of perspective. I've been very curious though (in opposition to everything espoused in our present philosophy of The Now) to try and understand our place in the context of historical Art movements/Scientific revolutions. This a moving target however. . . .

Recall that the classical, ordered, and clockwork Newtonian way of experiencing the universe gave way to the **chaos** of *relativity* and *modernism* near the beginning of the 20th century. There still existed objective truth, but it became relative. Einstein's addition to physics—his Theory of Relativity—still was classical in that **certainty** was still present, but became relative. I like to think of this in terms of Nietzsche's (prophetic) statement that "God is dead." The monotheistic "God" understood as truth—that is, **absolute truth**—became relative. The world agreed that noon absolutely exists, but that my noon isn't the same as yours. This Modernism led to an awareness of a much bigger world than we'd ever known, but we had just begun to become aware of ourselves. This chaos was reflected in the art of the time. Modern Art was a jumble of lines and shapes, and simultaneously experienced different perspectives, but it aptly described its moment. (Wondering about our moment? Look at dance *Now*.)

Yet at the very moment the scientific paradigm was shifting, another interesting development was also occurring. It was during this same moment that the lexicographers creating *The Oxford English Dictionary* really became consciously aware of the relativity of words in the English language. "The Word," as captured in humanity's first technology—the written language—is defined (in text) in terms of other words, and creates a circular, interconnected yet incomplete structure. Words in text are abstract pointers pointing to other words, which in turn point to others, creating a solid, net-like structure of meaning. Yet language is organic and alive. It flows. Although one may be able to track its course, it can't be controlled or prevented from flowing. Thus, (though the goal of the *OED* project was to find with certainty, the definitive state of **every** word), the result was cloudy due to the relativity of words and the difficulty of pinning down the most commonly used words. (*Superposition* anyone?) The project's authoritative completeness yielded an interesting result however, as this is an early example of a system becoming self-aware. The unbounded, flowing English language found a mirror in the *OED* in which to preen and play with both sides influencing the other! (Of course, the **one** object both sides point to is the same: *reality*.)

Shortly after *relativity*, Quantum Theory invalidated the notion of the objective, and then Post-Modernism denied truth. God was officially dead! That which was left in these scientific-revolutions' wake (*Finnegans*), was a fragmented, isolated, subjective perspective. A quantum perspective lacks certainty. It's all about possibilities, making both A and B potentially true at any given moment. Post-Modernism was how a previous age, that was used to certainty, processed uncertainty. All truth claims became suspect. Everything is perspective and all perspectives are different and unique. God is dead because there is no God . . . and what we are left with is pure chaos?

But what of all the order? And seemingly spontaneous arising order? If the second law of thermodynamics basically states that everything falls apart, what's the deal yo? And shouldn't the idea of ever-increasing complexity from **Information Theory** somehow blow up thermodynamics, or negate itself in the face of thermodynamics? How do these conflicting dualities square? And what the fuck is *entropy*?—something I've seen defined as **BOTH** qualities!

An interesting little bit of Quantum Theory is the idea of *entanglement* which one could possibly think of in terms of the **Tao** (yin/yang)—a swirling system made of equal parts "order" and "disorder"—one part *creation*, and one part *destruction*. Quantum Entanglement is the notion that the matter of which the object is comprised, which the subject wishes to view, is the same matter of which the subject is also comprised. Thus, the type of tool used to measure the matter determines the type of answer one receives. Because subject and object are inseparable, using a particle tool yields a particle answer. Asking a wave question (using a wave tool) . . . we all end up on the beach anyway! (Finding our *Self* staring right back at our *Self*.)

(An interesting note here is the idea of the levels of sophistication present in children's thinking. Young children need the certainty of a black & white worldview. Things and situations are either "good" or "bad." Jung believed that our consciousness is formed in this perception and experience of opposites, first noted in the work of Pythagoras. In terms of us, I guess this means that Modernism was the beginning of *Childhood's End*.)

But is truth really invalid, or just a little more difficult to pin down? Cloudy, let's say. And should it be pinned down? Maybe there is something to be gained from an "&" paradigm. The interesting notion of Entanglement though, communicates a flowing, interconnectedness of all things. The famous Einstein—Podolsky—Rosen paper was an attempt by its authors to undermine the uncertainty of Quantum Physics—you know some people don't like the idea of *dogs* playing dice, or maybe it's poker. Anyway, they didn't like the seemingly unpredictability of matter in the new Quantum Theory—that its state was uncertain until you looked, and how that looking influenced its state as well as the state of its partner. (Like the Tao, particles have "partners"—you know, *Atoms* and *Eves*.) The authors of the scientific paper actually ended up achieving the opposite of their aim. They proved the theory by showing the relationship of entangled, but "separate," particles that were somehow in SYNC, communicating faster than the speed of light—***instantaneously***.

Over this past year or so, I've recognized interesting similarities between the basic tenets of both Buddhism and Quantum Physics.

Buddhism experiences the world, reality, and life through its principles of **Emptiness, Impermanence,** and **Interconnectedness**. Matter, now seen through the lens of Quantum Physics, is comprised mostly of nothing, is constantly changing, and has a relationship to everything else. Reality is uncertain and so is matter. The Superposition principle is the part of Quantum Theory that explains this—how a particle could be anywhere at any given time, but that, through repeated observation, one can get a sense of a **Pattern** and of its general state. "I might do this, I might do that, I guess it depends." (It flows and syncs.)

One of the results of modern physics has been modern computing which yielded another tool for understanding The Now via SYNC . . . the weaving of the Internet, or should I say Indrasnet—a place where, with a little awareness, one is able to see the interconnectedness of everything; a literal window to the universe! *Indra's Net* is an Indian cosmological explanation of an interconnected existence. The idea is to explain both our connectedness and our individuality. This was achieved by a metaphor stating that heaven is comprised of jewels hanging in an infinite net, each jewel reflecting every other hung in the net. By venturing out into our own Internet, we see our Self reflected in the many other heavenly jewels we gaze into. We see patterns occurring simultaneously in macrocosms (nation states) and microcosms (individual states of being). At first we thought we were crazy for seeing a pattern, now we think everyone else is for not. . . .

So then, if *SYNC* is basically the waters of life, the air we breathe, the electricity that powers our tech, how does one get 'N Sync? One need not *get* in SYNC, one already is. One merely needs to become more aware of their alignment to **The Now**, what's happening right now (which is the paradox of simultaneous creating and experiencing the dream in which we all share).

But then what is **The Now**? How does one relate, describe, explain, and understand **The Now** if it is a beautiful, flowing, ever-changing scientific dance of something and nothing? Impossible, right? Actually no, but I do think that's for another time, maybe a whole book in fact. . . .

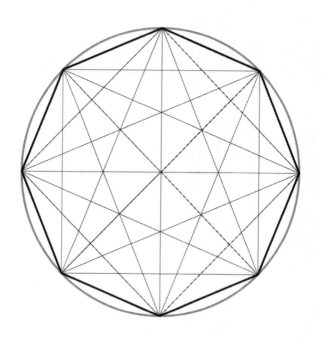

ANDRAS JONES
RADIO8BALL

Andras Jones created The Radio8Ball Show *on KAOS 89.3 FM in Olympia in 1998 and has developed the format for a variety of media (radio, stage, TV & interactive gaming). Jones is a film actor who has played starring roles in cult classics like* Nightmare on Elm Street 4 *and* The Attic Expeditions. *His band, the Previous, toured and recorded extensively in the 1990's. Jones currently makes his home in Olympia, Washington, where he is at work on a book exploring the town's sacred architecture.*

radio8ball.com
myspace.com/radio8ball
facebook.com/radio8ball

THE POP ORACLE

1. Ask a question.
2. Pick a song at random and listen to it.
3. Think about and/or discuss the answer.

Simple, right? It's like calisthenics for the part of our mind which recognizes synchronicity. The more we exercise this part of our mind, the more we are going to have the experience of synchronicity in our daily lives. Where this will lead you, I know not, but it may feel something like Walt Whitman's "Life immense in passion, pulse, and power."

To the outside observer, leading a synchronistic life may appear as a brand of madness or enlightenment or simply as being "lucky" (good and bad luck included). From inside of the experience, I can report that synchronicity does not change the fact of Buddhism's four noble truths, but it does open us up to a much larger playing field in which to experience the joys and sorrows which make human existence, well, human. Synchronicity expands the possibilities while cutting off most of the psychological escape routes. Once we realize that the world as we experience it is singing our reflections back at us all the time, it makes it very hard to blame anyone else for our predicament or, for that matter, to deny our own power (although most of us still try).

The Pop Oracle makes all of this truth palatable by using music as the vehicle. It doesn't even have to be a "good" song. As long as it is randomly chosen you will be able to find your answer in it, and in so doing, reveal the song's genius. Even an innocuous pop song carries a tremendous amount of cultural information which makes it an ideal vessel for divination. The music, with its natural rhythms and melodic organization creates an inherent sense of order. Poetry, even at its most juvenile, also adheres to some basic universal structures. Within these sonic mandalas, the artist's performance fills the frame with the color of their humanity and influences. And then there are all of these seemingly trivial details like the year the song was recorded, or the name of the record label, or the kind of hat the artist's girlfriend wore on the cover. It's all code. Anything that we notice with our synchronistic sense will be relevant to interpreting The Pop Oracle's reflections. Noticing what we notice and why, is one of the more revelatory aspects of integrating this practice.

Self knowledge is at the core of the synchronistic pursuit, which is probably why the most important element of the communication between The Pop Oracle and the listener is whatever psychic mapping we may have already done with the song or the performance or the artist or their influences beforehand. This is amplified when two or more people share similar psychic mapping around the song. Familiarity with the song and its structures will determine our comfort level, and the more comfortable we are, the better able we will be to perceive our "answers." This is why I call it The Pop Oracle; because we are using the comfortable container of pop culture to explore the unknown psychic terrain into which the oracle, any oracle, will necessarily thrust us.

My father, Richard M. Jones, spent his professional life writing about how to improve education by incorporating methods which engage the student's playful and imaginative self in the classroom. His obsession with this was based upon his experience as a clinical psychologist and as a university professor. He found that the learning functions of the brain perform better when we are entertained by what we are doing while learning. The primary method he used to access the playful mind was the dream seminar, in which students would write down their dreams to be read in class. The rest of the class would interpret the dream "as if it were their own dream." This trying on of each other's dreams "as poetry" had a profound effect on his students and fellow educators. It also seems to have had a profound effect on me because, unbeknownst to myself when I created *Radio8Ball*, I was trying to do for pop culture what my father spent his lifetime doing in his classrooms: Create an environment in which our brains can play together and, in so doing, become more conscious of ourselves, each other, and experiential reality as such.

If I had a reason for creating *Radio8Ball*, besides the pure fun of it, it probably had more to do with my frustration with the corporate takeover of the music business than with any sense of filial piety. I recognized in the 1990's that most venues, live and broadcast, favored background music and empty spectacle over music with content. I knew that the music that the best of my peers and I were creating was lost in a media landscape where active listening was discouraged. Active listening, and the art which rewarded it, is what made rock and roll the engine of cultural revolution that it was in the middle part of the 20th century, but by the 1980's the media corporations were figuring out how to reduce expectations and make the same kind of money as the Beatles without incurring the same kind of risks. By the millennium, the hottest market for songwriters was TV soundtracks. No one was listening, at least not in public. Radio, as anything but a pipeline for generic big releases, was practically dead and even the most intimate concerts were marred by the din of chatter from the jaded audiences. The internet was yet to change the whole game and I was already there.

I wanted, with *Radio8Ball*, to inject something into the culture which might trick us all into paying better attention to the music. Within its scope of influence The Pop Oracle has done just that. People don't talk during the songs at a *Radio8Ball* show. We are not silent out of respect for the artist but because we are listening intently for the answer to the question. We are looking for and finding synchronicities because that is what our minds do best and most happily. We find these synchronicities, not just in the songs but in the questions which are asked by the intimate strangers with whom we share the experience.

The personalization of the concerns and questions of others is one of the sweetest natural outgrowths of The Pop Oracle process. For me as a host, tending to the myriad ways the questions of others reflect my own deepest concerns provides some of the most pleasurable moments. Though it was unintentional on my part, *Radio8Ball* doesn't just generate good attention for the artists, but also for each other. This is what I believe my father was after. He knew that the group mind can nurture the individual mind, as long as the environment is conducive. Music. Synchronicity. Good attention. Maybe even a little booze or smoke or a good endorphin inducing jog or orgasm, what have you. All of these ingredients support this conductivity. Not just at a *Radio8Ball* show either. These are the contents of a happy home and a happy head.

The attentive reader may notice that most of the positive aspects of The Pop Oracle were not goals which I consciously intended or pursued. I've pretty much stumbled into everything good associated with The Pop Oracle while simply enjoying myself playing with music and synchronicity. *Radio8Ball* started as a lark, with me and a friend being funny playing CDs on shuffle function on a local community radio station in the wee hours of the morning. Next thing we knew the synchronicities started popping. Then the calls started coming in. The Pop Oracle wanted to be. It screamed out, "I am!" For some reason my buddy didn't get seduced like I did. That was 13 years ago, and what started as something to do "while I was busy making other plans" has become my life's work. Not that I didn't try to jettison it a couple of times, but every time I did, something happened which "pulled me RIGHT back in." I have often imagined myself as a more empowered Seymour to The Pop Oracle's benign "Feed Me" plant, or as one of those vision-mad characters from *Close Encounters* who can't get Devils Tower out of their head. There is no escaping it, and why try? We are all sick with the disease of culture. If we can't purge it then maybe we can find the medicine in it.

When I started *Radio8Ball* in 1998 I felt alone in the pursuit of the synchronistic arts. Out there in the wilderness Terrence McKenna and Robert Anton Wilson were talking a good game but nobody seemed to be doing anything about it. Some people dug *Radio8Ball* but most people thought it was goofy. As late as 2005, KAOS in Olympia, where the show was originally broadcast, gave *Radio8Ball* the dubious honor of naming us the "dorkiest" show on the air. Now, less than a decade later, a compendium like this can feature a wide community of kindred seekers working in a variety of diverse mediums all devoted to exploring synchronicity, regardless of the risks of appearing mad, enlightened or stoned.

Speaking of which, and in closing, I would like to share the craziest idea I have about synchronicity. It is almost entirely unfounded, and yet I would even go so far as to say that I believe this vision to be true. Synchronicity may be an untapped energy source. Not only that. Synchronistic exploration could lead to something which would look very much like time travel to those of us who are still hamstrung by our attachment to the illusion of linear time. I imagine the kids who grow up playing with *Radio8Ball*, watching Jake Kotze's films, and enjoying other forms of synchronistic media unraveling the mysteries of time at an organic level. In so doing, the science geeks and materialists among them may develop the technologies which reflect this understanding, leading to time travel or something very much like it.

I like to imagine that even now the children of these time travelers are sneaking in to *Radio8Ball* shows dressed like late 20th century civilians just to see where it all started. Crazy talk, right? I warned you. Synchronicity is not for the dull or the cowardly. It may lead us to proclaim utterly impossible and embarrassing things. The hope is that a synchronistic practice will also help us to develop discretion, humility and a sense of humor with which to balance our wild hopeful visions. With the awareness that each moment offers a unique and glorious opportunity to perceive what loveable fools we are, we may even recognize foolishness as a brand of wisdom, which is the true lesson of synchronicity, is it not?

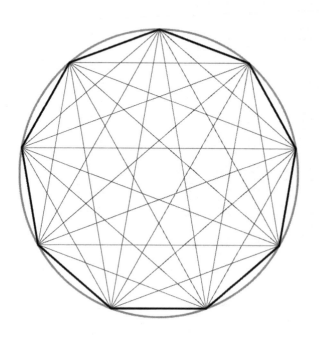

Jim Sanders
SyncWinnipeg

Jim Sanders is a filmmaker, media-arts educator and Ayahuasquero based in Winnipeg, Manitoba, Canada. He is a student of the Peruvian-based Ashanincan healer and Maestro Ayahuasquero, Juan Flores Salazar. Mr. Sanders is presently completing the feature-length documentary Nosis: A Cinematic Vision Quest, *to be released in 2012. In collaboration with Maestro Flores, Sanders is developing an institute for the study of plants and culture to be based in Manitoba.*

Twitter: @SyncWinnipeg
g8ors.blogspot.com

Mayahuasca

"Maestro, what is ascension?" I asked
"It is a strong cup."
Answered Maestro Ayahuasquero Juan Flores Salazar

This essay is inspired by the teachings of the Ashanincan plant healer Maestro Juan Flores who has taught me the art of being an Ayahuasquero. Most of all, much of what I have written is inspired by my own personal work with the plants.

Ayahuasca, which is Quechua for "vine of the soul" is the marriage of two plants, the Ayahuasca vine and the Chacruna leaf, both found in the Amazon basin of South America. Ayahuasca is considered the Father of all plants and Chacruna the Mother. Together they are mixed into a medicinal brew, their combined chemistry generating incredible power and healing potential. When Ayahuasca is prepared well and experienced in the right ceremonial setting it can become a powerful tool to help humans transcend the trappings of duality. When we perceive the world around us as separate it leads to suffering and fears that restrict our freedom and paralyze our spiritual evolution. Ayahuasca can help us see through the illusion of separation that dominates human consciousness on Earth at this time. When experiencing Ayahuasca, we can attain a higher, non-temporal perspective of our lives and those around us. We experience our past, present and future. We get to see ourselves for who we truly are, which can be painful at times—and at times feel like death itself. However, Ayahuasca comforts us with love and helps us accept and forgive the memories and emotions that are holding us down. Ayahuasca teaches humility, compassion, forgiveness and love.

This ancient medicine can help us wake up to the fact that our inner world and outer world are reflections of each other. Ayahuasca teaches us that peace must be attained within before it can materialize in the world around us. This attainment of union consciousness (that transcends the pendulum of duality) is the child born through the union of Father Ayahuasca and Mother Chacruna. They give birth to their Son/Sun in us. At its fullest potential, Ayahuasca helps us shine bright like a star. When we learn to channel the light of pure awareness, to incarnate the spirit of

God, to express the infinite in matter, to tap into the fountain of inner gnosis, to be humble—we then become a human bridge anchoring Heaven on Earth. Any time an individual achieves this state of being while on Earth, it triggers a flood of awareness and love that spills into the hearts and minds of all people. It is this kind of work with Ayahuasca that can become a path to attaining the Garden State on Earth. When humans attain a peace of mind and an open heart, so too does the Earth transform to reflect this collective inner state of being.

Anything is possible in the Garden if it is fueled by love.

Mayahuasca

Maya is the goddess of illusion, the veil of the world of experience and duality. Ayahuasca helps us see Maya for what she is—the face of our Creator. Our fear of Maya and the world we were born into becomes a love for Maya and all her creation. When we love Maya we become one with our Creator. No more are we slaves of the illusion, now we've become the Masters we are all destined to be. The Garden is a reflection of this mastery and love for Maya. With our collective hearts healed and minds at peace, an infinite amount of creative possibilities emerge for what we can do and where we can go as we experience the world of Mayahuasca.

Sync Don't Swim

Observing and attuning to synchronicity, or "sync," is one way of mapping and accelerating the process of gnosis (Inner Knowledge). Seeing synchronicity helps us perceive the world in a meaningful way. By observing sync, everything you experience develops meaning to you. Seeing synchronicity can lead us in many directions. It can lead us towards fear or love and many places in between. Often we forget that this meaning originates in us. We forget that we have the power to perceive the world in the way we choose to. When we consciously choose to see sync from the perspective of love then an interesting thing happens to us—we learn to die while "living." Instead of trying to keep our head above the waters of life, we let ourselves sink/sync into the infinite depths of being. We drown ourselves in our environment. To realize that everything "outside" of us is one with us means we must die to our limited identity of self. Fear dissolves under the power of love and sync. The world around us, that seemed separate and often threatening, now becomes the greatest teacher we could ever have—ourselves.

Sync is a way to love all of Creation. Through sync we may love every moment that unfolds. When we consciously choose love as the source of all existence then we can begin to see everything that happens within us and outside of us as an expression of love. When we see love in everything, the message of love is then transmitted *from everything* for all to see. The path of sync then becomes a vehicle for greater love here on Earth.

Regularly drinking Ayahuasca, together with daily sync/love work can act as a powerful engine for the transformation of consciousness. If one individual or, even better, a group of people do this "personal" work, it can affect us all. Distance between us is an illusion. We all share the same space. There is only one heart and one mind. In the infinite there can only be unity. The more individuals that attain this state of awareness, the easier it is for others to awaken to it as well.

When one drinks from the cup, we all drink from the cup. When one follows sync, we all follow sync. When one feels love, we all feel love.

StarG8ors

Cinema and Pop culture, when studied through the lens of sync, can energize the ascension power of Ayahuasca. In the global high-tech matrix that Earth has become in 2011, Cinema has risen to the status of a global religion. The theatres are the temples where we go en masse to worship the stars. In the cinematic temples around the world we gather to watch the same movies. Mainstream cinema has become a significant focal point for human consciousness. When movies are experienced through the lens of sync and empowered by work with Ayahuasca, the experience acts as a powerful gateway into the whole. Through pop media culture we all plug into each other. If we find synchronistic meaning in the movies we watch, our level of conscious awareness (spirit of God/gnosis/light) will be shared with all those who watch the same movie. We communicate non-locally with each other via movie, TV and computer screens.

The question then becomes, "what message are we communicating?"

If we watch movies with the mind and heart of God, then all those who watch movies will begin to understand the mind and heart of God.

The Plantenna

As we work with Ayahuasca, we can rise into a state of non-dual awareness that begins to pervade all aspects of life and not just in ceremony.

The power to see unity in everything is the awareness of the heart. Awakening to this awareness often inspires people, like myself, to begin to sing. Before I began working with Ayahuasca, singing was what I feared most. Ayahuasca has now made singing my favorite thing to do.

Song is the language of the heart. The power of an Ayahuasquero to heal lies in their ability to sing from the heart. Song can be a bridge between Heaven & Earth and, as it is brought into ceremony, it becomes the most powerful fuel of this ascension process. Songs used in Ayahuasca ceremonies are known as *icaros*, which translates as "songs of gratitude for the plants." We sing to the plants as they are the earthly roots of those souls that have transcended earth in their infinite exploration of the spirit world. We are all destined to become plants as we work towards transcending life on Earth. The *icaros* bring down this divine consciousness into matter, which, if done with the heart and good intentions, lifts us all up. When we ingest Ayahuasca, we become part of a global *plantenna* that receives the energy and gnosis from on high. Everyone, regardless if they drink Ayahuasca or not, feels the benefits of this work.

We build the bridge to Heaven and we flood the Earth with spirit all through song.

With Ayahuasca, song and cinema, we can build a *plantenna* ready to receive the Kingdom of Love on Earth.

Let me share with you some of the *icaros* that I have been graced with over the years, and which are the key elements to any Ayahuasca ceremony.

In rite we write the book with the songs we sing and the words are read in everything.

Peace

JIM SANDERS: SYNCWINNIPEG

Photos by Dustin Leader

Icaros
2008-2011

Light Switch

There is a light switch on top of the mountain

And we're going to turn it on

We climb this mountain fueled by song

We might be right we might be wrong

But our heart's on fire

And we climb higher and higher

Until the day we're gone

Turn on the magic, turn on the love

Become electric and plug into above

Let's keep this light going strong

Come on everybody and join song

Come on everybody and sing along

Eternal Father, Mother Nature

Eternal Father, Mother Nature

King Sun, Queen Moon

Give birth to a Son

Named Peace and coming soon

Jesus Christo

Sumi Runa

Healing plants

Teaching trees

I give thanks through my prayers

I get down on my knees

Ayahuasca, Ayahuasca, please heal me now, give me spirit, heal my soul and make me whole

Ayahuasca, Ayahuasca, please heal my friends, give them spirit, heal their soul, and make us whole

MAYAHUASCA

Eternal Father, Mother Nature

King Sun, Queen Moon

You fill my heart with your love

I rise to the sky, I fly like a dove

Jesus Christo

Sumi Runa

Guiding spirits teaching me

I give thanks through my songs

To the plants that help me see

Ayahuasca, Ayahuasca, please heal me now, give me spirit, heal my soul and make me whole

Ayahuasca, Ayahuasca, please heal my friends, give them spirit, heal their soul, and make us whole

Ayahuasca, Ayahuasca, please heal the world

Give us light so we make it right

Ring the Bell

Ring the bell
It's time to tell
The story of Hell

Why do we come to the land of fear?
Why doesn't God seem anywhere near?

Ring the bell
It's time to tell
The story of why the angels fell

For the love of all, the light had to fall
Into the dark
Oh, I yearn for my precious divine spark

I'm so lonely
I'm so sad
My heart is broken
And I'm raging mad

I run into the night looking for a fight
It's in the night that I find the light
And I realize in that moment
That everything is going to be alright

Follow me, rise with me to the Heavens above
Come on and join the army of the King of Love

Your Heart is your weapon
You got no opposition
Peace is your mission
You return to the Earth flying on a dove

I'm so happy
I'm so glad
My heart is awoken
And I sing with a voice I never knew I had

There's nothing to fear
God is near
Just look in the mirror
You've always been here

Ring the bell
It's time to tell the story of how we rose out of Hell
This is story of why you and I fell
This is the story of how the pearl is made in the shell

And that is why the healing of the world will never be done
Until each and every one of us realize we are one

The Cosmic Tigger

I'm walking through the Hundred Acre Wood
I'm frozen with fear, I'm not feeling very good
I'm stumbling through the Hundred Acre Wood
If I could leave I surely would

I'm lost in the Hundred Acre Wood
I'm singing a song, I'm searching for friends,
I'm making it understood

Winnie-the-Pooh, Winnie-the-Pooh
Where are you Winnie-the-Pooh?

Winnie-the-Pooh, Winnie-the-Pooh
We need you Winnie-the-Pooh.

You're a bear of little brain
And an atomic heart
Some people think you are a little insane
But you're the fool with keys to the Ark

Winnie-the-Pooh, Winnie-the-Pooh
Whatchya gonna do Winnie-the-Pooh?

You can climb a tree in search of Hunny
You can march in a band and sing "Yes we can!"
You can go to the North Pole with Christopher Robin
Eeyore, Owl, Rabbit, Roo, Piglet, have not been forgotten

You're Winnie-the-Pooh, Winnie-the-Pooh
Whatchya gonna do Winnie-the-Pooh?

You can save the day
Start a parade, Sing some praise
Makes some mistakes
And show us the way

Winnie-the-Pooh, Winnie-the-Pooh
He's got no idea what to do
But his heart's so big he always makes it through

Winnie-the-Pooh, Winnie-the-Pooh
Lives in a tree inside of you
Say hello, he'll open the door and pull the trigger
It's time to unleash
The Cosmic Tigger

KA-Boom, boom, boom,
Boom, boom, boom,
Boom, boom, boom, Boom, boom, boom,

With a tummy full of Hunny and a soul that's bright and sunny
Winnie-the-Pooh is here to save the day
Once I was lost, now I've been shown the way
The Hundred Acre Wood ain't so scary now
I've joined the band, I'm singing out loud
"Yes we can!"
I'm singing out loud
"Come join the band!"

Cosmic Tigger

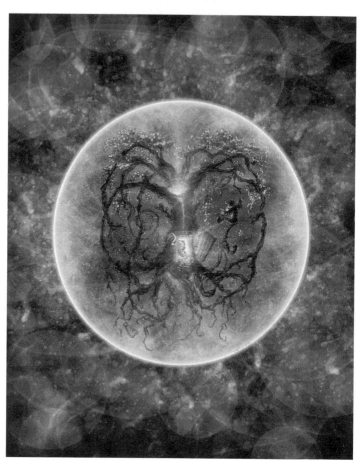

Illustration by Darcy J. Watt

DirtyWett.com

Hey Hermes!

Hey Hermes, where did you get your shoes?
How do you move so fast, where did you learn your moves?

Hey Hermes, run around the World
Like a snake up your spine that rises and twirls

Hey Hermes, show me a thing or two
Like how to find peace and
light the fire of knowledge inside me and you

Hey Hermes, your love spans the Heavens
Your Heart is made of Gold
And you're the only story that's ever been told

Hey Hermes, you played a trick on me
I spent most of my life not knowing of Eternity
I spent most of my life not knowing of our Destiny

Hey Hermes, come join me and my friends
We're ready to learn from you
And for your Spirit to descend

Hey Hermes, I thank you with this song
You've shown us the way
And now victory won't be long
Victory won't be long

White Bear

Since the beginning of time and the very first rhyme

Your song is the dream of eternity

Your song is the love between you and me

White Bear, White Bear, you show the love
through the way you care

White Bear, White Bear, we thank you
for the wisdom you share

And the light shines through your crystal hair,
White Bear, White Bear

Since the beginning of time and the very first sign

Your Mother made the mountain that got you there

High up in the air, White Bear, White Bear

You reach for the sky, you're ready to die

And the stars fall into you

And light up your hair

White Bear, White Bear

There is plenty of joy to share

You just have to care for your Mother and her White Bear

Oso Blanco y Pachamama

Illustration by Darcy J. Watt

DirtyWett.com

Top of the Mountain

It's been a long time

It's been a hard climb

But we're together again on top of the mountain

On top of the mountain where we can see forever

On top of the mountain where we can touch heaven

We're dancing on the stars, howling at the Moon

We're reaching out to Mars and singing Jupiter a tune

We're soaring like a bird, we're traveling with Mercury

We're breathing the living word, we're sailing through infinity

We're sliding down rainbows, we're yearning for Sirius

We're learning what the Lord knows
and we're kissing with Venus

MAYAHUASCA

We're praying for our Father, we're crying with our Mother

We're rising with our sisters and our brothers

We're blooming like a flower

We're dreaming of the Milky Way

Ayahuasca gives us power

We're waking up to a brand new day

We're shining like the Sun, we're feeling like the One

On top of the mountain where we can see forever

On top of the mountain where we can touch heaven

Rejoice in the Kingdom on top of the mountain

Peace in the Kingdom on top of the mountain

Love in the Kingdom on top of the mountain

Children in the Kingdom on top of the mountain

You and I in the Kingdom on top of the mountain

And we're together again my friends

On top of the mountain

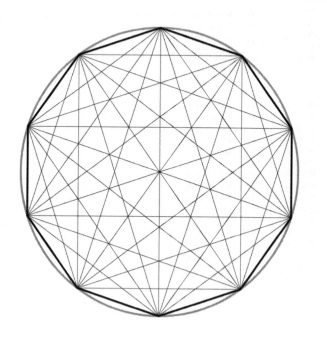

JON KIDD
ACCIDENTAL ALCHEMIST

Jon Kidd was born in Calgary, Alberta and his roots are planted firmly in a working class, small town setting. A father of three, he spends time researching many topics—anything from conspiracy and art to geometry and synchronicity. He was brought into the realm of popular conspiracy by an abstract lifelong fascination with the Giza pyramids, which eventually led him to the work of Steve Willner and Jake Kotze. His first video, Jokerman Saturn Pattern, explored a bombardment of syncs in relation to jokers/hexagons/dogs/money/fire, which, in his mind, held significant meaning. Jon went on to make another video, inspired by Kotze, which highlighted the many 'headshot' deaths Brad Pitt sustained in his movies, tying Pitt to the archetype of Death/Chronos/Saturn. Now Jon spends time developing his self-taught skills in drawing, writing and video editing, hoping to branch out as a professional one day. He currently resides in Drumheller, Alberta.

For this collection, Jon wanted to share a powerful personal experience he documented back in 2008 which he said, "represents my initiation/intention into this realm of thought, this sync. My newer exploits into sync are really layered and not fully formed enough for me to lay it down on paper. That is why I work with the videos more often."

jfdk1982.blogspot.com
theaccidentalalchemist.blogspot.com

Robin Hood and Little Jon

I did nothing today at work except sit in a truck, read, and bullshit with fellow slackers. This enabled great amounts of thought. I gotta say, my trade resonates my persona. Welding resonates the **Great Work** as it is the mastery of manipulating metals. I'm working in Fort McMurray Alberta, Canada. Away from home for 10 days at a time and then I get 4 days off. It's called a *10 and 4* shift. Anyhow . . . I'm sure upon arrival to this town, most minds would see it resonates very much with the 'Nature of the Beast' theme. Most of you sensitive synkkers would also notice that this town is a strong, concentrated cluster of synchronicity that relate to things discussed at *The Blob*. This place is far from my physical home. Home for me being Three Hills, Alberta, which has a town logo resonating the Giza pyramids. This will have to be a story of its own . . . very interesting town consisting of a couple thousand . . . AAAAANYWAYS Alchemist get to the arrow, I mean point!!!!!

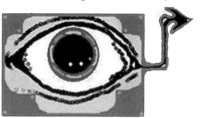

In medieval times Knights, Wizards, and Journeymen had an apprentice. I'm an apprentice—a sluggish, but ambitious one, for the record. This day gave me an opportunity to discuss some very interesting 'thatness' with my Journeyman Welding Wizard, but for now. . . .

A QUIK HISTORY: I started working with this man a couple years ago and by a series of 'coincidences' ended up being trained by him as an apprentice welder. Funny thing, before I had even a glimpse of this synchromystic art form, I had a habit of connecting people I know and work with to cartoon characters and movie stars from my nostalgic past. For example, this welder resonated

ROBIN HOOD AND LITTLE JON

Robin Hood to me because he wore a green hoodie, wore a Robin Hood resembling welding hat, and lived in . . . hahaha . . . Sherwood Park, Alberta! I guess I should mention, cast ye stone, at the time I smoked weed regularly. Fast forward. Today, while writing this, I realize that I fucking resonate Little John! Ahem . . . excuse the profanity . . . Well I've been called 'Little Jon' by a number of clever folks in the past.

But with these new, slightly open eyes, I see some fair facts to argue this point (arrow) . . . And for the first time I'll be looking into the repetitious nickname. . . . I do resonate with this fractal archetype of John Little.

- My name of course being **Jon F.D. Kidd**
- I weigh 360 pounds (163.293253 kilograms)
- I'm 6'3" tall (3 sixes—spooky)
- My friends tell me I am a big kid and a friendly giant (teddy bear)
- Being an apprentice under Robin Hood ties this all together . . . in my mind

I Google "bear constellation" . . . and . . . climb another rung on this special proverbial ladder to find Ursa Minor within my sights! I ask the (arc)hive Wikipedia Queenbee, "who is Ursa Minor?"

*Ursa Minor is a constellation in the northern sky, the name of which means **Little Bear** in Latin.*

A further retracting of the looking glass zooms me in further to examine this dynamic web . . . leaving me . . . well, quite thirsty actually. I'll take a drink from the 'little dipper' and find that this constellation contains a important star (all stars having importance eye know). This Bear cup constellation consists of se7en stars. The brightest star here is our familiar circle cutter, Polaris! At this point I find it necessary to add an image I have been thinking about for a couple days. So I projected it to pixels while writing this. . . .

Polaris connects to the goat through this little tidbit of info from Wiki and a little synchromystic alchemy. . . . To the Bedouin people of the Negev and Sinai, Polaris is known as al-jadiyy, "the billy goat." Time to use the 'Ferrismoon' technique in which he makes 'NY' into 'OZ.' We take the **yy** at the end of al-jadi**yy** and shift it over one to make **ZZ**. Then we take the **'al'** at the beginning of **al**-jadiyy and make it **all** meaning **Pan** of course. YY = ZZ = 2 × a(l) = a(ll). Stretching it a bit I know. But in alchemy you can't make something out of nothing! So I'll add a splash of color to the equation. al-**JAD**iyy JAD = JADE = Green = OZ. To further this Goat/Pan/Oz/ZZ theme we close it with a circle that is created by Polaris. The precession of the equinoxes over tens of thousands of years causes the Earth's axis of rotation to become perturbed and Polaris points to other regions of the sky, tracing out a circle. We'll leave that there for now and let it distill into something more pure. . . .

So could it be agreed I'm a Little John/Jon resonator? Then the Welder I work with is Robin Hood. Well let's just say for now I'm acting out this story of Robin Hood in some strange, sorry to say, bizzaro **evil** scenario. EVIL being LIVE spelled backwards. GASSP! Whatever do you mean, Alchemist?! Well, I work in the oil patch, or the energy sector if you wanna be nice about it. The force that is quite literally sucking the mako energy from the planet. Up here in the NORTHERN heart of Alberta I work in the tar sands, which is basically a gaping earth wound. A mix of . . . you guessed it . . . TAR and SAND. Which connects to previous DNA themed posts. Tarsands = STARS DNA, STARS AND, RATS DNA, etc.? TARSAND is processed and turned into many hydrocarbon products. *Rob the Rich planet's heart to feed the poor roops?* In a way we Rob the Earth of its dead organic matter (DNA) and turn it into a copy of *Arrested Development: Season 2* or maybe that spoon you're using to stir your coffee.

This 'right now' is where I stop writing for the night. Its appx. 2:00 a.m. I lay in bed going through the day I finished and the day that lay ahead. At this Point a post from *The Blob* comes to mind, and I ask myself some 'quest'iOZs. . . .

Can we take a symbol and manipulate it with our thoughts?

I continue to ask, "Will I ever achieve such a deliberate influence?" . . . "I'm gonna pay attention to this Robin Hood theme tomorrow. Let's find something at work, Jon. A color, a name, anything subtle. I could put it in the post and . . ." I drift to sleep finally.

The next day I get up for work. At 5:30 a.m.! Amazingly I feel quite well. I get to work and for some reason feel sociable. I turn into professor beer without the aid of alcohol! I'm chatting to people. Giving advice. Telling stories. Feeling pretty fucking confident! I'm not usually like this. . . . I feel full of Joy. Early in the morning the work crews meet in the job shack for our 'tool box' meeting. After we hear the game plan for the day someone usually sparks up a conversation piece. Usually this is done to stall the inevitable truth that awaits us out on the cold snowy job site. The topic of the day is workplace injury. At this point our crew is consisting of a few people telling their own little stories of injury. Finally, the welder I mentioned earlier tells *his* injury story. He tells us . . .

"This one time in high school, while in gym class, while practicing **arc'hery** . . ." My face flushes pale white as he looks over to me and acts out a scenario where a dude draws his bow and arrow and proceeds to release this arrow that, in turn, rips right through his hand! . . . He goes on to say. . . .

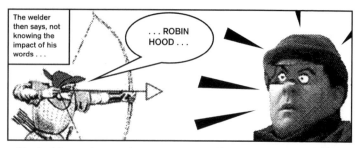

Yeah this guy in our class was acting all cool like he was ROBIN HOOD and proceeded to shoot himself right in the fucking hand!

Roaring laughter follows and I sit silent as time slows down to a crawl. . . . I'm looking at this Journeyman, who I earlier connected to Robin Hood, watching him 'Air Archer' (mime) . . . and say the words ROBIN HOOD.

As my face drains of blood I feel a slight touch of vertigo move through my whole body. This fully formed Welding ROBIN HOOD notices my quickening condition and with his eyes he says, "what, did you see a ghost?" A ghOZt indeed. I'm speechless at this point. I can't even laugh at the funny violent punch line end to his story. Not even a courtesy laugh . . . nothing . . . Which is rare for this yappy Alchemist . . . Maybe I spent too much time trying to turn lead (PB) into gold (AU).

I leave the room and then head back to the truck to think about this. . . .

Can we manipulate the symbols around us with our minds?

I try to remember the last time Robin Hood was even discussed by me or anyone else I know. Nothing in the past 2-3 years comes to mind. This leaves me in a bizzaro state of déjà vu.

I found many other Robin Hood syncs that relate to the post. But if you want to . . . go find them. Seven comes up a lot. So do other stars in relation to Polaris. One more thing about "Welding Robin Hood"—his trusty steed, would indeed, be a snowmobile (a constant conversation piece with this guy). Not too many companies manufacturing snowmobiles these days. **Polaris** is one of the last ones. . . .

Weeeeeiiiiirddddd!

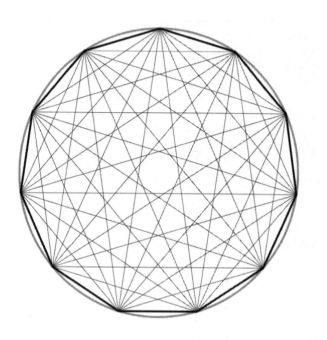

JENNIFER PALMER
REALITY SANDWICH

Jennifer Palmer is a producer of Reality Sandwich, Evolver *and* Evolver Intensives—*a family of sites dedicated to activating transformational communities, both on and offline. She is also a writer, DJ, and philosopher who goes by the name TRUE out on the internets. Her piece about interdependence, telepathy and Twitter was featured in the anthology,* Toward 2012: Perspectives on the Next Age. *Her blog,* BrandTrueBoy.com, *started as an art experiment in 2002, in which she posted as three fictitious characters that she passed off as "real" people who emailed, commented and chatted with other bloggers. Her current projects include working to build the (r)evolution; writing a book about online telepathy, social media and spirituality; honing her Twitter battle rhyme skills and being blissfully entangled in beautiful webs of synchronicity and magic.*

realitysandwich.com
evolver.net
brandtrueboy.com

THE FEELING OF SYNC

A Synchromystic lives in constant awareness while being awash in pop culture—always open to uncanny connections between the divine and the everyday. The sync is simultaneously discovered and created; it only exists because someone is there to experience it. It happens when a scene comes on the TV as you enter the room depicting the exact circumstances of a secret you harbor from everyone present, or when you run into your best friend from childhood in a non-descript town hundreds of miles from where you grew up. The more unlikely and tangential the connection—you pulled off the highway into the town's lone strip mall with engine trouble just as your friend was walking out of the 7-Eleven—the more bliss that's likely to be felt. (It goes up another notch on the *Twilight Zone* scale when you realize you've been seeing 7's and 11's for the duration of the trip.) Sync tells us: nothing is random, even the most insignificant seeming action fits into a universal plan.

By posting detailed accounts of their syncs online (via the Blue Bird of Twitter, which operates at nervous system speed according to the magical flux and flow of the synchronic order), Synchromystics create a feedback loop in which the awareness of sync can increase exponentially. I read a tweet about someone else's sync and am astounded to realize that I've had the same one. I tweet about this and it gets retweeted. Someone in a parallel stream reads the RT and has his mind blown before tweeting his own version of the sync . . . and so it goes . . . on and on like this, all around the world, hijacking frequencies and channels with blog posts and video added along the way. We realize that each one of our stories is a part of a larger, organic whole. The purpose of this text is not to broadcast and amplify more sync content, but to focus instead on the feeling of sync that is a result of it—a truly awesome, ecstatic experience—a mix of zooming in and zooming

THE FEELING OF SYNC

out that goes beyond the range of normal expression, like listening deeply to music, or falling in love. Synchromysticism, as taught by Jake Kotze and Jim Sanders, emphasizes the essential Oneness of all things—the joy of revealing connection in all its forms. You learn (not by reading in a book, but by the day to day of doing and feeling) that your consciousness is just as real as the trees and dirt. Through sync, I've been reintroduced to parts of my femininity that had been covered up due to fear or ignorance. It's a healing modality sprung out from the intersection of pop culture and spirituality—a cyber-shamanic cornerstone for a new mythology of Being that's building itself.

I was overjoyed and relieved when I found blogs devoted to synchronicity in early 2008, reveling that there were people out there who had noticed the same patterns in pop culture involving occult symbols. I noticed that the bloggers were all men but I didn't care—I was just happy they existed, as it meant that at least I wasn't alone in my craziness. Given their collective subversive nature and the prominent use of code names and celebrity headshots for avatars, it's possible that more than a few of them were women anyway. Whoever they were/are, they painted a picture that (quite brilliantly, in many cases) revealed the possibility that the secret order unveiled by sync was created and maintained by the Freemasons and/or the Illuminati. Sync was evidence of the Matrix: a system of control that may also have alien origins—either as willing co-creators with the reptilian blue blood elites or because of their technology being stolen by the American government. The narratives differ on the point of origin, but they all share the idea—seemingly random events meant something in a grand scheme of mind control. According to some, the only way out was through revolution—others felt this would be impossible—our enemy was everywhere, and watching everything we did at all times.

I felt like these secret sync comrades were all getting closer to something, but were unable or unwilling to see the forest for the trees. To be fair, it was a forest of red herrings—each one branching out with more plots than a Hitchcock film. These were the pioneers—discovering a new way of thinking and talking about life's myriad design. Their work was energetic and inspired, but they used their findings to build labyrinths spiraling infinitely inward. An anarchist destruction vibe permeated some of the sites—the layouts and language were punk-tinged and aggressive. A part of me felt very at home with all of this, but in a way which no longer felt authentic, like walking past a building where you used to live. I'd gone down some of my own conspiratorial rabbit holes, but had the hunch that there was something more to all of this—that the sync trail was leading us to answers other than who killed Kennedy. I remained invisible to the community until I discovered Jake Kotze and his blog, *The Blob*. Jake was my portal *in* because he emphasized the bliss of experiencing sync—and not only the possible conspiracy that it seemed to unveil. This would be a position he would continue to gravitate towards in his writing over the next years: it wasn't that he ceased to understand certain events, such as 9/11 as Masonic "mega-rituals," it was that he moved the emphasis from the occult elements and questions of agency to its status as a mythical event staged by and for the collective unconscious:

In my mind . . . 9/11 synchronicities dwarfed the possibility of conscious human orchestration leading to the letting go of paranoia and conspiracy as key dynamic that governs world affairs. The new ruler of the Earth had to be something bigger than any human or material agency and had to involve my own consciousness directly.
My attraction to spiritual matters moved into the affair and a new understanding of the 'non-local Self orchestrating organism of Being' awakened in ME/WE.
—Jake Kotze

This realization of Jake's really resonated for me. I'd had a personal set of syncs with 9/11, way before I would have ever referred to them as such . . . way before I started to pray again in earnest. I was an artist living in Greenpoint Brooklyn and working at my day job in midtown as a receptionist. I became obsessed with the Twin Towers during the year before the disaster. They rose over McCarren Park, larger than life . . . it felt like they were calling to me. They were in my dreams—when I wrote scenes that took place in the city I always worked them into the description. Sometimes when I was walking with someone I'd suddenly be filled with an overwhelming urge to point them out. "They mean something," were the cryptic words I used on many occasions.

THE FEELING OF SYNC

On 9/11 I ended up walking all the way downtown to the Williamsburg Bridge, passing zombies covered in white plaster dust along the way. A lurid calm had descended upon me. For many blocks my chief concern was buying a cold bottle of Gatorade. Some stores were closed . . . some were open, but no one was behind the counter. I don't remember exactly when the thought first came up, but somewhere between when I made it across the crowded bridge into Brooklyn and seeing the TV footage of the planes for the first time, it occurred to me that my obsession with the Twin Towers may have been some kind of message—a warning, a precognition like in *Minority Report*, a feeling in the wind. There had never been information specific enough to act upon, at least not any that made its way to my conscious mind. There had definitely been something persistent about the way the Towers kept edging themselves into my thoughts. When they were gone, I found myself missing them.

I remember the look on my ex's face when, several months later, I showed her notebooks filled with sketches and poems of the Towers that were dated pre-9/11. A recurring theme was that of bodies falling down a river with flames high above them. She nodded and changed the subject with an abruptness I'd only seen before on TV, when one character reacts to another character going crazy. It occurred to me that maybe it would be better if I didn't tell anyone else about the coincidental nature of my obsession.

I didn't really know what I was asking a potential listener to understand—that I somehow had foreknowledge of 9/11? Had something deep inside been employing me to create art and writing that would eventually get out a meaning that was too terrible for me to remember?

I considered the possibility that this was an initiation of some sort. I'd been called to a task . . . but to do what . . . and by whom was I being called? I went around with a vague feeling of being doomed before I realized it was because, although I hadn't found them yet, I somehow knew with a strange certainty that the answers to my questions existed outside of the secular materialism sensibilities I supposedly espoused. My atheist outer shell was beginning to crumble. It would take a few more years, but from

9/11 on the prodigal daughter was looking HOME. The reason for this—I would realize years later—was that despite the continued destruction of life and the awful wars and the repressive Bush Crime Family shakedown that followed, there was an undeniable sensation on that day of an opening up, not a closing down. I felt a hand steering me—not necessarily to safety, but to a higher vantage point, where I'd have a front row seat to the intergalactic shift.

It was from these heights that I learned a way of seeing and interacting with 9/11 through the everlasting NOW of sync. It has helped me to heal—not only from my guilt from that day, but from my distrust and even hatred of my penchant for prophecy. Jake's description of a "non-local Self orchestrating organism of Being" resonated with a new feeling of connectedness I had with the world around me. As wild as it sounded, it felt like I'd discovered a way in which to "see" the invisible—it was like revealing a half covered circle by imagining its missing piece. . . . It's no longer that the sun shines on me, it's that I express its light and warmth. I'm a poetic extension of the sun—like a ray of light shining through dust particles or a puddle of water that slowly vanishes over the course of a leisurely lunch. For many years I'd been the lurker, the plainly dressed person at the end of the real or virtual social table who quietly judges the reaction of others whenever she dares to look their way. A person is shy because they observe others so closely, they assume everyone is doing this to them. What Jake's conceptual framework allowed me to do was disseminate that guilty self, so I stood out less to myself. I went from a lonely little collection of experiences to being an entire network. The sense of standing outside of everything that *happens* is also a part of that whole. The I/Eye was a media creation—a broadcast from me to me. Psychic pixels blasted across the panoramic flat-screen in my head. Learning that this was how it worked liberated me to do what I did best: fake it so real with strange writings and experiments carried out simultaneously across the Internet online and the *innernets* in our minds.

Just finding Jake was a sync in its self—I'd been looking for others who examined the use of symbols in popular culture, and not only did I find someone who could do this in a virtuosic, mash-up style, but he also shared what I called the "and/or" theory of

9/11. Even if the conspiracy theorists were correct about some, even all, of what they proposed, it didn't change the fact that this event had also been an opening. I shared Jake's sense that the mega ritual had been staged by forces beyond those of a consciously laid scheme. This was the work of our dreams and hidden connections, speaking out to us against the bright blue of the sky.

I studied Jake's blog posts the way I used to study philosophy texts: 45 minute bursts with no music, good lighting and a notebook out. I caught up on his cosmology, which was a mix of RAW, Jordan Maxwell, Richard C. Hoagland and Jay Weidner, Jung, quantum physics, Masonic architecture, symbol literacy, and the pantheon of Hollywood stars, who are unconscious resonators associated with certain patterns and archetypical or esoteric symbols. His ideas about oneness were amplified by his friendship and creative partnership with the filmmaker and *ayahuascero* Jim Sanders in Winnipeg, Canada, Sync Capital of the World. Joining forces with Jim created the innermost ring of the Synchromystic order. Radiating out from their Sync Walks and time spent watching and making movies was a new form of art and a new way of being that experienced the divine as being just as present in a movie theater as in a temple or church. Along with others they formed the *Sync Whole*—members of a group blog that record the syncs experienced in current movies and television.

It wasn't about reading the future but reading the present in a new, fuller way—using sync and social media to understand the messages being sent back and forth between the conscious and unconscious collective mind. We were learning how to feel our way from the linear universe to a holographic one—a revolution on par with Copernicus and Einstein. Synchromystics chart patterns in pop culture—no matter how serious or silly. Judgment based metaphysical distinctions such as this (as well as *good and bad* and *right and wrong*) are observed and put off to the side. Sync awareness teaches that it's often the so-called bad movies that contain the wildest syncs. The act of watching a movie whose lame plot can't fully hold your attention allows for other things to jump out at you—you're already standing outside of the experience of watching.

This past winter (exactly at the solstice) a series of happy accidents and graceful gifts sent me to Winnipeg to meet Jake and Jim in real life and give a talk before a screening of *2012: Time for Change*. It came together suddenly, and with the kind of ease that sometimes shows up when you least expect it. There was the sense that I was planting seeds for a near-future harvest. The two guys showed me the sacred spots of the Peg, and (in one of the highlights) we went to the movies to see *Black Swan*. (As I just wrote that, I was compelled to check Twitter where the first tweet on my timeline was someone's Twitpic and the word "Swan.")

Although the chance to see a movie with the O.G. Synchromystics who had inspired so much of my thinking and personal transformation was already like being in a dream—the fact that Twitter was such a part of the experience made it even more powerfully uncanny. While I expected the occasional on-the-go tweet, Jake and Jim were especially tuned in . . . it was amazing to watch them weave in between clothing displays as we walked through a Canadian department store. They were constantly checking Twitter on their phones—reading tweets out loud and then silently typing some out when we stopped somewhere. The intensity of this had increased when we embarked for the mall in Jim's car. Unlike the United States of phone screen slaves, they seemed to be fully aware of their surroundings—making syncs with things they read and things around us. That was the trick—to do both at the same time. (Go all the way in and still be all the way out). We're all connected by a psychic subtext, I thought, looking around at the symbols in the store names and on the T-shirts of the people who walked past. It was at the food court that I started experiencing the amplification of these forces and the familiar feeling of sync at a heightened level. Like the first time in your clubbing career when the DJ reads your mind and drops your personal lonely loser anthem into the set—I felt at once integral and important, and completely disposable. I felt giddy, yet strangely at peace, surfing the white noise din of hundreds of conversations happening at once. In addition to it being solstice, a full moon and an eclipse, I was still negotiating the power of the Sync Capital super signal. My body had been turned into a tuning fork—from before I even took off. By the time we landed in Manitoba I was dialed into the satellite of love. I carried a special two-way to Super Me/We—

that version of humanity that's waiting for us to bravely step across the deep chasm in front of us. I felt heart palpitations and focused on my breath, the way I do before I have to speak in front of people.

Somewhere between the wraps place and the island of seats and chairs we stood around to eat, I crossed over into an admin role. I was now helping conduct the frequency. Although we never spoke about it, the three of us became a mobile army unit, carrying different pieces of psychic radio equipment in order to broadcast LOVE. Our signals merged like crossed beams in *Ghostbusters* and blew up into a zillion pieces of buckshot bandwidth. We were in sync like *Voltron*—each a part of a whole that consisted of everyone else who lived or had ever lived—all of us together, all at once.

The years of bad dreams and things that I couldn't tell anyone about were over . . . the premonitions and emotions—my fear as a little girl that I was cursed when I realized that not everyone felt the Earth and stars speaking to them with such intensity that it kept them up at night. I flashed through the years of doing battle against the tug of the tides in my moods—augmenting them with sugar and other self-medication. Suddenly it was the easiest thing in the world to embrace it all and let it go. I felt joy buzzing off the beat of the heart of the-heart-of-the-continent as I carried the popcorn back to my seat, just as the previews were ending and the movie was about to start.

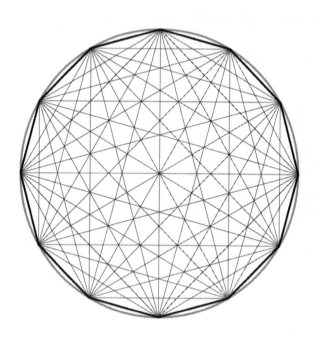

CHRISTOPHER "C" MYERS
MERCURY'S MESSENGER

Christopher Hunter Myers is known in different circles as Mercury's Messenger, The Quark Observer, M Trismegistus and/or C. Goddess worshipper, a practicing chaos magician and, on occasion, the human host to the gods. He enjoys the pursuit of knowledge, and spends most of his free time learning about the multiverse that surrounds (and sometimes revolves around) him, everything from contacting the spirits of the dead to quantum physics. He is a part-time actor currently on hiatus to raise his two sons. He resides in his hometown of Baltimore, Maryland.

synchronize23.blogspot.com
mycosmicstardust.blogspot.com
mtrismegistos.blogspot.com
facebook.com/christophermyers23

THE MAGICK OF SYNCHRONICITY

Synchronicity for me goes way beyond Carl Jung's definition of synchronicity: the experience of two or more events that are apparently causally unrelated or unlikely to occur together by chance and are observed to occur together in a meaningful manner. I will start with the first profound experience I had with synchronicity. Back in 1996, I was 18 and high as a kite reading the Bible in my bedroom. The Steve Miller Band song "Fly Like an Eagle" came on the radio just as I was reading a passage about an eagle. Stuff like this happened to me a lot as a kid, but this time synchronicity was a little more punctual, as my mom came in the room with a letter that had come in the mail from a "Brother" at the church I attended. I opened it up and there was an eagle flying on the front of the card.

In 1999, I got my foot into Hollywood's door as an extra and then as a double for a main character (Pam) on a John Waters movie here in Baltimore. I had just recently lost all my friends and almost lost my father who had to have a seven time bypass surgery to fix his heart. With a ton of depressing downtime I delved into lots of fact-based books about "why?" One in particular was a kids' picture book and it explained questions like "Why is the sky blue?" . . . "Where do rainbows come from?" . . . "Where do stars get their colors?" You get the point. That had me already making what some would call Synchromystic connections with the concept of *"as above, so below; as within, so without,"* even though at the time I had no words to explain what I was experiencing.

There was a point where I had hypothesized on my own that we, and everything around us, are made of stardust. Little did I know this was already a known fact among scientists at the time. In my defense, the information highway wasn't what it is today. In a very "classic" Synchromystic way, I remember putting together that line from John Lennon's "Instant Karma" . . . *"We all shine on, like the moon, and the stars, and the sun,"* with a simple thought of us all being stars in essence, especially the "stars" on TV. This was long before my personal discovery of Aleister Crowley's quote

"Every Man and Woman is a Star." Right after I had processed my Synchromystic hypothesis in 1998 about the "stars" on TV being related to the "stars" in the sky, I caught a documentary on the "Big Bang" and it went on to say that a percentage of the static on your television is caused by radiation left over from the Big Bang. Years later, I would learn to combine all of this information with the fact that spiritualist William Crookes had invented the Crookes tube after scrying in a black mirror as a way to communicate with spirits. Now besides the Crookes tube leading to the discovery of electrons and later X-rays, it was used to invent the original standard TV. Spiritualist John Logie Baird (born 1888), who invented the television itself, had said in his own book that he was in contact with the spirit of Thomas Edison.

Now back to my foot getting into "Hollywood's door." I was on the set with many "stars"—Melanie Griffith, Stephen Dorff, Alicia Witt, and Maggie Gyllenhaal. At the time, I think I may have been preaching a good bit about my newly acquired knowledge of the stars in the sky. There was something to this day that I can't really put my finger on, about talking about stars in the sky and how they work with people on a movie set full of "stars." There were connections to that movie that have had a profound effect on my life; I explain most of these in my blogs. There was a scene where I was doubling as the character "Pam" and Alicia Witt was next to me with a torch (*à la* Lady Liberty, Isis, and the torch of illumination). I didn't think much of it at the time, but in retrospect, when I connect the dots, I assume there is something that has had a hold of me since birth and synchronicities are the only way I can make sense of any of it. *Donnie Darko* and *The Dark Knight* star Maggie Gyllenhaal is a Satanist in the movie. She has the filmmaker Kenneth Anger's name tattooed on her chest. Anger is a self-proclaimed Thelemite and was close friends with Church of Satan founder Anton LaVey. The connection between some of these main figures in the occult pop-up in synchronistic ways with me frequently, as you will see. Some Synchromystics pick a "star" as a "resonator" for their absolute point of all of their movie synchronicities. I am my own resonating "star." Let's leave it at that and move on.

This is me with my 23necklace circa 1996. I was obsessed with Michael Jordan (#23) and the Chicago Bulls.

Ever hear of Robert Anton Wilson and "The 23 enigma?" (My blog address is *synchronize23*.) The 23 enigma refers to the belief that many incidents and events are directly connected to the number 23. I'll start with when I first started to phonetically sync my nickname "C" with "sea" and "see." I got the nickname in 1995 from a friend after we watched the movie *A Bronx Tale*. Well I got two nicknames from that: "C" and "Zero." "C" stuck so much that I even changed my middle name from "Hunter" to Christopher "C" Myers on my S.A.G. (Screen Actors Guild) card.

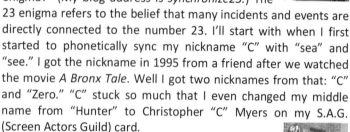

In 2002 I did some work with the actor Domenick Lombardozzi who played "Zero" in *A Bronx Tale*. This is him behind me in the hat with #23 on it.

You can imagine my surprise when I discovered synchromysticism on the internet in 2008 and went to the blog *The Blob* and saw the stuff about C/Sea/See. Another one I was connecting phonetically since 1999 that *The Blob* included was the "I" and "Eye" connection. This is stuff I never spoke about openly to anyone except my wife and ex-girlfriend at the time. Who knows who opened the door to synchromysticism; I am just glad I am not alone, even if my brand of synchromysticism is different. Mine seems to be more personal, also mixed with magick and communication with spirits.

I guess the first numbers (besides 23) I got into were triple digit numbers. 111, 222, 333, and so on. My birthday is 7778, and not until I discovered Aleister Crowley did I ever think much of the 777 part of my birth date.

I got into the occult ("knowledge of the hidden") through my research on conspiracy theories. The general research for me into conspiracies started in 2002, but not until a few years ago did I take it as far as getting myself personally into the occult. You can learn more about my views on all of that through my blog since I want to stick to synchronicity here, though it does all tie together.

THE MAGICK OF SYNCHRONICITY

In the movie *Space Jam* where Michael Jordan (#23) gets trapped in the cartoon universe, my birthday is the final score when the "TuneSquad" and Michael Jordan beat the Monstars (77 to 78 aka 7778). I can't share some of these images due to copyrights or else I would. Visit my blog for screen shots etc. . . .

At some point I remember embracing the whole 777 Aleister Crowley thing. I was watching a documentary on the Great Beast (666) and a guy named something "Hunter" came on and mentioned Crowley had passed away at the age 72. Well long story short, I asked Aleister Crowley's spirit if he could go by 72 (the age he died) and I could have 666 for myself. I hoped that some way through synchronicity he could confirm this for me. The next day my friend that works for NASA posted a video with this plane in it.

666-72. I believe that this was my synchronistic sign from Aleister Crowley's spirit giving me the green-light.

Then, in late 2010, while I was telling my girlfriend about how meaningful that number 66672 had become to me, not more than 5 minutes later we saw this bus.

The Crowley 72 sync was so profound that I use the age that people pass from this world onto the next to communicate with their spirits. I found out that my grandfather (who shared my middle name, his first name) "Hunter" had also passed at age 72 . . . more synchronistic confirmation for me.

I recently got my four main sync numbers tattooed on my arm: 23, 42, 37 & 72. Along with "I Bring the Light," which translates into Lucifer. Plus an Aleister Crowley quote below "Do What Thou Wilt..." The pentagram represents the path of the planet Venus in an 8 year period.

Both my uncles passed at age 42. And the 37 is the number I received by the spirit of Anton LaVey instantly when I asked for it. I explain this experience in detail on my blog. I later found out that it was also the age at which the occultist (O.T.O. member and friend of Crowley) and NASA rocket scientist Jack Parsons passed. You see how this plane makes even more sense now?

In 2009, I watched a documentary about occultist, ceremonial magician and comic book writer Alan Moore where he explained how he had declared himself a magician on his 40th birthday. Now, I had been sending things out for years into the ether of the atmosphere with a noticeable butterfly effect of sorts. I have been doing something I would call for lack of better terms "Personal Quantum Experiments" since about 2000. Once I discovered Quantum Physics and learned about Quantum Superstition, I realized that even a small conversation and exchange of information  between a random acquaintance and me would send vibrations of my being, opinions and will. Perhaps much more so if it was a celebrity, such as Martin Sheen. In 2003 I talked NWO, Gandhi and JFK with him. I even gave him a pin (button) of George Bush with a Hitler mustache.

After I read more about Magick, it seemed that I had been doing it anyways, under the guise of Quantum Physics. Once I realized I was a Magician to start with, and after seeing what Alan Moore had done, I proclaimed myself as a Magician.

MAGICK is the Science and Art
of causing Change to occur in conformity with Will.
—Aleister Crowley

My own brand of Magick is mainly chaos magic. This basically boils down to: as long as the method works, I will use it. The main thing with my brand of Magick is that the results/product is/are synchronicities. I always know when a method is working, as it will show up in profound synchronicities.

THE MAGICK OF SYNCHRONICITY

Now it wasn't until I read the essay "Pop Magic!" by another occultist, magician and comic book writer Grant Morrison that things got very profound. I created a magical sigil like Grant said to.

This is what I came up with. It was a tad different, as I interchange the word sometimes. I didn't even intend for it to look like a witch stirring a caldron. That was happenstance.

This is my second sigil, which I call "sync bombs." I believe you can make one or two and continue to charge them with whatever intent you need at any given time, instead of making a new one every time you have a new intent. My preferred method is masturbation/ejaculation (read more in Grant Morrison's "Pop Magic!").

Now after I launched that first one, I went outside to see if I could see something in the sky. Hopefully a comet or something odd. I waited about 10 minutes staring as widely as I could into the night's sky. Nothing happened so I went to go inside the house, took a turn back for one more look, saying my sigil's meaning in my head. Right then, a comet burned through the sky, starting as I began my sigil's meaning and ending exactly when I was done reciting it. As if that wasn't crazy enough, I went inside to grab a bowl of ice cream and watch some TV, being satisfied with my results. I turned on my kids' TV and sat to eat my ice cream. As the TV clicked on it was what looked like stardust in outer space, kind of odd and digital. It started to spell out my last name MYERS; you can imagine my shock at this point. I looked for some rational explanation. First I clicked info and found out it was the animated science fiction film *Titan A.E.* (Later I found out that one of Crowley's nicknames was "Titan." Some say NASA even named a rocket after Aleister Crowley.) I searched the credits on IMDB in hopes to find an explanation, like maybe someone in the animation department with the same last name as me or something similar . . . and nothing. I would share images here if not for the copyrights. So be sure to check my blog for that screen cap.

As if that weren't enough to take in, I was drinking coffee like crazy, as per Grant Morrison's suggestion in "Pop Magic!" to contact Hermes, Mercury, Thoth or even The Flash: "Call fervently upon Hermes. Luxuriate in his attributes. Drink coffee . . . Fill your head with speedy images of jet planes, jet cars, and bullet trains. Surround yourself with *Flash* comics and call down Hermes." The result was I was reading a book a day or two later called *Alchemy & Mysticism*. Lots of pictures, the kind of shit I dig. When on page 13, I came across a picture of Hermes-Mercury that looked almost 100% like me.

This is from Achille Bocchi's emblem book *Symbolicarum quaestionum de universo genere* from 1555, which takes as its subject the whole of universal knowledge: physics, metaphysics, theology, dialectic, Love, Life and Death; packaging them under the veil of fables and myths.

The picture above said "Hermes-Mercury . . . urges silence . . . The experience of the effect of the spiritual centre (Unit or Monas) is inaccessible to the expressive possibilities of language." In the margin next to it, it continued, "In the cosmic visions of Giordano Bruno the monads, the divine nuclei of all living creatures, correspond to the gravitational centres of the earth." The reason I mention this is because Giordano Bruno proposed that the Sun was essentially a star, and moreover, that the universe contained an infinite number of inhabited worlds populated by other intelligent beings. He was burned at the stake by civil authorities in 1600 after the Roman Inquisition found him guilty of heresy for his pantheism. When researching him, I found another picture that someone painted of Giordano Bruno burning at the stake that looked like me. Again, I can't share this here due to copyrights, so check it out on my blog.

Enochian is a name often applied to an occult or angelic language recorded in the private journals of John Dee and his seer Edward Kelley in the late 16th century. The men claimed that it was revealed to them by angels. I later learned how Aleister Crowley thought he was Edward Kelley (born 1555) reincarnated. Sometimes I really wonder if I am Crowley reincarnate. But if that were true, then all the communication with his spirit wouldn't make much sense.

I would love to be able to fit into this some "how to" methods on magick and synchronicity, but I am limited for space. You can find me and my websites in my bio. I have a million other great stories I would share if I had more space, so add me on Facebook or something and we can chat it up about synchronicity, magic or anything. Remember to always try to stay grounded when dealing with these synchronistic experiences and if you ever need someone to share your experiences with, I am easily found in cyberspace. I once wound up in a mental institute shouting about the Illuminati being pussies for not gold-capping the pyramids, all because I had no one to share my experiences with and the synchronistic connections had festered in my mind too long. The thing that got me to come back down was when they were handing out the meds (keep in mind there were only about 15 of us in that ward at any giving time) and I saw a last name on one of the medicine cases that read CROWLEY!

With all of that being said, I don't think you need Magick to bring about synchronicity, but it will make you more in tune and connected to it to the point that you won't need to do much but charge your sigil every once in a while to see a ton of numbers or symbols that remind you of things in your life, past or present. I was once in a used book store and picked up a book called *How to Communicate with Spirits,* and flipping through it I noticed the previous owner had highlighted some of bits they wanted to remember. I flipped straight to a page with just this highlighted, "It is important to pay attention to the synchronicity of events in our lives." It went on to say, "Synchronistic events are just another subtle way that the spirits have to communicate information to us." Subtle my ass.

I would have also loved to have shared with you my story of yellow balloons that have followed me since my childhood.

The "Everyman" Egyptian statue that looks like me, that has the God Horus and the God Set on each side of the "Everyman."

There are multiple pictures I couldn't share here cause of copyrights. One in particular that some artist who has no clue who I am (as far as I know) painted of the god Osiris that looks like me. Also how I gave solid numbers to the 7 colors of the rainbow.

About how I have been on hiatus from acting since about 2005 raising my two sons, but got called to be in a movie *Unstoppable* with Denzel Washington and Chris Pine. I would have been hit by a train called the "Crazy 8" (train number 888) and killed in the movie. I turned it down, based on a tarot reading I gave myself . . . only to find out that when the movie hit theaters they changed the train's number to "777" and called it *The Beast*.

Or how my hometown of Baltimore, MD is host to tons of synchronistic events such as the release date of this book. On September 11, 2011, a dedication ceremony will be held at Baltimore World Trade Center (the tallest pentagonal [PENTAGON/PENTAGRAM] building in the world) to unveil the memorial containing the steel beam artifact from the twin towers and limestone from the Pentagon crash site.

You can find details of all of these on my blogs.

I truly believe in my heart of hearts that synchronicity has been moving from the unconscious mind to the forefront of our conscious exponentially in the past 10 years or more. Soon the world will not be able to deny that synchronicity is universal consciousness itself.

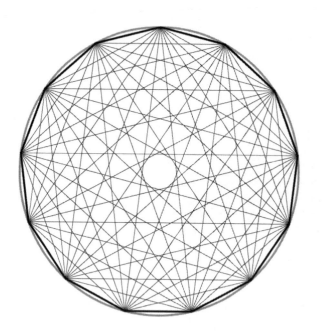

Kyle Hunt
Star Theory

Kyle Hunt is an artist, writer, and entrepreneur. He is now known as the man behind the Star Theory *blog and radio show, but Kyle began his wild writing adventures while working for Google in 2007, first getting an article published by* LewRockwell.com *and then writing op-ed pieces for other outlets under the pseudonym and avatar of "Ferdinand the Bull." Kyle's intellectual interests vary but will often include mythology, linguistics, science, alchemy, astronomy, popular culture, current events, literature, and revisionist history. Kyle was interviewed by Henrik Palmgren of* Red Ice Creations *in 2009 for* The Gods of Technology. *On his own radio show Kyle has frequently collaborated with* The Celtic Rebel, ViølatoR of The Stygian Port, *and Dennis Fetcho of* The Illuminatus Observor. *Kyle recently launched a community publishing platform,* Great Minds of Today, *which he invites you to join.*

startheory.wordpress.com
blogtalkradio.com/star-theory
greatmindsoftoday.com
& search "Star Theory" for everything else

THE RAINBOW ALPHABET
An Alchemical Study of the English Language

And as he spoke of understanding, I looked up and saw the rainbow leap with flames of many colors over me.
—Black Elk

ABCDEFGHIJKLMNOPQRSTUVWXYZ

Signs and Synchronicity

Laid atop the natural world are layers of names, structures, and symbols. Long before the current generation of human life came upon the planet, there were already established languages, religions, myths, and histories dating back many thousands of years. They seem to all be carefully crafted so as to connect in very profound ways, if one cares to look with discerning eyes. Our current culture of movies, books, television and other media is created by those who seem to be very much "in the know"; possibly initiated in ancient mystery schools. Because of this, it is important to make a distinction between what I consider to be organized, crafted connections and organic synchronicity.

When an observer reads and interprets the stories and symbols, organized synchronicity can become organic synchronicity, a very powerful component of life. You may experience this kind of synchronicity in any number of ways. Perhaps you have a song running through your head and then suddenly it's playing on the radio. Did your thoughts create the reality or did you pick up on some invisible energies and have a prophetic moment?

Musing upon this topic a bit further, consider whether or not much of what we call synchronicity is actually the unfolding of our own genetic coding in some hitherto unknown way. DNA is analogous to a language of letters which make up words, forming phrases, sentences, paragraphs, chapters, books, and libraries in increasing complexity. Who's to say if this story really ends or begins somewhere? Even the most primary components of language or DNA are formed by smaller parts. Each letter has curved and angled lines which can be seen as visual metaphors, just as each base pairing of DNA has component chemical bonds of atoms which are themselves made up of smaller relationships. There even appears to be an intelligence which knows the big picture and is able to fill in and correct the deletions and mistranslations that occur over time, as long as the code is not too badly damaged. This leads one to the concept of God and divine intervention.

The Gift of Angels

The origin of the English language is still shrouded in mystery, with little attention given to how or why such a late-comer could spread throughout the entire world in only a few centuries. It was able to move past national borders and cultural boundaries, conquering vast lands without much brute force. Much of this expansion could be attributed to the dominance of the American-Anglo trading empire. Could there be some hidden mathematical or even divine elements within English which have aided in its easy acceptance around the world?

Before the current version of the language was "set in stone," there was Old English, which dates back to the 5th century AD when Germanic tribes invaded the shores of England and pushed back the Celtic tribes. The era of Middle English started around 1100 AD. After the Normans conquered the island in 1066, the ruling and business elite spoke French, while the commoners spoke English. Eventually, French words became incorporated into the language and English dominated once again. The genesis of modern English came about in the mid to late 16th century when alchemists like John Dee and his disciple Sir Francis Bacon, the likely author of the Shakespeare folios, were doing their complex mathematical, astrological, theological, and linguistic work.

Though the phonetics of English might have remained the same, it seems that there were important changes made to the spellings of words so as to make them mathematically "perfect." There are many ways in which this could be accomplished. A good example is that of gematria: the process of adding up the numerical values of the letters found in one or several words. Various forms of gematria date back thousands of years into linguistic history. It was used by the Greeks, Jews, Phoenicians, and others. Nigel Pennick's *Magical Alphabets* covers the different systems available.

Markings of Magic

In simple gematria, each letter is equated to its sequential position within the alphabet. It's as easy as ABC, 123, Do Re Mi (to borrow a line from the Jackson 5). An example of how gematria is used to divine hidden connections is found in the analysis of the word "God." G = 7, O = 15, and D = 4, which gives us GOD = 26. Not only is this the number of letters found in the English alphabet, it is also the sum of the letters, which in Hebrew, spells the common name of God: YHWH, or Yahweh. Two other English words with a value of 26 are GAME and FLAG. Both are things which have been worshiped like gods. A hunter hunts "game," and a flag is the object one hunts in the classic game of Capture The Flag.

The number 26 relates to the Precession of the Equin**ox**, The Great Year, which takes almost 26k years to complete. The 26th element in the periodic table is iron, which is labeled as Fe. We are *fe*rociously coming out of the Iron Age as I write these words. Fehu (or Feoh) is the first rune of the Elder Futhark, and esoterically represents the cow. Our first (Fe-hurst) letter, A (Alpha to the Greeks and Aleph to the Jews), when inverted, can be seen as the head of a bull. The cow, a beast of burden, was a primary source of milk, horn, hide, and meat, making it a symbol of moo-vable wealth to our ancestors. Real moo-la or moo-ney comes in bars or rounds made of precious metal—it is known as bull-ion.

> *I am the Alpha and the Omega, the First and the Last,*
> *the Beginning and the End.*

This celestial crafting is integrally tied to our Western system of stellar reckoning. An example of this can be seen when taking the

25,920 years for one complete precession of the equinox and dividing it by the 12 signs of the Zodiac, which gives us exactly 2,160 years for the completion of one sign or age. The diameter of the moon happens to be 2,160 miles. 2,160 = 6 × 6 × 6 × 10. The 666 commonly associated with "The Beast of Revelation" also represents a ratio of ⅔ (.66$\bar{6}$). This ratio is significant when considering that our investigation is of (and written in) Anglo Angle-ish, and that ⅓ (.3$\bar{3}$) of the Angels fell from heaven in the great rebellion against God. Other significant 33's are the number of vertebrae in the human body, as well as the honorary 33rd degree of Scottish Rite Freemasonry. The number 666 also represents the element carbon with its 6 protons, 6 neutrons, and 6 electrons. Carbon is in the charcoal found after a (car)bonfire. Carbon is the basic element found in all the organisms of this world as well as the stars in heaven, making us all char-actors in the great play of life.

> *All the world's a stage,*
> *And all the men and women merely players;*
> *They have their exits and their entrances;*
> *And one man in his time plays many parts*
> —As You Like It, *Act II, Scene VII*

Translating the 216 (6 × 6 × 6) into English letters, we get BAF which may be a nod to the Goat God of the mysteries—BAFomet. Also spelled Baphomet, this god is Hermaphroditic, having masculine features while sporting a pair of breasts. He sits with the double helix (of the dual-snake Kundalini) rising up his torso while indicating the hermetic axiom: as above, so below. Goat, good, and God all seem to derive from a similar phonetic root.

Circles and Spirals

The protagonist of Darren Aronofsky's film *Pi* searches for a 216-digit number which serves as a code for the name of god. According to the Hebrew mystics this name, known as the *Shemhamphorash*, is made up of 72 separate 3-letter names (3 × 72 = 216).

Dennis Fetcho, discoverer of what's known as the *Isisian Codes*, served as inspiration for much of the work which led to this author's uncovering of The Rainbow Alphabet. He asserts that most of English is based around the concept of Pi. He demonstrates how the word ZODIAC, re-arranged as CADOIZ, decodes as: 3,1,4,15,9,26, the first 8 digits of Pi. Dennis has also shown that "epiphany" holds E, Pi, and Phi—ratios which are found in DNA as well as in the proportions of the human body.

The golden ratio (1/0.618), represented by the Greek letter Phi, forms the golden spiral (S-Pi-Ral) found in nautilus shells, the face of sunflowers, and the shape of some galaxies. It is also found in the length of the sections of a pentagram's arms. The magic **phi**re of the **phi**ve-sided pentagram can be found in words and phrases like re*pent*, car*pent*er, *pent* up, and *pent*house. **Phi**guring that this ratio may decode somehow into English, we'll write out the Fibonacci sequence in which the quotient of consecutive numbers approaches Phi:

1,1,2,3,5,8,13,21,34,55,89,144, . . .

We'll go another step by moving a few commas around:

1,12,3,5,8,13,21,3,455,89,144

And by direct transliteration of numbers into letters, we arrive at the following:

ALCEHM U C DEE HI ADD

Note the "DEE." Did occultist John Dee have a made-up name? John Dee could possibly be the basis for the name John Deere, which adds the "Re" of the sun goddess of I-Re-Land to the name. John Doe is the name given to unidentifiable dead men. The deer is an incredibly significant symbol, seeing as how some men hunt for "bucks and doe (dough)" (male and female deer, or slang terms for money). Speaking of male bucks, Pagan cultures give us The Great Horned One who is similar to the satyr Pan, a stag(e). Matt Groening has his animated creation Homer exclaim, "D'oh." Before Re and Mi is Do. The active verb "do" is used before other verbs. Children might make a "doo-doo," while dew forms on plants in the early morning.

The John Deere company produces tractors, which are used to maintain a person's tract of land, taking the place of oxen. Land has officially become the property of a person or group when someone takes a rule and protractor and angles off a section in some ledger. Pro-Trac-Tor. Deer are also "tracked" through the woods. Continuing with this breakdown, the Tor relates to Thor who is another form of the god Horus (THORus). A radiator (Ra-Dia-Tor) indicates how the heat of the sun god Ra came through (the Greek prefix *dia-*, "through") Thor's crafting. Thor can be found in AuThor (Au represents Gold in the periodic table of elements). He is also seen in HaThor, the cow goddess of Egypt.

Revealing the Beast

You keep thinking when you're throwing a dart, it's just going to keep hitting the middle of the bull's eye. No matter, you throw left-handed or one-eyed or whatever, you just feel comfortable that things are very much within you.
—Stuart Appleby

C = 3, O = 15, W = 23. By reducing 2 or more digits into a single digit (1 + 5, 2 + 3), COW becomes 365, the number of days in a year. We live in the Milky Way. The "cownting" system for digital technology is binary, being made entirely of 1's and 0's. IO was a Greek goddess who was turned into a cow by Zeus. The Greek symbol for Phi, Φ, is a combination of the Greek letters Iota and Omicron; an "I" laid over an "O." Zeus transformed himself into a bull to steal Europa.

You should now be properly prepared for a tour of The Rainbow Alphabet (The RA).

He found him in a desert land, And in the wasteland, a howling wilderness; He encircled him, He instructed him, He kept him as the apple of His eye.
—*Deuteronomy 32:10*

Each pairing of letters is equal to 26. Z is the completion point, where 2 become 1. Each letter of the alphabet should be analyzed for its own symbolic importance, but I will only be analyzing the sets of letters.

AY - Spoken like "eye," it is an affirmation. It can be circled around to form YAY. It is found in words like: bay, day, gay, hay, lay, play, stay, may, nay, way. It is seen as **YA** on the bottom.

BX - This seems to reference the cube or box of sacred geometry. The X-Box is a gaming console. Perhaps it is Pandora's Box. Pi can be approximated by 22/7 = V/G, like Video Game or VaGina (a girl's "box").

CW - This is the sacred cow. CW is a yellow band in the rainbow, like the Golden Cow worshipped as Ba'al (bell, ball). Looping it, we find WCW. Perhaps **WC** is the wick of a candle's golden flame.

DV - This could form the basis of DoVe. If looped, we find DVD, as in DaViD or DiViDe. Visual and audio information can be stored to a DVD disc. **VD** is an STD.

EU - This pairing of letters means "Good" and is in blue, which is also the color of the **E**uropean **U**nion flag. The US is known to the Spanish as the EU: los Estados Unidos.

FT - FaTe, FaT, FiT, FaiTh, FoughT, Full Time.

GS - Guess. **SG** is the StarGate, perhaps.

HR - Her, HeaR, HeRa, Human Resources. **RH** is an important component to blood-type and RHea is the mother of gods.

IQ - Intelligence. QIQ (quick) thinkers only, says HR.

JP - JaPan, JiP, JP Morgan, **PJ** is PaJamas, Peanut-butter and Jelly.

KO - Knockout. KO at the **OK** corral. The fatal blue KO may represent sleep ("the blue pill" of *The Matrix*), sedation, and death (turning blue from suffocation). *Chao* is latin for chaos and is pronounced as "KO." *Ordo ab chao* is order out of chaos.

LN - Lion, lawn, line. **NL** could be Nile or Nil.

M - M&M's. The M shape can be broken into I V I, revealing the V in the middle, a feminine symbol for the mother sun or moon and also the Roman number for 5. If an M overlays another inverted M (W), it creates a diamond between two pillars.

Over the Rainbow

Some people will see the rainbow alphabet and wonder why there are 6 colors in the rainbow and not 7. This is natural, since we learn the acronym ROY G BIV at an early age. However, when the rainbow of white light was found, there is a story that since 6 is the devil's number and 7 relates to the big G and heaven, the seven band rainbow was formed. If you try to separate blue from indigo, you will find that the two colors really shouldn't be listed as individual. Some scientists have refined the rainbow to 6 colors recently and the rainbow flag of the homosexual pride movement features only 6 colors. In web coding, colors are defined by hexadecimal values, which many of you are probably aware is a set of

6 letters and numbers that define a color value. It's paint by numbers.

There are other things that led me to this specific coloration, like the recent phenomenon of "double rainbows," which I attribute partly to the excessive amount of particulates in the atmosphere due to geo-engineering or chemtrailing. Nevertheless, it helped inspire this configuration which seems to have a great deal of validity. 26 letters, 2 bands of 6 colors. 6 × 6 = 36, like 360 degrees. 36 + 35 + 34 + . . . + 2 + 1 = 666. Six is the number of Saturn, the planet with a hexagonal feature at its north pole. When many die, they are placed in hexagonal coffins and put six feet under. The Latin for 6 is "sex." Sex and death.

By analyzing the similar colors in one column of the alphabet, some more pairings can be made, such as: AG, BH, CI, DJ . . . PV, QW, RX, SY. Similar bands of color can also be combined to form new words or phonetic phrases. The orange bands can sound like "HeR BoX" or "BoXHeR," which fits within this model as KO, a boxer's knockout punch, is represented in one of the inner circles.

The Ring Box

Boxing and wrestling take place in a ring shaped like a square: a "squared circle." Squaring the circle is one of the great riddles of mystery traditions such as Freemasonry. The circle of the alphabet is O and it is the 15th letter. If 15 is squared, 225 is the result, which is about the number of days it takes for Venus to travel around the sun. 225 is coding for V(22) and E(5) of VEnus, with NUS being the reverse of SUN. Perhaps this could also be the shell of the gorgeous goddess, as B(2) and Y(25) are on the outside of BeAutY. Five consecutive inferior conjunctions of Venus trace a pentagram in the heavens.

In Einstein's famous equation of $E=MC^2$, the C stands for light which is what we "see." We "see" the world in two different ways: with our two eyes and two hemispheres of the brain. We get depth (perception) when the two streams of light are combined, combining with **M**ass and forming **E**nergy.

When looking at the inner circles encompassed by KO/OK, a cubed circle can be found.

K L M N O
11 12 13 14 15
KaBa π Star Theory

In the above diagram, the middle of the alphabet is translated from letters to numbers and then back to letters to form KaBa (11,1,2,1) and the first 5 digits of Pi. To Ancient Egyptians, *Ka* is the Spirit and *Ba* is the Soul, in a generalized sense of the words. A Cabal (Ka Ball) is a hidden group of conspirators. This area of research would be termed Kabbalah (Cob-Allah of the Corn God) and could tie to the cube-Allah found in Mecca, known as the Kaaba stone, around which many pilgrims form their concentric circles.

26 is the magical number of the Cube. For the Cube has 6 sides, 8 points or corners, and 12 edges or boundary lines. The Cube is said to contain the Great Secret of the Universe. In Alchemical terminology it is the Stone of the Philosophers. It is a symbol of the Sanctum Sanctorum or the Cubical Holy of Holies that contained the Ark of the Covenant on which rested the Holy Shekinah. The Cube is a symbol of the World and the Throne of the Deity.
—*Instructions on the Middle Pillar,*
The Thelemic Order of the Golden Dawn

A 2-dimensional hexagon (⬡), in sacred geometry, is seen as a 3-dimensional cube, which you can visualize by connecting 3 corners to the center in a "Y" shape (⬢). "Cubed" numbers of great importance: 2→8, 3→27, 4→64, 5→125, 6→216, 7→343. Perhaps the translations of the results are significant: H, BG, FD, ABE, BAF,

CDC, and so on. I could go off a number of tangents here. Instead, let's move into the bull's eye.

Holy Cow!

The Norse creation myth tells of the primal cow, named Audhumia, whose formative function was to lick the cubic block of crystalline salt which contained the progenitor of humankind.
—*Magical Alphabets*

It is truly elementary, this L-M-N-Taury Toroid TarGet. LMN8 could be said as "eliminate" or "illuminate." LyMaN Frank Baum wrote *The Wizard of Oz*, an alchemical narrative about going over the Rainbow, walking the golden brick road to the M-erald City, which is in the middle of Oz, and getting back to Aunty M.

Perhaps MN could represent Man, or the emanations (MN8ions) of God. The M in the middle of the rainbow alphabet may be a MinoTaur in the labyrinth. The bull's eye in the sky is the red star Aldebaran (Alpha Tauri), and has long been associated with the "diamond consciousness" of the Buddha. Aldebaran is allegedly where the Vril Society believed their ancestors had come from and seems to be where George Lucas looked for inspiration in his naming of Leia's home world Alderaan.

The Bible (Bi-bull) is likely the most important fusion of books of the past two thousand years, the Pope issues decrees and this is known as the papal bull. BULL = 47. 47 is an important prime number, being the number of silver (Ag) on the Periodic table of LMNts. An AK-47 fires *bull*ets. By punching 4747 into a touch-tone phone, you either spell IRIS or ISIS, the goddess. The myth of Mithras involves the sun goddess, with the same crown as Lady Liberty and Hera, slaughtering the sacred cow in order to ensure a good harvest. Perhaps the blood of the bull is spilled every night when the sun sets and the red colors give way to the darkness.

Judaism is based on the Torah, which ties directly to the Torador and tAROT, which has 78 cards. Subtracting the 26 of god, you are left with 52 cards of a traditional deck (not counting the foolish joker). 26 × 2 = 52 cards of the Bi-cycle deck, as 52 is the number of weeks in a year. The Tower card of Tarot features a tall building ("a taur") being struck by a lightning, relating to the fall of the tower of Babel, and more recently the fall of the Twin *Two*ers.

Perhaps this relates to the en-*lightning* nature of Zeus, whose primary weapon is the lightning bolt. The Tower is card XVI (16), which is the letter P, both Powerful and Phallic.

And he said to them, 'I saw Satan fall like lightning from heaven.'
—Luke 10:18

The Apis bull of Egypt was said to have been struck by a lightning *bullt*, making him a representative of the spirit of the god Osiris (O's Iris). ACOW = 42. Zeus is equated with the planet Jupiter whose astrological symbol appears to be a combination of the shapes 4 and 2. A golden cow could be also been seen as an Or-a-Tor. Ore being the rock from which metals are derived. Even the word "star" breaks down into S-Tar, relating to the Babylonian cow goddess Ishtar, and breaking down simply into S-Tar. To get our light at night, we switch on light *bull*bs.

To further illustrate to you the power of the cow, even its excrement produces holy sacraments. I am referring to magic mushrooms, which grow on cow **pi**es. This mushroom may have played a crucial role in activating parts of the human mind, and the myths and symbols of many religions are found to have encoded their reverence for this sacrament. Light is taken in through the concentric circles of AY/eye, is absorbed by the body, and the waste gets pushed through the "KO LN" or colon.

God of the Underworld

In Ancient Egyptian mythology, a soul was weighed against a feather (Fe-at-her) on the scales of Ma'at in the Underworld. Ma'at would likely be where we get words like matter and mother. Ma'at had 42 principles by which a good soul was supposed to live their lives. The red band on the rainbow is white light refracted at 42 degrees to the observer. The outer red band of the Rainbow Alphabet is AY on top and YA on the bottom. Red is the color associated with the base chakra. Perhaps a person is *weighed by YA*: YA-Weighed. In Exodus **3:14,** God was said to have declared I AM WHO I AM, which has been written as YHWH.

In *I Am Legend* (the Legend of I AM), Will Smith's character speaks about Bob Marley,

He had this idea: It was kind of a virologist idea. He believed that you could cure racism and hate . . . literally cure it, by injecting

music and love into people's lives. When he was scheduled to perform at a peace rally, a gunman came to his house and shot him down. Two days later he walked out on that stage and sang. When they asked him why, he said, 'The people who are trying to make this world worse . . . are not taking a day off. How can I? Light up the darkness.'

In Ridley Scott's *Legend,* the Prince of Darkness has bull horns and he describes the magical unicorn to his minions:

It has a single spiral, reaching like an antenna straight to heaven!

The unicorn is featured a number of times in The Bible.

For the Lord hath a sacrifice in Bozrah, and a great slaughter in the land of Idumea. And the unicorns shall come down with them, and the bullocks with the bulls. —Isaiah 34:6-7

God brought them out of Egypt; he hath as it were the strength of a unicorn. —Numbers 23:22

With the GS band of red on the inside combined with AY, it can spell GAYS, a group which now uses the rainbow and unicorn as their symbol. Ridley Scott also directed *Blade Runner*, which begins zoomed in on one blue eye and also has unicorns as a major part of the narrative. The unicorn seems to not only indicate one horn, but also one eye (Uni-Cornea) which could tie us to popcorn or Pop-Eye, who would say, "I yam what I yam." Odin has only one eye. ODIN = 42. He hung upside-down from the world tree for nine days to gain access to the nine realms and recover the runes. NINE = 42.

The Bridge of Noah's Arc

The Vikings sailed about on what were known as Dragon Ships, made of wood with serpents carved on front. Ships **steer**ed from the wheel, but commanded from the Bridge. In Yggdrasil, the Norse Tree of Life, there is a burning Rainbow Bridge, called the Bifrost, which leads to Asgard. This tree can be seen in movies like James Cameron's *Avatar* and holidays like Christmas—"*Feliz Na'vi-Dad*" as people exchange boxes of presents under the tree, while the Na'vi aliens commune around their world tree.

It seems the mother figure of Ma'at is something of a counterpart to the father God Odin, Saint Nick of Time, or Jehovah. This may explain why Eve was demonized for her eve-il act of eating the red apple from the forbidden tree. Still, children are fed Mott's apple sauce. Neo takes the red pill to see *The Matrix*. "A pill" to see the Ma'at Rx. (R&X are orange)

> *Keep me as the apple of Your eye;*
> *Hide me under the shadow of Your wings.*
> —Psalm 17:8

The pupil of an eye acts as its aperture, adjusting according to the levels of light in the outside world. The word "aperpture" derives from the word apple. A pupil is also a student, like a disciple. There are 12 discs surrounding the M in the Middle, sort of like how Jesus had 12 disc-iples.

The Colorful Serpent

By **apply**ing some knowledge of the Aboriginal culture of OZtralia, one can see that perhaps the tales of the tailed Rainbow Serpent could relate to the serpent in the Garden of Eden. The serpent (SirPent) was giving Adam (Atom) and Eve the light of knowledge. It was literally opening up the apertures of their eyes for them to see their place in the world, not as something outside, disconnected from the source of all things, but a fractal representation of the cosmos made in the image of god, with the ability to create new life and make "things."

The Apple of Knowledge could be related to the worship of the Sun Serpent, the Golden Cow, the single open eye of God which seems to coil about the world as we move through the seasons. It can be a giver and taker of life; creator and destroyer. Just like the people who spread this language of ours.

There is even an ancient practice known as sun-gazing, which involves allowing increasing amounts of light into one's eyes over time during the safer periods of the first and last hours of sunlight. Both Max from Aronofsky's *Pi* and Superman were said to get their incredible powers from our yellow sun, but only Max explicitly said he had stared at it, en-lightening himself, whereas it is only implied in the case of the Man of Steel. Steel is Fe+C.

A B C D E F G H I J K L M N O P Q R S T U V W X Y

The Bavarian Illuminati was founded on the symbolic date of May 1, 1776, May Day. This is the dawning of the "May Sun." Money is being S-Pent as the one dollar bill. The ONE in the middle of M-ONE-Y can be translated as the first letter A, revealing MAY. By using the above diagram, which draws out the hidden M, A, and S of the illustrious pyramid (Pi-Ra-Mid), we can form the MAS of Mason, Master, Mast, etc. The eye can also be *seen* as "I"—resulting in I AM. There is even a movie titled *I Am Sam*. Reversing the letters of I AM results in MA I, like the eye of the mother, or the beginning of Maitreya, the Buddhist world teacher of prophecies. No wonder the pyramid has become such an important AMerIcan symbol! The IS and AM could also be separated to show different forms of "to be." Saying that something "is," creates connections, defining the world around and within us.

The diagram above also shows how straight lines can be drawn to connect the pairings of the Rainbow Alphabet, still resulting in AY at the top. The eye atop the pyramid is often known as the Eye of Providence. The city of Providence is IN RI (Rhode Island), which could be sounded out, "in our eye." INRI are the letters atop Jesus' cross. INRI adds up to 50, like SNAKE, APPLE, AMERICA, JOY, and some other important words. The 50th element is tin, the metal associated with Jupiter and Zeus, which is represented

THE RAINBOW ALPHABET

by the letters Sn, the beginning of Snake. If you cut an apple in half horizontally, you will see a pentagram of seeds. There are 50 pentagrams on the American flag. The Serpentine S can be found in the middle of the Yin-Yang symbol, which equally divides the black from the white, much like 50 would do in our base-10 system, as in 50 + 50 = 100. The "SerPent" gave the apple as a "PreSent," and these words are anagrams of each other.

The Power of Creation

26 has something of a counterpart in the number 74, as these two numbers complete each other by equaling 100 when added together. 26 × 74 = 1924, which could be SX, as S is 19 and X is 24. In this same way, 74 could be seen as GD. Out of respect for God, some Jews write the name as "G-d." There are 7 days in a week and roughly 4 weeks in a month. 74 is the value of: ENGLISH, HAND OF GOD, MASONIC, SIMPLE, GEMATRIA, HEXAGON, THE KEY, LONDON, MESSIAH, LUCIFER, JESUS, MUHAMMAD, ENERGY, OCCULT, RULER. 74 itself could be flipped to reveal 47, which is DG, again representing ISIS, as she is connected to the Dog Star, Sirius.

The AY of the rainbow is in red, which is the hair-color of Vulcan (or Hephaestus) the red-headed god of armaments, husband to Venus, who was "cast" from Olympus. When volcanoes erupted it was said to be because she was away and the red god was hammering in his forge (forge could be seen as 4-G or 4-7). The Red AY (R-AY) is also the color of blood, due to its iron content, and red is the hue of the root chakra of the hue-man. The red chakra likely relates to the *rub*edo of the alchemists. Iron gives blood its magnetism which leads to the eruption of Heph's volcano, the one-eyed pyramid crowned by the serpentine 'one-eyed monster' of men, with its slit-eye atop the e-rect red rod. The AM of morning hours could be the "dawn wand," the morning wood, or the tree of life. It can also relate to the Ma of FeMales, as well as MaN, with the one-eye representing the woman's vagina which looks remarkably like an eye. The AY is atop the two pillars of the Rainbow Alphabet, which can form the triangle of the pyramids when one's legs are spread apart.

Then I saw another mighty angel coming down from heaven, wrapped in a cloud, with a rainbow over his head, and his face was like the sun, and his legs like pillars of fire.
—Revelation 10:1

It should be no surprise that we can write with a pen(is) and get our words from dick-tionaries, as the names of these definers tell this same tale of bull gods, I AM, and the bridging of words: Ox-Ford English, MerrIAM WebSter, and CamBridge. The writings of humanity have been scribed in the sands of time, set in stone, inked on the hides of animals, printed on the flesh of trees, and now are the visual representations of 1's and 0's in the digital realm.

The Light of Lucifer

In order to have words on a page, there must be both light and darkness. We need contrast in order to communicate. Light is opposed to darkness, but even within the color wheel of white light, each hue has its opposite.

How art thou fallen from heaven, O Lucifer, son of the morning! how art thou cut down to the ground, which didst weaken the nations! —Isaiah **14:12** (14 + 12 = 26)

I Jesus, have sent my angel to give you this testimony for the churches. I am the root and the offspring of David, and the morning star. —Revelation **22:16**

Venus is known as both the Morning Star and the Evening Star because at different periods she can be seen before the sun rises or after it sets. Is Lucifer the hero or the villain? Perhaps it's a little bit of both and depends on who you ask. Without night, the sun would be a brutal enemy burning us in its light. Without the sun, we would freeze in the coldness of night.

Our DNA is changing all the time according to the energies with which we interact. There are many organizations and people who would like to put themselves and their images in the way of the light, as it is such a powerful force. There are also great imitations of light, projected from sets in homes all over the world. These can be tools for great enlightening or great destruction. Unfortunately they have become little more than the idiot boxes of today's world, encouraging passivity and obedient servitude instead of real creation and natural wonder.

There are still many great questions to ask, and ideas yet to be explored. Was our DNA crafted by a higher intelligence? What about the mathematical proportions of life and the planetary orbits of our solar system? Can we change our genetic structure for the better through language, tones, light, and harmonics? And how can we best use this immensely powerful language as a tool for liberation and illumination?

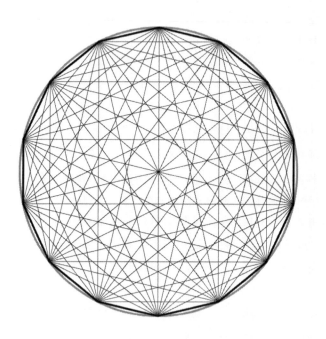

CRYSTAL KANARR
CONSTELLATION CONTEMPLATION

Crystal hails from the Pacific Northwest, currently residing in Seattle, Washington. She was born when the sun was traveling through Aquarius and as the Virgin was rising. Previously trained to put pieces together as an apparel designer, she presently spends much of her day analyzing the symbolism and patterns within the world around her. In winter of 2009-2010, she started the blog Constellation Contemplation, *as a way of integrating and sharing the connections she makes throughout her own personal development. Her favorite form of expression of ideas are collages, as she feels pictures really are worth a thousand words—at least. Crystal also enjoys collaborating with others on subjects of synchronicity and symbolism at another blog,* The Mask of God, *and looks forward to further learning, growing and exploring of the Universe.*

constellationcontemplation.blogspot.com
themaskofgod.blogspot.com

TWISTS OF FATE
Synchronicity and the Birth Chart

The stream of creation and dissolution never stops... All things come out of the one, and the one out of all things.
—*Heraclitus*

One of my favorite delights (unfortunately I have only experienced it a handful of times) is to open a "non-fiction" book and read the author's introduction which disclaims that everything they have written is a work of their own imagination and they made it up through the use of their own senses, intellect and intuition. This is probably one of the most honest statements, and I wish that doctors, scientists, other 'experts,' writers and creators of all sorts were only so honest. I have come to know in my own heart (at this point in time), that a person's truth is only a compilation of their inheritance, individual perspective and patterns of experience; how they see the world, and what they have gathered through their faculties of perception and then integrated into a belief of what one "knows." So, I would first like to begin by following suit and saying that everything that I have written below and in my blog is my own magical tale thus far, based on associations that my mind creatively ties together and inspired by others' tales that have made their way into my heart and mind.

I think this is an important statement to make, as I have come to feel that it has everything to do with the subject of synchronicity. I will attempt to show in the telling of my own journey with "syncing," that it is the arching bridge that shows us the way to experiencing wholeness; a tool for healing the fragmented perception of the world as black and white and the illusion that every creature, person, place and thing is separate. After all, we have two eyes, but we don't see two separate pictures; the two eyes work together to show one vision.

Some may say that another person's associations made with the awareness of a synchronicity seem like a bit of a stretch, as if they performed an act of *bending* the "truth" to make pieces of the puzzle fit together. But when I think of bending, bowing, arching, I naturally think of the practice of Yoga. The Online Etymology Dictionary says the word *yoga* comes from the Sanskrit word *yoga-s*, which literally means "union, yoking" (with Spirit/Higher Self/God), also possibly rooted from ancient Indo-European *yeug-* which means "to join."[i] This is precisely what a moment of magical, meaningful synchronicity does, it shows the unity of two or more *seemingly* separate things.

In my own personal journey, the awareness of synchronicity has risen on the heels of my growing awareness of astrology. In my relatively short time of studying such subjects, I have experienced that astrology and synchronicity really go hand-in-hand. The language of astrology has been deciphered through the use of the same pattern recognition that synchronicity alerts our attention to. Ancient sky watchers noticed cycles above and made associations between those cycles and events happening below, just as we see connections between two or more outwardly unrelated things due to curiously timed "coincidences" that draw our attention to them. These unexpected events and combinations show us that mind and matter are not separate.

One way that we can consciously make connections is to follow the trail of the etymology of words. I often do this when a word keeps 'popping up.' When we look at the root of the word *synchronicity* we see that it is the quality of being (-ity) synchronic/synchronous, which means *simultaneous* and comes from *syn* which means "together" and *khronos* which means "time."[ii] *Khronos* is the name of the Greek god that ruled time, and was linked with *Kronos*, otherwise known as Saturn. Mythological Saturn shares the name with the famous ringed planet, which is astrologically associated with . . . yes, *time* and matter. The roots of the word *time* lead back to "to cut up, divide."[iii] Synchronicity, in its very etymological breakdown, shows unity in time, a quality of bringing pieces together to be viewed as a whole. Astrology is a language and study of the archetypal patterns of energy and cycles of time. So both astrology and synchronicity are intimately tied to our perception of timing, and are tools to alert the Self explorer to connections between pieces of the whole that are *in sync*.

Synchronicity is the relatively modern term for what people throughout the ages have called signs and messages from the god(s). Most (if not all) spiritual paths throughout time and culture speak of a Higher Self that is working through the individual, with the common view of signs, messages and synchronicities as a way of communication between the higher and lower Self, or Spirit and the persona, to align the individual with their true path/purpose/will. I like to think of synchronicity as a process of pollination. The pollen being symbolic messages from the Universe that are continuously being released, so that we might catch the drift, the seed might be planted, ultimately for the intent of creation and embodying the soul. The means of communication between the inner genius and our brain is through the universal language of symbols. This is why the arts of language, astrology, tarot, Qabalah and numerology are invaluable to our quest, so that we can become more symbol literate, enabling us to better understand what is being communicated. Finding meaning in the unexpected repetition of symbols in our daily life is our waking dream work.

Years ago I read *The B∞k: On the Taboo Against Knowing Who You Are*, by the great philosopher and writer Alan Watts. In the book, the author relates his version of the Vedanta story from the Hindu tradition. The story being that God or Self plays hide-and-seek with self for all eternity by pretending to be you and me.[iv] If you have not read this work, there is nothing I recommend more highly. I tend to forget time and again, yet I am always led back to the realization that we are each the divine spirit, playing, creating and adventuring toward knowing thyself again. A different perspective begets a different experience. If the purpose is eternal creation, what better way to perpetually create than to peer through infinite eyes? This is the importance of each individual, that each experience is absolutely unique, telling a distinctive story about a different facet of the diamond.

In the modern view of astrology as a psychological language, a person's astrological natal chart is a map of an individual's psyche/soul/mind; it describes their perspective of the world. You might say it is a map of symbols describing what Timothy Leary and Robert Anton Wilson called an individual's "reality tunnel." The birth chart is a snap shot of a moment in time. The individual embodies the energies of that moment. The planets and stars are not above us causing those energies, they, like us, are manifest *symbols* of archetypal energies that are within. So I think it's important to mention that the "body" is everything that is perceived and experienced, not limited to the physical person.

There is much that could be described about the astrological natal chart and I apologize that I cannot go into the details of terms and symbols here, but there are many great sources for such information. However, for those who aren't familiar with the natal chart, it is a wheel chart that shows the zodiacal sign and house positions of *all* of the planets at the exact moment of a birth, be it a birth of a person, pet, business, country, event, question etc. I am not a professional astrologer, just an admirer, so I will do my best to describe briefly what I have learned about the natal chart in the Western astrological tradition. (I make that distinction as there are some differences in Eastern systems of astrology, which I have not studied much as of yet.) The chart is a flattened image of the ecliptic (the path that we view the sun travel in the sky), which is then divided into 12 pieces of the pie, known as "houses." There are different systems for calculating the houses, but in widely used modern systems the first house begins at the degree of the astrological sign that was rising on the eastern horizon at the exact time and location of your birth—known as the Ascendant. From that point the entire zodiac circles your chart. Depending upon the area of the sky where the planets are currently traveling at any given moment, they will fall in the corresponding sign of a chart, which if the Ascendant/rising degree is known, will place them in a house. It is the Ascendant that sets the tone and uniqueness of the chart; this is why the precise birth time (to the minute) and location, in addition to the date, are required to make the most accurate map. The houses represent realms of life experience, the planets are the different forces of archetypal energy, and the signs represent the flavor of how that realm of life and force is expressed. So the natal chart is a starting point, but just as an individual does not stop developing at birth, the chart evolves as well.

Throughout the course of a lifetime, the planets, being *symbols* of parts of the psyche, keep circling the center of the natal chart, the center being you. We see them going forward, and then retrograding (appearing to move backward from our point of view on Earth), which I like to see as a giant piece of fabric folding backward, and then folding forward again, adding new layers to the story. The story is you; you are the whole of the story. Synchronicities that we experience are like the needle and thread penetrating the layers of fabric and stitching them together, having meaning because they bring awareness to the story, to who you are. If life is a journey, then the astrological birth chart is the map, and synchronicities are the road signs. The landscape may appear to change over time, yet the location is always the same.

> *You must put the arrow to the bow,*
> *but do not draw to the full extent of your power.*
> *Where the arrow falls, dig and search!*
> *Trust not in Strength,*
> *seek the treasure by means of piteous supplication.*
> *—Rumi, "The Treasure Seeker"*

Admittedly, I wasn't sure how I was going to go about putting my experience with synchronicity into words for this book. I follow my sync nose in combination with astrology all the time to make connections in my journey to "know thyself," yet now I was challenged with the task of actually describing what synchronicity is to me, what it is saying, and the relationship with the natal chart. Of course, as it turns out, all I needed to do was follow the flow of sync. I would like to share with you that whirlpool I've been traveling the past couple of months.

A little while ago I woke from a dream with the sentence in my mind, "The fall of man was a divorce." I had heard statements made like that before in regards to stories about humanity's fall or separation from unity consciousness and/or God. But out of curiosity I decided to look at the etymology of the words. "Divorce" is related to "divert" and has its roots in the word *vertere*, meaning "to turn." "Versus" also comes from the word *vertere*, and/or the Old English *weorthan* meaning "to befall," and *wyrd* "fate/destiny, what befalls one." Turn comes from the Greek *tornos* which is a "lathe, tool for drawing circles."[v] This was all significant to me because my attention to the circulating planets had been leading me to the same concepts of turning and destiny. Later that afternoon, on the same day that I was looking at the origin of the above words, I was talking with someone about the difference between introvert/extrovert and she began talking about the "vert" base of the words and how it meant *to turn*. This amazed me considering I had spent my morning researching that very word! Later that evening, a post at the blog *Look at All the Happy Creatures*, brought my attention to the turning connection within the tornadoes that were ravaging the Midwest. At the time I still wasn't quite sure what the significance was of the synchronicities to *turning*, so I kept them in the back of my mind, hoping that at some point there would be more clarity.

A seemingly separate flow of synchronicities and connections began through the study of astrology. I started to read about the comet Chiron[Δ] in Barbara Hand Clow's resourceful and insightful book *Chiron: Rainbow Bridge Between the Inner & Outer Planets*. Chiron is a small planetoid, thought to be an asteroid until recently a faint tail was detected and it was classified as more of a comet. It has only just been discovered in 1977 and is said to be the bridge between the inner and outer planets, as it orbits in the space between Saturn (which was classically known as the outermost planet of our solar system) and Uranus, the first of the outer planets, discovered only 230 years ago. This is significant as it is symbolically seen as a link between the structure, form and time of our present reality (Saturn), and the intuitive, electromagnetic energy, higher mind (Uranus). In Greek mythology, Chiron is a wise centaur, son of Saturn and a nymph. He is an astrologer, archer, healer and teacher, and taught many heroes these skills. He is called the "wounded healer" due to an accident with a poisonous arrow that left him in eternal pain; he was immortal yet could not heal the wound. Eventually he sacrificed his immortality so that Prometheus could bring mankind the knowledge of the fire of the gods. After giving up his immortal life, it is said that Zeus/Jupiter placed him in the heavens as the constellation Sagittarius.[vi] In keeping with his story, astrologers consider Chiron to be a symbol in our own birth charts of where we have a deep wound, where we are misfits and a bit of a rebel, pushing against limitations, and where and how we can be a healer and teacher to others and thus our self.

The astrological symbol for Chiron looks like a key. I had been noticing keys and even dreaming of them, so I took note of that connection. During the time that my attention was focused on Chiron, an email from a friend included an image of the 5th card of the Tarot, with the wise centaur depicted as the Hierophant. I was amazed, as I had not even made the connection of Chiron the teacher and healer as the Hierophant. I began to look at other Tarot decks and noticed that many of them show the symbol of the key on that card. The Hierophant is the bridge between Higher Self and Lower Self, or God and Human, shedding light on the mystery about our true nature. The key is to learn via the intuition, to listen to our inner wisdom and speak our own truth. The Hierophant is not someone outside of us, but a part within that has access to the treasure trove of knowledge. A little research into the card revealed that it is associated with the sign of Taurus, the sense of hearing, and the Hebrew letter *Vav*. The letter *Vav* means "nail or hook" as well as the word "and."[vii] These are tools for making connections, linking two or more things together. Sounds like the role of synchronicity to me!

It was only later, after writing down the connections between Chiron and the Hierophant, that I was amused to remember that these connections are of course reflected in my own birth chart. Chiron is in the sign of Taurus, and in the 9th house (the house of higher learning). This is one example, but as these things go, it's not unusual to see a mirror between synchronistic experiences and the natal chart. This makes sense, as both are speaking of the same energetic blueprint.

Another interesting tidbit that I took note of about Chiron was that *chiro* means *hand*.[viii] I probably wouldn't have been so tickled by this, had I not also just learned that the Hebrew letter *Yod* also means hand, the ultimate creative instrument. *Yod* is depicted as a little flame, and is said to be the basis from which all other Hebrew letters are formed. A video presentation I watched recently, of the amazing and groundbreaking work by Stan Tenen of the Meru Project, shows this connection clearly. Through his mathematical research and study, he discovered that a shape derived mathematically from the surface area of a Torus (a doughnut shape, "a surface of *revolution*"[ix]), fits exactly into the palm of the hand. He then demonstrates that the shadows that are cast from looking at this shape at different angles reveal the letters of the Hebrew alphabet.[x] In essence, one of the oldest known languages is derived from the combination of turning and spiraling, and the hand.

So it was precisely all of this attention around the HAND that caught my attention when at a book store, I picked a dictionary of occult symbolism off of the shelf, and as 'coincidence' would have it, opened it randomly to the page describing the symbolism of the HAND. I then noticed that the shelf that I grabbed the book from was the PALMistry section. I was amused, but still didn't think much of "palm" in particular. As I walked to the checkout my mind was certainly running with the hand theme, "There are 5 fingers on a hand—like a pentagram! . . . The HANDS of Time!," and so on until, as I was paying for my purchases, a book on display near the register caught my eye. Across the front of the book was the author's name in big bold letters: PALMER. Later that same evening my husband, unaware of the palm sync, shared a news story with me and the individual on which the article was written also had the last name of PALMer. (Yes, Palmer is a fairly common surname, but it was the precise, synchronous timing that urged me to pay attention.) The next night while doing some light fictional reading, I see mention of "palm trees" and shortly thereafter look down to my side where I see the sign that has been literally in my palm all along, as the style of my cell phone is a PALM Pre.

So these synchronicities led me to start thinking about not just the hand, but in particular the *palm*. I was contemplating the palm, thinking about the divinatory art of reading a person's destiny in the lines of the palm, when I wondered if there is a Hebrew letter that specifically means "palm." Indeed there is; the letter is *Kaph*, meaning "palm" or also "grasping hand." It is represented by the planet Jupiter and associated with the 10th card of the Tarot, the Wheel of Fortune. This card depicts that "wheel in the sky," the zodiac, the wheel of stars above and within that are continuously turning, spiraling, cycling.[xi] These symbols are expressing the archetype of destiny/fate/fortune. The palms of your hands and the wheel of your birth chart both show the same evolving pattern of your soul.

As is shown in the collective of blogs at the *Sync List*, Jupiter is a planet and mythological god that has proven to have an undeniable relationship with synchronicity, as it emerges time and again. Astrologically, Jupiter is the force within that presents opportunity and urges us to seek meaning, to *grow*. The spiraling geometry of the manner in which nature *grows*, mathematically shown by the golden spiral, can be seen in the far out galaxies and in the smallest of pine cones. This innate geometry is sometimes referred to as the "fingerprint of God" as it shows us the pattern of creation that underlies the material world. Alice O. Howell is a well-known leader in linking psychology and astrology. In her book *The Web in the Sea: Jung, Sophia, and the Geometry of the Soul*, she describes her "aha moment" in working with the golden rectangle, revealing to her the nature of how symbols are layered and lead to growth through spiraling insights.[xii] Interesting when we think back to the Hierophant card and its connection to the sense of hearing, as the cochlea of the inner ear is also a manifestation of this sacred geometric spiral.

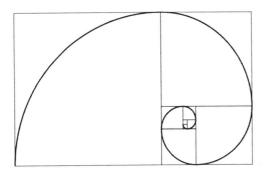

So the synchronicities to the word *vertere* and *turning* have been spinning a web, expressing the inherent nature of synchronicity, the pattern that is always there and the invisible hand of the inner guide that ushers in the chance to see it. By following the symbols that have been with us all along, that seemingly arrive out of nowhere all at once, we are listening, climbing the arching bridge or spiral staircase between the seen and unseen, noticing that the layers are all formed from the original fabric, and syncing with our purpose to be whole and fully embody our soul.

Shortly after following the *palm* sync down the rabbit hole, I realized that all of these connections lead back to what motivated me to start blogging in the winter of 2009-2010. I had recently been re-inspired by the beauty and mystery of the world, and was curiously noticing the pattern of vibrational energy that makes its mark on the magnetic field of the earth, trees, fingerprints, etc. I actually spent a good portion of a day staring at the swirling and branching lines on my *palm* in wonder. One of the very first posts I made to my blog, *Constellation Contemplation*, was a collage of these curving, vibratory pattern associations titled "in the beginning there was the word (sound) . . ." Around that same time I had looked at the Tarot for the first time. The very first card that I ever held in my hand and contemplated was the Hierophant. It's all so perfect, although not surprising, that the synchronicities I've experienced during the period of writing these pages, have circled me back to the beginning of my journey. This is the flawless delivery by the adept and well-versed cosmic comedian (Divine *Cosmedian?*), efficiently ordering each bit, dropping punch lines at the perfect moment, and always bringing the act full circle. It still gets me every time.

Δ *Editor's note*: Chiron should not be confused with Charon, which is discussed in Chapter 3, Jeremy's *Reflections on the Cinematic Underworld*. They are two distinct and separate heavenly bodies, as well as mythological figures (although both appear in the *Inferno* or underworld of Dante's *Divine Comedy*).

---

[i] Harper, D. (2001-2010). "Yoga". Retrieved April 2011, from *The Online Etymology Dictionary*: http://www.etymonline.com/index.php

[ii] Harper, "synchronic", *ibid*.

[iii] Harper, "time", *ibid*.

[iv] Watts, A. (1989). *The B∞k: On the Taboo Against Knowing Who You Are* (pp. 14-16). New York: Vintage Books.

[v] Harper, "divorce", *op. cit*.

[vi] Clow, B. H. (1987). *Chiron: Rainbow Bridge Between the Inner & Outer Planets* (pp. 1-4). St. Paul, MN: Llewellyn Publications.

[vii] Moore, D. (2007). *The Rabbi's Tarot* (pp. 85-107). Palm Bay, FL: Hughes Henshaw Publications.

[viii] Alli, A. (1999). *Astrologik: The Oracular Art of Astrology* (p. 190). Berkeley, CA: Vertical Pool.

[ix] "Torus." (2011). Retrieved May 2011, from *Wikipedia: The Free Encyclopedia*: http://en.wikipedia.org/wiki/Torus

[x] Stan Tenen, M. F. (Director). (2006). *First Light: An Overview of Meru Research* [Motion Picture].

[xi] Moore, *op. cit.*, pp. 193-205.

[xii] Howell, A. O. (1993). *The Web in the Sea: Jung, Sophia, and the Geometry of the Soul* (pp. 200-204). Wheaton, IL: Quest Books.

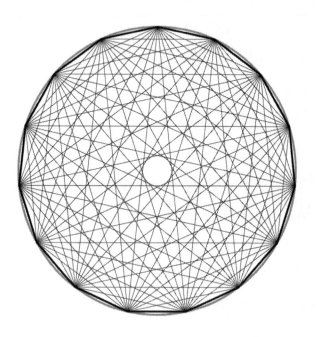

Kevin Halcott

Live from the Logosphere

Kevin Halcott is a lover, synchromystic, multimedia artist, occultist, writer, musician, psychonaut, student, and dishwasher living in upstate New York. He writes under the name Indra's Net on a small handful of blogs on the internet. Kevin started his own blog in 2008 called Live from the Logosphere which began as an exploration of synchronicity, popular media, conspiracy, mythology, and astrology. As Kevin's work progressed, he began to believe that it is not only people that are conspiring on planet earth, but that the Earth and the Universe itself are constantly conspiring together intelligently, and that synchronicity is the means by which this can be demonstrated. "In a world that is constantly being disenchanted by modern science and the illusion of 'normalcy,' synchronicity allows us to acknowledge that all is part of a story bigger than any one person can tell. It is the Synchromystic's joy and job to turn these mazes into mandalas. There is nothing in every star of screen and sky that is not of you and I." Kevin has also been contributing to The Sync Whole since 2009 and has recently been holding public viewings of his short documentary entitled Film: A Thin Skin or Membrane.

liveinchapelperilous.blogspot.com
youtube.com/kevin23420
vimeo.com/user1814089
g8ors.blogspot.com

The Synchromystic Aura
Opening the 42fold Stargate

Obscure metaphysical explanation to cover a phenomenon, reasons dredged out of the shadows to explain away that which cannot be explained. Call it parallel planes or just insanity. Whatever it is, you find it in the Twilight Zone.

Art as a Language

They say a picture is worth a thousand words. Art is indeed a language of its own, one that we may use to convey things that we cannot communicate with just words. We acknowledge this quality of art when we consider the advent of language, as many posit that mankind first communicated with the use of drawing symbols that were inspired by the external environment. These pictograms would become the building blocks of the symbolic language of a culture's understanding of its placement and navigation in the universe, eventually forming the unique alphabets through which information could be passed on through time. We can think of art and storytelling as vital organs in mankind's understanding of our relationship to the external universe, in that they transmute new experiences into symbolic representations of the wisdom gained therein. In our culture, and historically in many tribal cultures, as people traverse the many stages in the human experience, these stages are celebrated with dramatic artistic ceremonies or initiations. Often particular markings will also be made, whether temporary or permanent, on the body to denote the level of development that has been accomplished.

I propose that the pop-films that we share and enjoy in our modern time are also metaphoric initiatory tattoos or expressions denoting our dramatic movement into deeper union with the infinite and ourselves. Just as we used to embed our initiatic mythologies of the Gods or the forces of nature into the Stars of the night sky, we now have our dramatic mythology supplied to us by the movie *stars* of the silver screen. The Art of Synchromysticism acknowledges the significance of what we call movie "Stars" on planet Earth as being intimately and symbolically connected with the same dramas that have been recorded in the stars above since the dawn of storytelling. Let's consider that this is the journey of cinema and mythology, the externalization and documentation of the mythic, spiritual, and social drama of self-realization and celebration of the spectrum of the experience of life in symbolic form. Just like the tribal cultures weekly ritual drama under the starry night, we in the West have Friday nights at the cinema, where the movie stars of the silver screen now provide us with up to date reflections of our lives and times.

Cinema as Large Scale Cultural Initiation

The word Tragedy etymologically descends from the Greek "Goat Song." We can think of the Goat as symbolically linked with initiation. Since the Goat is an animal that can climb to the heights of hard mountains, if we consider the mountain as a metaphor for life and initiation, we can see the Goat as a perfect symbol of the earthly life journey. In Aristotle's *Poetics* he defines Tragedy as such: *"Tragedy is an imitation of an action that is admirable, complete (composed of an introduction, a middle part and an ending), and possesses magnitude; in language made pleasurable, each of its species separated in different parts; performed by actors, not through narration; effecting through pity and fear the purification of such emotions."* Tragedy and drama are the Goat songs we sing together as we climb the wHoly mount-*in*. Acknowledging cinema as a dramatic developmental mythology can empower us with new avenues of understanding the purpose and process of art, drama, and our human experience.

Pop art informs the depths of our self awareness, at least on an unconscious level for most of us. As children we find our identities in that which we resonate with most—whether it's *Spider-Man*, *Superman*, *Macho Man Randy Savage*, *Cat Woman*, or *Wonder Woman*. Our unique self becomes attracted to that which we truly resonate with. We can think of these mythic passions of ours as the development of our own personal Totems. Our popular culture and the many characters of its history has provided us with a rich pool of totemic mythic reference, highlighting our expanding spectrum knowledge as well as inspiring us and guiding us toward what brings us our own unique joy. The worlds and characters of films have become mirrors of aspects of ourselves and the infinite universes to be brought to light, constantly updating our lives with new meaning and understanding in our fast paced times. We use these films and metaphors to describe how and who we are, and the metaphors only work because they sync our environment with ourselves.

When we feel full of valuable energy we say, "I'm feeling golden!" And when we are feeling drained of that valuable energy we say, "I feel like shit." When a person is smart we say, "He or she is really bright!" Do we really know what it feels like to embody gold, shit, and brightness? No and yes. We have an understanding of the Value of these things external to us, and we define and make relationships between our human functions and these functions of nature. We are informed about aspects of ourselves through metaphor, and these metaphors provide examples of how we use symbols from our external environment to dramatize the internal experiences we want to communicate.

It is no surprise then that we will find around the world many similar symbols, deities, stories, characters, and so on—though these have been produced by cultures that are separated by vast distances. This is because we as humans are bonded by the language of nature and art, and languages are molded out of the use of metaphors that bring us closer to what we are specifically trying to communicate. We can group symbols and mythologies from these seemingly separate cultures to demonstrate this bond that we all share with nature.

Myth speaks a language of its own and communicates through characters. Recurring types of mythological characters like the Egyptian child hero Horus and the modern Luke Skywalker and Harry Potter myths are great examples of the recurring world mythos of the hero child who is destined to avenge his father's death. We can also see this child's vengeance as a multi-contextual parable of the formula of life, the symbolic drama of genes being passed on from father to son and so on. Here we have a natural formula, translated into human expression, demonstrated in cultures distanced by time and place. This is a Synchronicity in itself, and a good place to start exploring the Language of Synchromysticism.

When we look at nature we see patterns—the seasons, cycles of the moon, and motions of stars and planets are all patterned. This is also true of the movement of people, including movie stars. When we acknowledge a pattern arising in pop culture (like Horus, Luke Skywalker, and Harry Potter), we see that, beyond the surface appearance of forms and names, the same drama can express itself. These patterns cross time and place because all cultures are subject to the same forces of nature and are all symbolically transmitting mythic language that is beyond words and forms.

The great thinker Carl Jung proposed that all humans share what is called a collective unconscious, a deposit of stored genetic data that informs the conscious minds of all of us seemingly separate individuals and manifests in the form of shared cultural behaviors. Jung called the common forms that arise from this collective unconscious Archetypes. Archetypes are the common figures or concepts encountered in the human experience: Gods, Demons, Heavens, and Hells. These archetypes are rich with information about our collective unconscious. We encounter the feeling of being informed by archetypal information when we are unreasonably afraid of the dark or the unknown. We also encounter archetypical beings in our daily life such as family, elders, healers, priests, priestesses, saints, devils, workers, tyrants, and leaders.

Art is a tool which takes the more dramatic, exaggerated, and rich experiences that occur on the inner Spiritual or Archetypal plane, and projects them out into the external environment. When we are engaged with a film we are encountering representatives of living spiritual and archetypal forces that have been communicating with all humans through time. They are the ever-changing Earthly reflections of living principles of the spiritual world. Art is the story that we bring back from our very own hero's journey in the inner and outer worlds. The landscapes and characters of our dramas are our "Goat songs" of Ascension, coming from the shared inner landscapes and the pantheons of our collective psyche.

Pop culture is our own spiritual compass of anagnorisis (meaning to "know again" or "knowing back" or "knowing throughout") about human destiny and the will of the gods. Aristotle terms this process "a change from ignorance to awareness of a bond of love or hate." All of this talk about the power of metaphor, the collective unconscious, and language isn't synchronicity—but I believe we can come to understand the role of film and drama, and therein understand what synchronicity is teaching us from its source of origin. Then we can set out to understand it as a language that we are already familiar with.

Film: A Thin Skin or Membrane

One of the definitions of the word "film" is "A Thin Skin or Membrane." I do believe this is true, even of the Cinematic definition of a film, that it is a membrane or medium through which greater intuitive knowledge of the self and the universe are expressed in symbolic form. In the world of film and popular culture at any given time, there is what we can imagine as an alphabet of similar roles and themes that are being called into the spotlight generally to mark some kind of new collective understanding of our experience. The world's deities and characters in stories are used the same way: good is good, whether you call it Horus or Luke Skywalker or Harry Potter, we just have different names for "the good guy" all over the world. There is an Archetypal Alphabet, or Deity Soup, always swirling around our consciousness, picking up new representatives for who will be the Hero this year—as well as the Villain, the Queen, the Stargater, etc.

This kind of understanding of reality on a symbolic level is not new. The sciences of Kabbalah and Tarot, for example, put forth that the universe is built with 22 elements. These "Forces" are then represented by letters of the alphabet. Every culture has a pool of symbols for the ever-present forces that sustain the economy of the universe.

This is the same with movie stars. When a spiritual force or archetype is being highlighted, we call upon particular stars to represent it in the drama. When a movie star is cast in multiple roles that resonate with each other we can see there is a law of attraction at work—resulting in what we call typecasting. However, beneath and beyond that, we associate people with whatever they would naturally be fit to represent (our intuition informs the selection process in who gets what role). This alphabet of forces takes on human form through the movie star and creates what we call drama, but ultimately these Stars are only vessels for the universal language.

There is a common belief among all cultures that there is a spiritual dimension which underlies the waking world. There are many names for this spirit world: Astral Plane, Afterlife, Underworld, Heaven, dreamtime and so on. Kabbalah details a concept of a Bridge uniting the Heavenly and Earthly planes of existence. This bridge, when represented on the *Tree of Life* diagram, crosses the hidden sphere of "Daath" or Knowledge. This sphere is where consciousness experiences heaven (the imaginable) and earth (the physical), as one inseparable condition.

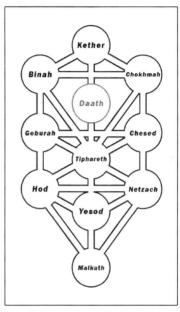

Viewing our dramas through this lens, we would experience a unity with the underlying spiritual language represented in the art (like when we feel as if we are really *in the movie* or a virtual reality). When we look at the archetypical or spiritual quality of drama we can begin to see actors as living archetypes, as representatives of mythic forces of spirit itself. I believe that art, and especially Film—the membrane or bridge—is our tool for exploring our own sphere of Daath, where we encounter divinity as dramatized by the earthly stars.

While Daath is the sphere crossed by the bridge, the bridge itself is known as the middle pillar—connecting the spheres of Kether (the heavenly crown) and Malkuth (the earthly kingdom).

The middle pillar has also been called "The Rainbow Bridge" and is directly analogous with the Vedic tradition's own Rainbow Bridge of Chakras. These Chakras run up our spine as energy centers—each with their own color and function. This Symbolism of the rainbow uniting Heaven and Earth is a common mystical, religious, and pop culture archetype.

And the bow shall be in the cloud; and I will look upon it, that I may remember the everlasting covenant between God and every living creature of all flesh that is upon the earth. And God said unto Noah, This is the token of the covenant, which I have established between me and all flesh that is upon the earth.
—*Genesis 9:16-17*

Here we see an early example of the Rainbow as an archetypical bridge between heaven and earth, between man and the divine. In modern times we have our own pop mythos communicating the same Rainbow Bridge: the *Wizard of Oz* and the "Over the Rainbow" theme. In this story, the rainbow is a bridge to the heavenly realm of Oz and here Dorothy must learn to see "behind the curtain" or through the film/membrane.

Synchromysticism and Building the Rainbow Bridge

So if there really are more subtle planes of consciousness that are parallel to our present Earthly one, there are probably stories and symbolism down here on Earth that point toward this other reality. "As above, so below," right? Just as we looked at above, the Rainbow is the perfect symbol of this bridge between the spiritual dimensions of our imagination, and the physical human world we live in. Thanks to science-fiction, the word Stargate is a term that many of us are now familiar with. In case you aren't, a Stargate can be defined as any time/space distorting event or object. We may consider that the Rainbow Bridge to Oz is a Stargate symbol too, a bridge from Earth to the Stars or Heavens, the higher "far out" worlds.

Alice Bailey, a popular modern spiritualist and mystic, believed that connecting heaven and Earth is the current spiritual task of humanity, to build the "Antahkarana" Rainbow Bridge and unite the Soul plane of existence and the physical. Alice believed that, if we are all true to ourselves, we are therefore true to our unique individual and Soul, thus uniting spirit and matter or heaven and

Earth. Author of the *Wizard of Oz*, L. Frank Baum was part of the same Spiritual Mystery School as Alice Bailey, which is called Theosophy. Baum wrote the *Wizard of Oz* at the same time that Bailey was working on her esoteric sciences of the Rainbow Bridge or Antahkarana. According to Bailey, the Antahkarana Bridge is activated in our human body when all of our Chakras (energy centers of our heart, mind, and body) are balanced and functioning in unison.

Of particular importance in Bailey's energetic constitution of this Antahkarana Chakra-bridge is the Dog Star Sirius, which some traditions believe to be our Spiritual Sun (in contrast to our Earthly Sun that brings physical life on Earth). The Antahkarana is the spiritual economy of life. We are all spiritual beings having a human experience. When we live in that knowledge, the Rainbow Bridge is activated and accomplished inside and outside of us. Now let's consider the Dog Star Sirius again, remembering that it is our Spiritual Sun and a highly important Chakra center in our spinal Rainbow Bridge. This Dog Star guide is a perfect fit: in Egyptian mythology the Dog Star was representative of the dog deity Anubis, the guide to the Dead as they crossed the bridge between worlds. Let's then consider the importance of the dog Toto, who goes over the rainbow in the *Wizard of Oz*. In all of these analogous myths, the Dog guides the human between the worlds, and even lifts the veil from the false Wizard creator of Oz, revealing the self as the center of the mandala. Sirius, Anubis, Toto, Oz, Astral Plane, Over the Antahkarana Rainbow Bridge between worlds. . . . did Baum and Bailey collaborate? We can only guess.

Down the Rabbit Whole

The Dog Star happens to be a keystone in the history of documented synchronistic high weirdness. In Robert Anton Wilson's *Cosmic Trigger: Volume 1*, he explores his personal experiences of contact, seemingly from an intelligence that he believed was communicating with him through the Dog Star Sirius. Bob had many wacky synchronicities, such as being informed while in a trance that Time and Sirius would be important in his life—later realizing that he had that experience on July 23rd, the only day of the year that the Dog Star rises before the Sun. Robert Anton Wilson is certainly a forefather and an original inspiration to the Synchromystic. Wilson, along with William S. Burroughs, popularized the synchronistic number 23 in the 1960s. The film, *The Number 23*, would later re-popularize this number. When Wilson began having his strange synchronicities in the 1970s, he attributed these cosmic coincidences to what the Irish called the "Phooka." The Phooka is said to be a human-sized White Rabbit trickster-deity that is responsible for high weirdness in the lives of folks—causing them to question the limits of their reality. He would later attribute many other metaphors to his strange synchronicities, such as the guidance of Secret Chiefs, ET Contact, Guardian Angels, the right brain, and quantum knowledge.

To the Synchromystic, the White Rabbit brings to mind stories like *Alice in Wonderland, Harvey, The Matrix, The Last Mimzy,* and Frank from *Donnie Darko*. So here we have a pool of symbolic narratives where the White Rabbit serves as an initiator of the trippy-trip down into a hole, that is a (w)hole new narrative. Interestingly enough, the Rabbit constellation *Lepus* was believed by the Egyptians to be the Boat to the Spirit world, and believe it or not, this constellation is right beneath Sirius the Dog Star (Toto-Anubis, the guide to the dimension of spirit).

To demonstrate *another* Synchromystic association, I will note the recurrence of the Number 42 in relation to this Rabbit theme. To begin, the Egyptians believed that the Rabbit Constellation led one's soul to the courts of the Goddess Maat and the 42 assessors of the dead. Alice, led by the White Rabbit, ends up in the Queen's Court where she is cited for breaking "Rule Forty-two. *All persons more than a mile high to leave the court.*" Now even further along these lines, *Donnie Darko* features a White Rabbit who tells him, "28 days, 6 hours, *42 minutes*, 12 seconds. That is when the world will end." Then there is *The Last Mimzy*, wherein a Mandala Stargate opens—via a mystical White Rabbit sent back in time—called the 42-triangled Sri Yantra mandala, further entraining these two forms.

Not just the White Rabbit, but also the Rainbow Bridge, our other symbol for uniting worlds, is associated with the Synchromystic 42, since Rainbows are created when Light and Water are married at a 42-degree angle. This gets better when we see the White Rabbit and the Dog Star come together again: Keanu

Reeves plays bass in the band Dog Star, goes down the rabbit hole in *The Matrix*, and here he even interacts with a television playing the film, *Night of the Lepus*, in one scene.

While editing this article, Facebook's Thelema group just so happened to post a link to Aleister Crowley's *Liber 242 Aha*—wherein he perfectly mentions the Hall of Death and the Rainbow veil while talking about spiritual aspiration. In Egyptian and Thelemic mythology, the Hall of Death refers to the spiritual underworld, the Duat, and its 42 assessor deities, as well as the 42 confessions of Maat. Remember that the rainbow is light and water meeting at a 42-degree angle.

> *Fashion thyself by austere craft*
> *Into a single azure shaft*
> *Loosed from the string of Will; behold*
> The Rainbow! *Thou art shot, pure flame,*
> *Past the reverberated Name*
> *Into the* Hall of Death. *Therein*
> *The Rosy Cross is subtly seen.*

This is highly cool synchronicity at work. The Rainbow Bridge, the Dog Star and Rabbit (w)Hole appear to be aspects of the Spiritual Architecture—architecture that we are noticing as the worlds of spirit and matter unite.

Opening the 42fold StarG8

Now we can see how our symbolic/archetypal alphabet soup can take form with the aid of movie stars. We can perceive an economy of dynamic narratives, forces, and symbols that reveal the language of synchronicity. Next, I would like to offer some of my personal experiences with synchronicity and powerful movie-star/heavenly-star associations that I believe offer validity to this synchronistic language concept.

Two weeks before Michael Jackson passed away, I was deep in the throes of understanding the Antahkarana Rainbow Bridge and writing posts about it over at my blog, *Live from the Logosphere*. While surfing the net on a break from researching, I happened randomly across a blog featuring Jackson 5's "Can You Feel It" music video. This was immediately a synchronicity for me, as Michael Jackson actually lifts a Rainbow Bridge up and over humanity in this video. This blew my mind. I had just been exploring the Kabbalistic and Norse Rainbow Bridge myths; the Rainbow Bridge of Daath and Asgard. Within a few days, I had collected all sorts of rainbow synchronicities in Michael's career: from his glowing Rainbow shirt, his bringing Light and Color to the world in *Captain Eo*, the Rainbow featured right behind his name in the credits for the musical *The Wiz*, to the Rainbow behind him on both the movie and video game posters for *Moonwalker* and even his Spiritual Advisor, Reverend Jessie Jackson, being the head of the Rainbow Push foundation.

Here we have a beautiful example of how synchromystic resonation works by creating an aura which informs us to the nature of any star we have focused on. Stars are attractors—when you think "Sylvester Stallone," boxing and semi-automatics come quicker to mind than flowers and Rainbows, right? So here we can see how typecasting and resonation both appear to arise from intuition. We associate stars with roles and forms that we perceive with our spiritual or inner vision. Michael Jackson was a Rainbow Bridge himself, uniting the spectrum of illusory racial, sexual, social, and even spiritual differences that block the Antahkarana or Rainbow Bridge from being built on Earth. Michael's aura thus attracts the archetype and symbols of the union of opposites and the unity symbolized by the Rainbow, making these synchronicities seem more than meaningless. Synchromystic vision can allow us to perceive the symbolic auras that surround us: those of actors, places, ideas, or even ourselves.

Just two weeks after I had taken my first personal interest in MJ ever, had just published numerous blog posts and videos about him and the rainbow bridge between worlds—Michael literally returned to the Soul, crossing the Rainbow Bridge that I was writing about. So, when I heard Michael Jackson had passed away, it was one of the weirdest days of my life.

I was even more amazed when I watched the *South Park* episode that followed Michael's passing. The episode featured Zelda Rubinstein, the exorcist from the hit film *Poltergeist*, playing a spiritual guide who helps Michael Jackson cross over into the spirit-soul plane. I decided to do a synchromystic star chart of Zelda's career to see what symbolic aura might be attracted to her. "Will

THE SYNCHROMYSTIC AURA

there be rainbows?" I wondered. I was given immediate synchronistic confirmation that her association with Michael Jackson, the Angel of the Rainbow Bridge, was meaningful and proper indeed.

Zelda Rubinstein strongly resonates with the bridge between worlds, firstly by her opening the gate to the Soul plane in *Poltergeist* and *South Park*. She is also the narrator of the Skittles "Taste the Rainbow" commercials. Zelda's Rainbow-Aura shines brighter when we realize that she plays "Iris" (Latin for *Rainbow*) in the film *Under the Rainbow*, and plays (White-Rabbit-resonating) "Bunny" in *Unbeatable Harold*. Remembering again, that a rainbow is made from light and water meeting at a 42-degree angle, it's wild to note that the house address in *Poltergeist*, where Zelda opens a stargate, is 4267. The icing on the cake here is that the star child actor of *Poltergeist*, Heather O'Rourke, had done a few commercials in her sadly short life, some of the most popular being the *Rainbow Brite* commercials. *Rainbow Brite* is a show about a girl who must bring light and color back to a dark world, very similar to Michael Jackson as the angel of the Middle Pillar-Rainbow Bridge in *Captain Eo*. Also, if you do your homework, you can see that Zelda Rubinstein in *Poltergeist* is actually the spitting image of Alice Bailey from her Theosophy era (I wouldn't doubt that that may have had some level of influence on the film, conscious or unconscious). These connections, particularly Zelda Rubinstein helping Michael Jackson cross the bridge to the spirit world on *South Park*, are more examples of seemingly random associations (of characters to people and to themes), actually containing a meaningful synchronistic mandala, one rich with the residue of our collective unconscious and the architectures of other planes.

Bridging the Gap: Tweenwave Zero

In the film *Ghost*, Patrick Swayze plays the disembodied soul of a man seeking to contact his widowed wife. In one scene, we see Swayze as a ghost in the subway (underworld) of 42nd Street—in perfect sync with the aforementioned 42 deities of the Egyptian underworld and the 42-degree angle that takes us over the Rainbow. In further sync symmetry, we can note that Swayze is in *Donnie Darko*, and first appears in shot with Donnie as he acknowledges the mysterious number 42 written on his arm. Patrick

Swayze is also the star of the film *Black Dog*. In *Black Dog* we see Swayze having hallucinations of a Hellhound, a common mythic dog from the underworld (reminding us of Anubis-Sirius). The truck that Swayze drives has a 42 on the license plate *and* he even works for a character played by Meat Loaf, who appears in *The Rocky Horror Picture Show* right after Rocky creates his new-man in a rainbow vessel.

The truck in *Black Dog* can be related to the Egyptian Duat Boat, which transports souls from this plane to the next. The Duat Boat is also analogous with our energy body, or body of Light, known to Hebrew mystics as the Merkaba. The Merkaba is also known as the Chariot and is the means by which our spirit travels out of our physical body. The Merkaba Chariot is also the archetype of the Chariot Tarot Trump, known as the Child of the Powers of the Waters, which brings to mind the Duat Boat again.

We can see a boat to the underworld in the chapter "Anchors Aweigh" of the film *Waking Life*. In this scene, we see the main character enter a boat with a pirate flag and the numbers 424242 repeating on the side of it. As we might guess by now, the archetype of entering another dimension is also a major theme in this movie, further associating the number 42 with the uniting of the spiritual and physical dimensions.

The year 2009 was the year that the Rainbow Bridge was established, in my opinion. In July, I had my synchronicities that preceded Michael Jackson's crossing of the rainbow bridge, and, to my further amazement, one of the forefathers of the 2012 phenomenon, José Argüelles, announced his mission to create a collectively-visualized Rainbow Bridge around the Earth. José believed that, through visualizing the rainbow enveloping the Earth, we could all activate and communicate within the Noosphere (the Sphere of all human consciousness, thoughts, and concepts). José believed that building this bridge was vital in attaining world peace, very much like what Alice Bailey had said about the Antahkarana Rainbow Bridge in the 1930s.

In 2009, both Michael Jackson and Patrick Swayze—strong rainbow and rabbit hole resonators—passed away. In 2010, Zelda Rubinstein passed away. And now, in 2011, José Argüelles did too.

THE SYNCHROMYSTIC AURA

As I was writing this article, *South Park* aired a new episode called "You're Getting Old." In this episode, a cultural timewave is acknowledged and termed "The Tweens," a nickname for the years between 2009 and 2013. It is my opinion that something in the collective unconscious kick-started the activation of the Rainbow Bridge, creating the next wave of enlightenment. The "Tweens" timewave concept highlighted by *South Park* is a perfect metaphor for the bridge between the *pre-* and *post-*2012 era, and highlights some of our own unconscious understanding that a period of great change has begun. It's up to us now to build this Rainbow Bridge in ourselves, and as a planet. As the great Occultist and Prophet of a new golden age, Aleister Crowley, said, "For the colours are many, but the light is one."

What's a Meta-For Anyway?

We navigate our world with the use of symbols. Badges help us find people who uphold the law, the caduceus helps us find the Hospital, and Rainbows can remind us that we are spiritual beings having a human experience. What symbols attract you? To what surroundings has your love brought you?

Art is an act of love and union. Films are a highly complex form of Bhakti (love/devotional) Yoga, in which we honor and glorify life by reproducing it and celebrating it. Synchronicity arises from our natural inspiration and celebration of life. It allows us to acknowledge the unifying animating force that flows through all different forms, narrating a larger story that houses all contexts, cultures, and narratives. The force, which is consciousness beyond time and place, acknowledges us/itself through us/itself. Consider that maybe we all have symbolic auras that we express through our surroundings—maybe we have seen fractals and patterns in our Life Narrative already. Consciousness—the force of life and love that has guided us through all of our stories and stages—is all there is . . . so there is only our own territory to tread.

We can now begin to perceive the synchromystic symbolic aura as something real and observable. Understanding that synchronicity is always at work around us can help us treat life as if it were our own meaningful mandala rather than someone else's meaningless maze. It's our job in these times to piece/peace the world together. When I decided to blog about synchronicity, I chose to write under the name *Indras Net*. I chose this name because the Vedic god Indra was said to maintain a giant web of jewels connecting the whole universe, reflecting any influence upon one jewel through the rest. Long after using this as my name on the blog, I began to have the above-mentioned rainbow synchronicities. I was amazed to later find out that I had chosen the shortened name of *Indra*. It turns out that the full name of the god is Indradhanush, meaning "Indra of the Rainbow." It would appear that the Rainbow and Rabbit are now a part of my Aura too. Just as we can perceive synchronistic fractals in people's careers, we are all fractals of ourselves-to-be as well. Synchronicity occurs when we get a wink from our non-local self that is beyond the changing times and forms. Synchronicities are kisses from "somewhere over the Rainbow."

> *Our birth is but a sleep and a forgetting:*
> *The Soul that rises with us, our life's Star,*
> *Hath had elsewhere its setting,*
> *And cometh from afar . . .*
> —William Wordsworth

If we can acknowledge the patterns that have arisen in our lives, we can then use synchronicity as a compass, to bring us closer to knowing who we have been, who we want to be, and what we are here to do. There is nothing in any star of screen or sky that is not of you and I. It is of us and we are of it. I leave you with some thoughts from Albert Einstein. He said it well when he said, "*Coincidence* is God's way of remaining anonymous."

Namaste

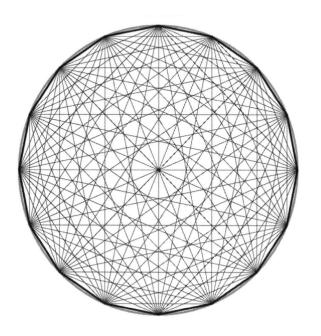

Douglas Bolles

*Douglas Bolles is a writer working in sync. (As a form, "sync" is less concerned with what's real, i.e. fiction or nonfiction, because it's **all** real—though none of it is.) He is currently working on a novella called* Winter's Labyrinth, *of which a portion is featured here. The story is told in four parts and what's presented here is Part One and a portion of Part Two. Look for this work's completion early next year. D.B. is a self described MOTHERMAN and Snake River Phoenix. He is a fruit vendor by trade and may be responsible for the revolution. (Sorry.)*

Winter's Labyrinth
A novella in four parts

In the high branches of the Central Tree perched a regal Golden Eagle. It was teased and taunted by a Serpent in the roots. This place was *every* place and *no* place. It was the Hollow where time and eternity met; where something and nothing came together. . .

The Serpent loved trying to get caught. It put itself in ever more compromised positions, reveling in the chase, and exiting the trap—of course infuriating the Eagle in the process.

In the branches were others as well. An odd, red-breasted Robin had a way of capturing the attention of those at the Tree. Two Owls often were present, and the Robin was somehow able to bring together a Condor from the south as well as a Black Shuck from the highlands. They would all gather in the Hollow listening to the Robin as it communicated the nature of being.

Naturally the Serpent challenged them. . . .

One day when they were all gathered and listening to the Robin, the Serpent interrupted. It asked them if they had noticed the Smoke coming from the Man City.

The Condor replied, "Heaven is spread upon the face of the earth yet they do not see it."

"You think it that easy then?" questioned the Serpent.

The others at this point joined the discussion. They too were ashamed of the lack of consciousness in the Man City.

"They remove every tree, gouge the land with holes, destroy the soil, and fill the air with smoke," noted the Eagle.

"But what if it is not entirely their fault?" hissed the Serpent.

"They are unconscious to their place in Heaven," retorted the Condor.

"Well then friends—"

"Do you have friends, Serpent?" interrupted the Black Dog.

"I have a proposition . . . I have learned of a way to save Man."

"Just in time," screeched the Owl.

"Of course, you know, there is a catch," explained the Serpent.

"Yeah, yeah. Out with it, Serpent!" continued the Owl.

"Is it really Man that needs saving, or the land?" questioned the other, hairier Owl.

"Can one separate Man and the Land?" answered the Serpent.

"So it is paradox rhetoric you're after this day, Serpent?" glared the Eagle.

"To save Man you must become Man."

"Now *this* sounds like another of your tricks, Serpent," intoned the Eagle.

"No. . . . No trick; this is participation in the mystery."

"Yes. We become Man, and lead them to their true Self."

"That's the idea, Condor," reassured the Serpent.

The Robin finally spoke, "How then do we become Man, Serpent?"

"Do I hear a willingness to take on this noble cause? To leave the high branches of Heaven and walk upon the land?"

"I'm still considering whether or not I should bite you," glowered the Dog.

"If you follow the flow of the Stream that runs through the Hollow to its source, you will reach a spring, a fountain. A tree here grows which produces a kind of fruit that will put us on our way."

"You care *too*, Serpent?" questioned the smaller, less hairy Owl.

"Can I let you have all the fun?"

"How do we not know that this isn't another trick, Serpent, and that this so-called fruit is not *poison*?"

"Oh, it is poison, Eagle, and you *will* die. You will die to your animal nature, but you then will have the opportunity of coming alive to your *human* nature."

"Opportunity?"

"That is up to you Eagle. There is a process in becoming Man."

"The proposition then, is for us to stay here, conscious in an ever diminishing Heaven, or to play an active role in this as Man, attempting to save Heaven from its unconscious destruction," stated the Robin.

"Interesting you should note the idea of *consciousness*. In becoming Man, you will have a journey to undertake to become conscious again. It will be many man-years before you can remember who you are and why you came, if you do at all."

And there was silence in the Hollow. All the animals grew contemplative save one, the Black Shuck, the large black Dog. It growled, "So we've become a suicide club? Trust a Snake do you? What other kinds of trickery is involved here? I want nothing of this—"

"This Adventure?"

"This exile from Eden, this fresh death. Oh I believe the Serpent's words about your death, only I doubt very seriously that any of you will be born again. Perhaps this will make a lovely tale someday, how the Serpent won the Hollow."

"I will eat of the fruit first," announced the Serpent.

It was at this moment that the Condor, the Eagle, and the Robin appraised the Serpent's eyes. The Robin addressed then the group, "I will partake of the fruit after the Serpent." He paused and again looked into the Serpent's eyes, "When should we undertake this journey?"

"The daybreak of the morrow. Let us meet at the Fountain at first light."

A strong wind then began to blow lifting dead leaves and the fur of the glaring Dog. It rattled the skeletal, leafless branches of the Central Tree and made it difficult for the birds to maintain their perches.

The Condor and Eagle both took to the air, and both cried in unison into the wind, "The Spring! Tomorrow!"

And all the animals departed the Hollow save two.

"I could end this foolishness right now, Serpent. I could kill you in 23 different ways."

. . .

"But you still have something to say. What is it? Why are you still here? Are we not similar things?"

And the Shuck strode off, responding not to the Serpent's questions, never again speaking to the Serpent again in this life.

Upon the first rise beyond the Hollow, the Dog stretched, straightening his front legs and bringing his chest close to the ground. A yawning/growling noise sounded as the Dog did this. The Shuck walked to a clump of grass, hunched, and shat. Upon finishing, the Dog bounded away, springing and leaping like a gazelle, running fast to the first ridge. There, the Shuck momentarily paused at the top looking down upon the Central Tree.

It had been a cold winter and the Shuck was ready for life to return to the Hollow. As the Black Dog paused, the faintest noise caused one pointy ear upon the Dog's head to rotate ever so slightly. The expression on the Shuck's face imperceptibly moved in the direction of a *Grim* grin and without warning, the Dog bounded off up the hills and toward the mountains moving deliberately and with an expression of what could only be called joy, ever upward through the diminishing day and toward the night.

A Red Sun rising began a new day. It had been a long night for the Dog though, and its rising had not been seen. The Dog slept on as the Sun began and undertook its adventure through the *vault* of heaven. When the Shuck did awake, the air was warm with a hint of moisture. The Dog's repose had been taken in one of the favored dens. This particular one shielded from rain should it do so, but was open enough to take in the entire southern sky, framed as it was by the snowy Southern Mountains. Paradise.

The Dog stood, stretched, yearred, and thought about the previous day's *foolishness*. "What was that asshole after? Did the Serpent find meaning in trickery? Leading dupes into unsuspecting and compromised positions?"

These musings piqued the Dog's curiosity, "What *would* be found at the Spring were a sojourn there taken?" The idea of a cool drink from the Fountain tickled the Dog's fancy, and the Shuck bounded away toward the Source.

What greeted the Shuck upon arrival was a bit of a shock though. Dead things completely surrounded the Fountain of the Spring. This large, shallow pool surrounded by smooth rocks, was fed by a spring, the Source. The flow of the Spring which ran down and through the Hollow began by cascading over a large, slanted, flat stone that formed part of the pool's bottom on its southern end. The Fountain was partially shaded by the Tree growing just north of the Source.

The Black Shuck viewed the grisly results of the Serpent's taunts. The two Owls lay dead, one to the east, and one to the west. The Condor and Robin both lay dead together, north of the Fountain. The Golden Eagle lay as dead as all the others but to the south of the Fountain.

And the Serpent's skin?

—was nowhere to be seen...

"Did he slither off to die alone somewhere in the wastes, or..." wondered the Dog whose initial suspicion of the Serpent's dare appeared well founded.

The Dog moved toward the Fountain and began lapping from the pool. It was cool, and invigorating. The Shuck then noticed its reflection on the surface as it drank. Halting, the Dog reflected upon the moment noticing the half-eaten fruit directly beneath its mirrored self.

Without a thought, the Dog's snout struck the surface of the water crashing through its image, opening and closing its mouth upon the fruit. It then yanked its face from the Fountain lifting its head in the air swallowing the entire bite.

The Shuck had no idea why these particular actions had just occurred. Before any time for thoughts though, the Dog staggered off far to the east of the Fountain and collapsed. As the eyes of the Dog closed and as consciousness was lost, the Dog noticed a pulsing, circular tunnel near the roots of the Tree, compelling entrance. And then everything went black . . .

Part II

As I became conscious again, I noticed how badly my head hurt. It throbbed, and I lifted my hand and found a bump, a tender "goose-egg." I opened my eyes and saw only the tiniest bit of light at the mouth of the cave. I was warned to keep away from this place, but I swear I had heard music. I must've tripped here over these boulders on the ground while not allowing my eyes enough time to adjust to the dark of the cave.

I could still faintly hear the music or voices—something—deeper into the dark of the cave. I could also *see* writing too, like it glowed somehow. On one side of the cave wall was written, "a big Kidder wuz here!" And on the cave ceiling directly above me, I read, "Tommy can you hear me?"

Strange. I have been called Tommy, but it is unusual. Mostly I go by my full name, Thomas. So, was this somehow a message for me? I was surprised, but what was the *information*? Did it speak of the music? Was that what I was to hear?

It was after a deep breath and another tentative touch of the growing egg upon the front of my head that I became aware of barking.

"Arrow?" Very little sound came out of me. I tried again louder, "Arrow!"

He barked louder, but did not enter the cave. I rose and gingerly walked toward him, toward the light, toward the mouth of the cave, toward my dog. He turned up last summer in July. I had dreamed all the kinds of dogs that I could possibly want—all the different qualities—and he was it all. All the things rolled up into one tiny, medium-sized dog. I called him *Arrow* because of his pointy nose and ears and because he could fly across the hills. When he showed up at the Market, the Market Lord granted him to me. Despite all I had lost, I was very lucky.

As I exited the cave, I was born into the light. It was blinding, and I held my eyes tightly closed. I stopped, sunk to my knees and took a deep breath. I felt wet tongue upon face.

"I'm so glad we found each other Arrow." He stopped licking and gave me a ponderous look. "You probably had a point in keeping out of the cave, boy."

I had heard stories and rumors about this cave, this so-called, "Cave of Voices." There was talk in the Market that one could find answers in its depths. Likely they were just having me on, and thus the joke was on me—the fool—stumbling on the rocks. I guess I *can* hear you.

I suppose I went in looking for some truth of what had happened to my parents. When I was newly born, 10 falls ago, my parents traveled to the *Capital* City but never returned. They were caught in some tragedy, a conflict that has never been properly explained to me. Since that fall, I have lived with and been brought up by an aunt and uncle—Emma and Ernie, and they have been unwilling to even hear my questions. I've heard stories of a "rebel alliance" and a plot undertaken by shadowy figures from lands far, far away. I don't know why these people should hate us?

I don't know if I understand the dealings of men. Or why wealth is so highly prized. Of course, I have nothing, save Arrow. Actually, that's not entirely true . . .

My friends from the Market do comprise a strange family. And two nights a week I'm part of the insular world of the Noodle House. I'm not of their family, the family that operates the establishment, but they treat me as if I were. Because I'm not *one* of them—I'm one of them, but not really one of them—I can see why they all behave the way they do. The old man, the son. His sister, and the mother.

The old man came to this land with a dream of abundance, yet through all his hard work, he has become a servant of material, of wealth. He has lost his family in his quest to take care of his family. He can do nothing but work, to achieve that ever-advancing dream of abundance. Although he speaks our language poorly, his children's tongues betray their looks. They truly inhabit two worlds, the old land, with its ways, and our land with its stated desire for equality and *progress*.

The best I can understand about the dealings of men and how they govern are the two views:

There are those, who like my Noodle House Family, prize the liberty of the individual as the highest value. These men believe that if everyone were to take care of themselves, that everyone would be taken care of.

Of course, there are those who disagree, like my friends at the Market. The Market, is a group of individuals who have banded together, sacrificing some liberty to the group for the benefit of all. Of course, there are those who think that the group breeds laziness and complacency with an expectation of the group to care for them.

Sometimes *I* feel like a group, like the whole world is me. Sometimes I just feel like a speck though, one mote in a sea of dust . . . a drop in the ocean subject to the waves, but usually I only feel this way when I'm questioning.

I tend to question. I like to understand why things are the way they are. What's the purpose of the order?—of the various systems of men. I have learned a secret though—often people do not understand the system that they are part of. There is unconsciousness. Since I've always been alone, I wonder where I fit in. . .

(much more to follow! thank you gentle reader)

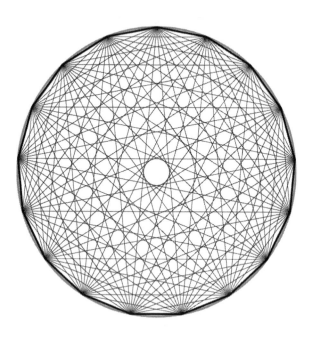

Peg Carter
Synchromysticism Forum

Peg Carter discovered that "the Shakti" (or what her former Guru-brothers and -sisters, thought and experienced and called "the SHAKTI") was "merely" Synchromysticism.

Being a student of Maha yoga since her teenage years, she became dissatisfied with her yoga teacher because of a lack of political engagement—"even apart from, as some would have it, the material fraud involved."

She found an incipient political community for a while and then became disillusioned with human groups altogether. Yet, she feels gratified, grateful and challenged. "It seems everything grew out of my disillusionment. Keen to learn when I was young, I knew every course of study would fail to lead me to where I wanted to end: with certain knowledge. So I decided to study Consciousness itself."

Her child, now a man, was deathly ill a few years ago, and is now recovered. The experience of his illness changed her life. "My chapter here is for him."

She is an administrator for the Synchromysticism Forum.

synchromysticismforum.com

Sweet Earth or Chthonic Underworld
Oracle for the Kali Age?

I salute Ganesh! Elephant–headed son of the banished Goddess.

From a "Hindu" scripture I read in my yoga days, in my youth:
> *Because I was not satisfied with less,*
> *I have come this far.*

This is a bit similar to the theory of Darwin and materialism, though it is not . . . take away what doesn't work, and there you have it: Michelangelo's David.

The saying also appreciates the "loose ends" of *not* having the answer: Only from the honest admission of limitation, one will be open for the next answer, when it presents.

My interest in Synchromysticism grew from an intense interest in 'the subjective' and from many years of yoga meditation practice. I found the video of Jake Kotze's called "The Itsy Bitsy Illuminati Propeller Heads" in 2007 and found real information embedded in the stream-of-consciousness narration. Each point of connection led to many others. I had found a vein of intellectual ore to mine.

In my years of yoga practice and study, I learned about yantras, which are geometrical glyphs, forms or maps. The associations in the yantra arise to the surface when focused upon. They are the equivalent of a bija or seed mantra, which is often a single syllable, but in the form of a graph. Synchromysticism reads signs, symbols, graphics, letters, numbers: as a springboard for freeform associations.

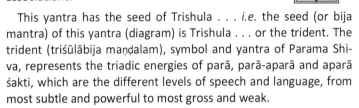

This yantra has the seed of Trishula . . . *i.e.* the seed (or bija mantra) of this yantra (diagram) is Trishula . . . or the trident. The trident (triśūlābija maṇḍalam), symbol and yantra of Parama Shiva, represents the triadic energies of parā, parā-aparā and aparā śakti, which are the different levels of speech and language, from most subtle and powerful to most gross and weak.

But all language has its limits?

From the *Tao te Ching*, the first aphorism of the Tao (variously translated, but here it is by my favorite translation):

The Tao that can be spoken is not the Eternal Tao.

So with the Synchromysticism attitude, one plays with language; flows, rather than wrestles with it, having no need to force a definite meaning or worry for a lack of the same.

Language is playful. It points to things and is not definitive. (I learned this from a philosopher, Arne Næss, who studied directly from the philosopher Wittgenstein.) Do not be deceived. Language only points. Language suggests.

And the deepest language of all will create, according to the Kasmir Shaivite monistic yoga tradition.

Monism is any philosophical view which holds that there is unity in a given field of inquiry. Thus, some philosophers may hold that the universe is one, as opposed to dualism or pluralism.

So maybe if the "synchronicity" is pinned down, it can no longer function as synchronicity? Or maybe that is wrong too.

I've been meaning to define what the "syncs" ultimately mean or where it's all taking us. . . .

For me, the whole process is so miraculous, I just (perhaps naively) accept it. It has to do with subjective signs and oracles. I feel that if the sign is really a sign it will come to you and "hit you over the head." There is no reason to scratch around for it, if it's truly a sign. So, there is a gracefulness inherent in the process; a movement, a swinging-like movement from ring to ring on a gymnastic swing set. You grab the next and let go of the last. You can go back to a favorite, but don't get stuck on the meaning of any one (since you know the meaning or sign itself is just a mask, a prop).

My "Guru," Swami Muktaananda, taught us, his students, about a kind of yoga which contains a similarity to the Synchromystic stance. It is an effortless yoga. He advised us, "a Yogi does not strain."

Baba called it "Anupaya"—the method of no method. It was the first method to try in the series of four methods for the attainment of the Self. This teaching structure derives from the Kasmir philosopher and aesthetician, Abinavagupta.

Abhinabvagupta starts in his Tantraloka with the highest type of yoga and comes down gradually to lower type of its practices. He is of the view that aspirant should catch hold of the highest practice and should try it.

ANUPAYA
The first one is Anupaya. It is immediate through speediest descent of grace. Therefore, Diksha (initiation) has practically no role. In this path to liberation no active process on the part of the individual is involved. An aspirant has only to observe that nothing is to be done. Be as you are: only reside in your being. This is attributed to ANANDA SAKTI [Bliss Power] of Siva and is also called ANANDOPAYA [Bliss Method].

Anupaya (NO METHOD) should be the easiest, since it requires absolutely nothing for it to be accomplished, yet, ironically, could be seen as the most challenging.

If that doesn't work, you get the second teaching, which is SHAMBHAVOPAYA (the method of the giver of Peace, Shiva) also called ICCHOPAYA (Method of WILL). It would be constant focus of the awareness on the Shiva Principle—"I Am That."

SHAKTOPAYA, the third teaching, is for those who do not succeed with Shambhavopaya. It is the path of knowledge and reflection, which would ultimately lead to the experience of the Absolute.

Lastly, ANAYOPAYA is for those who are in ignorance of the true nature of the Self. This fourth practice would include all the ordinary 8 branches of yoga.

Anupaya (no method) corresponds to Zen, in that the littlest simplest thing could trigger the insight/state. And the "accomplishment" of recognizing one's own true nature, might arise unexpectedly, from something one has seen or done or thought many times (to no effect previously), in one moment. Or, most likely, through constant or even just one moment's reflection upon the great statement: "All this is Consciousness."

The above sounds so self-contained as to appear selfish (if misconstrued?). I feel the *"nothing is to be done"* needs to be tempered. For instance, by the thought of other living beings? Being totally self-contained and in a personal state of bliss, even seems to be incomplete?

We need each other to help interpret the syncs?

The interchange among the Sync community via the online social networks amplifies the experiences. Each person has their own gifts for seeing winks and has their own story. When the insights ricochet throughout the community, we learn from each other.

This extra context, the unknown element, reminds me of the Tolstoy story "What Men Live By," which is a story involving a stranger coming to live with a family.

> *I have learnt that all men live not by care for themselves but by love.*

I feel the Synchromysticism point of view is basically one of grace and effortlessness, as the highest Maha yoga. And one of total subjectivity (which counterbalances the total alleged or claimed "objectivity" of the dominant culture) and one of a true scientific-like community of researchers.

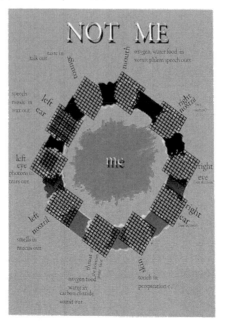

The Kashmir Shaivite philosophy of Maha yoga was very difficult for me when I first was taught it. This was in the first months and years after the initial experience of a Kundalini Awakening, called the descent of Shakti, which I experienced most likely as a result of the presence of the vortex of energies and traditional yoga practices swirling around my Guru. I was experiencing a lot of pain.

In the "Shiva Sutras" which are aphorisms of Kashmir Shaivism one aphorism states (in translation):

The Entire Universe is the sport of Cit-Shakti.

Everything Arises from Her Own Blissful Being.

(The Sanskrit words are technical, and there is a tradition that goes with the verses. You are supposed to have a teacher to tell you what they mean. It's not supposed to be just from a book.)

What I was taught violently contradicted my own "experience," feelings and perceptions at the time. To the point, I felt the aphorism *"Everything Arises from Her Own Blissful Being"* ironic. What I was taught was very counter-intuitive, even for a native Southern Californian who was brought up to believe suffering is a result of wrong thinking patterns.

To find my own health and take "responsibility" for my own suffering and "drop it [my suffering]" was a course I did not know how to unfold. Though it happened after a while by itself: my neurotic, un-supported suffering, the narcissistic (as I see it now) suffering fell away.

Now I see the issue of suffering and malevolence historically and politically: The planet Earth was meant to be a paradise. Yet the divine storyline has interference. The outlines of which are becoming, with research, more and more defined. I do not blame myself and my own nature for the condition of the larger world sphere *à la* "It's all me—a projection of my own distorted nature." Nor do I deny the reality of suffering when I say, "the Inner Self is pure Bliss." Historical reality is true on the human relative scale—just as is the weather, this keyboard, this city—the reality of the complexity and depth of creation.

What I came to read (and which helped me, since I wasn't satisfied with less, and kept searching) was that the Absolute Bliss, Pure Consciousness, Effulgent Self is the base reality to everything. The suffering issue is a cloud which passes. And it does pass. The true nature of the Self (Bliss and Wonderment) is that which self-manifests, which is true substance. The suffering-thing has no own-reality. No permanence.

Shiva Sutra Aphorism 1-18
"LokaAnandah SamādhiSukham"

My teacher translated this as: "The Bliss of looking into another person's face is the greatness of the Samadhi state"

Literally it is:
"The Bliss of this Place [Loka = World], is the happiness of Samadhi."

From another translation: "World-bliss is Samadhi happiness."

The flavor of the Synchromysticism enterprise seems to be to find ecstasy and joy in the mundane and ordinary. What is a greater miracle than a flower growing from a seed? It is still not explained. Yet the miracle is not commonly appreciated . . . nor is the miracle of human life.

I consider the veneration of "miracles" to be infantile. The fascination with things which are uncommon and therefore judged to be exclusive and special, combined with the ignoring of what is all around and which *is* so terribly special anyway, forms a blind spot, blocking happiness from humans, since nothing is ever enough. And the special is all mirrors and deceptive smoke.

Instead the Synchromystic projects the beauty and bliss of the pure inner Self, consciousness, onto the entire world. In that way, the Synchromystic resembles the Shaivite.

SWEET EARTH OR CHTHONIC UNDERWORLD

On the *Synchromysticism Forum* (of which I am an administrator), "The Donkey" wrote:

Can a Gnostic view of this reality exist harmoniously with the idea that nature is indeed perfect? A beautiful hell?

In the Hindu system, there is a "Kali" Age or bad Age, where everything is backwards from the way it should be. Some think we are in that age. The Kali Age, supposedly, started at the end of the war between the Pandava Princes and their cousins (detailed in the epic *Mahabharata*). All normal protocol and righteousness is mostly tossed aside during that time.

In the bad age, it is still all the play of divine consciousness.

So my teacher said:

This is really the bad age. The ignorance is so thick that yogic secrets which used to be guarded and only given to certain students believed worthy, can now be just said right out loud and given freely, because even then, they still remain secrets.

No one can grasp it, so even if it's right in their face, it's still a secret!

So how does one reconcile the beauty of this Paradise world—this Sweet Earth, the intelligence of Nature and birth from purity—with the raging Kali Earth Mother Demon who is only pacified by blood offerings?

How does one reconcile the perfection of the Universal Consciousness with the human diversity which made a place for the rise of the Psychopath in places of power?

In my tradition, Kasmir Shaivism, we are taught that the underlying stratum of reality is not just benign, but positively illustrious and full of ecstasy, bliss and grace. What runs counter is simply alike to the clouds, which may obscure the background sky for a time, but are impermanent and will not persist.

From "illegalbrain" of the *Synchromysticism Forum*:

What actually is this force, variously described as the universe, collective unconscious, hyperspace, voice of God, synchosphere or fairy land?

Is it real? Is it just in our heads? Is there a difference?

Personally, I have attributed these experiences to everything from basic biology to God/gods to Jungian archetypes to aliens to demons. This leads me to often wonder if these are all just ways of interfacing with the same thing, or if they are masks that hide something else. This in turn leads me back to the idea of being deceived, which then makes me think there must be a truth to be deceived about, which makes me think how could I distinguish between the truth and a lie, between the real world and the dream world?

As you can imagine, the whole thing is making me a bit dizzy.

For me, the experiences of Sync are a demonstration of the grace of the Whole and the mark of how I am embedded in the Universal fabric of Creation.

Some believe that suffering and malfeasances are necessary for humans to grow.

Here is "noob" from the *Synchromysticism Forum*:

As the 'evil' AI in Matrix *says it, humans stop 'being useful' if things are too one sided. There can be no free will, and no spiritual progress, in a 'perfect' world.*

Can any qualifications be made, prerequisites demanded, for spiritual progress or attainment? And if there were, would suffering be one?

> *There is no necessity or purpose to Suffering.*
> —Shiva Sutras

The notion that suffering is necessary, noble or good is part of how our dysfunction propagates and persists.

My personal belief: "suffering is necessary" is propaganda.

I feel this self-fulfilling propaganda notion is used by people who hurt others and mess up nature and society, and who do not want to do their duty. The statement: "This is the way it is; it will always be this way," is a justification. And I think it is also a propagated form of mental conditioning through thought contagion.

That so: Is there likely a certain structural necessity for *some* "imperfection" built into creation itself? I am not even completely sure of that! (It's even a possibility we live in a "perfect" universe/world!? Already!)

There are tradeoffs and compensations in nature—like a very good looking person is likely to be less skilled in erotic art (no motivation?). Or a white flower will have the best scent and a beautifully colored one will not (for reasons of conservation of energy). But these things wouldn't reach the level of tragedy we are presently seeing in our world. The level of benightedness we see is not structural or built-in. It's deliberate.

I reject the New Age notion that "if there is anything wrong with the world one should look within, listen to the tearing thoughts against the ego, and try to approach a perfection which our monkey mind establishes for us." The bar set by the monkey mind for perfection will always be wrong.

Does it make sense that by claiming: if one is actually "good," "pure," "enlightened," a "Thus-Gone, Tata-Gata," one no longer needs to . . .

. . . choose one:
1. Eat
2. Sleep
3. Have Sex
4. Breathe
5. Die
6. Get Angry and/or Fall in Love
7. Have Any Desire

and the big one (which should probably be addressed separately)
8. No Ego?

Is this impulse, to deny life and replace it with supernaturalism, itself a symptom of the degrading of Nature? Isn't the miracle of life enough? Why demonize its functioning? Is it possible that this attitude could be fostered by a "cult of death" since something dead is, under this system, finally perfect? Why do so many things have to be denied in order for so-called "perfection" to be realized?

To me, the focus on renunciation is really about attachment. We are subconsciously attached to things, so we believe that once we "got there," those things would, of necessity, go away or maybe have to go away? Does it make sense that the true renunciation has to do with a person's lack of inner attachment? And that all the "symptoms" of "enlightenment," upon which seekers focus, are actually distractions from the reality of the inner state?

"Peace follows renunciation," but it is of the inner station and posture, not of the external effects. Kundalini Shakti is NATURE, your body.

The Chthonic Goddess of Nature can be a vagina dentata, a scary octopus, Pandora, the source of all that is wrong with the world system.

SWEET EARTH OR CHTHONIC UNDERWORLD

Or she can be the divine Mother, the sweet earth, who nourishes and comforts us.

In the tantra yoga system in which I was schooled, she is called Matrka, the goddess of the letters, the Shakti (power) of the letters, words, sentences, ideas. The entire world in which we live is created by her vibration.

Matrka Shakti is the root of our bondage and of our liberation. Terence McKenna beautifully enunciated in his famous lecture "Eros and the Eschaton":

The world is made of language.

The Synchromystic (like the Kabbalist, Jungian dream interpreter or alchemist of the past) decodes the string of moments, the string of letters and concepts about which the fabric of our subjective experience is wound. The letters are said to be strung on a garland around the neck of the Universal Goddess, whatever the name you choose, which would embody some of "her" qualities.

According to my Guru brother Swami Shankarananda of Australia, there are two worlds, the Inner world and the Outer world. If you are a Monist, as we in our tradition are, you have two choices: You may say, "All this is material" (as do the present day material determinists). That is: consciousness arises as an epiphenomenon of the swirling around of matter . . . and basically has no substantiality apart from the material processes which gives birth to the illusion of Consciousness.

Or you can say, "All is Consciousness." Therefore, what appears to be this material world is nothing but an expression of pure consciousness, sometimes called "Shiva," the "Auspicious." "Shiva" reveals his/her auspiciousness directly to the Sync Head.

The purpose of yoga, the re-unification with the cosmic universal order, would be enabled by taking a second education: learning about one's Inner world, one's subjective space.

The centerpiece of that Inner world would be the Heart. It is from there the body of the fetus unfolds to a fully articulated multi-cellular creature. It is the top (4th of the bottom four chakras) and is the root chakra of the top four chakras.

Yet, if we are talking about the heart as a place:

[Nityananda of Ganeshpuri (my Guru's Guru)] tells us that the Heart is not the physical Heart, nor the heart chakra located in the area of the physical heart. He tells us that the Heart is the one, indivisible Sky of Consciousness that is the Absolute. This Heart is beyond the body and the senses and can be accessed through the Crown Chakra in the head.

In the relative world, though, we have the so-called Dark vs. Light expression of the Absolute.

In *Man and His Symbols*, Carl G. Jung explains:

Envy, lust, sensuality, deceit, and all known vices are the negative, 'dark' aspect of the unconscious, which can manifest itself in two ways. In the positive sense, it appears as a 'spirit of nature', creatively animating Man, things, and the world. It is the 'chthonic spirit' that has been mentioned so often in this chapter. In the negative sense, the unconscious (that same spirit) manifests itself as a spirit of evil, as a drive to destroy.

So how do the Inner world, the Outer world and the Cosmic world come to mesh? What is the unified theory?

Don't know. Yet, with the help of a research group of talented Synchromystic decoders, we are on the trail to reverse-engineer the answers.

The imaginal world is real. The world we think we know is born from that. And "That" speaks and winks at us, giving us bliss and a sense of Home at heart.

The "imaginary" ideal world of name, number and archetype is born before any of us. It may seem those two, "mind" and "matter," are forever separate, cannot touch one another . . . but they do, through our own subjective consciousness and being.

SWEET EARTH OR CHTHONIC UNDERWORLD

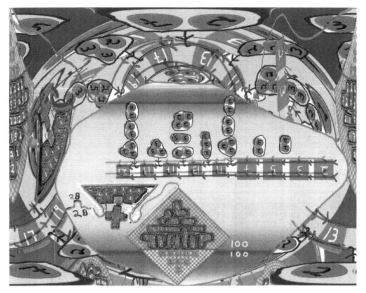

From James Farrington, the painter:

I side with those who feel that the miracle of creation does not consist in the creation of something out of nothing, but, instead, consist in the creation of nothing out of all that is.

Images courtesy of James Farrington and Albert Duffy

Photos by Peg Carter

Additional images courtesy of commons.wikimedia.org

Will Morgan
A Few Shots to Shaman

Known for his offbeat sense of humor and "raw" delivery on his blog, A Few Shots to Shaman, *Will Morgan (also known simply as Shaman) started his obsession with sync in early 2008. Will has experimented with video and many different styled posts in presenting sync. For example, only using pictures, only using text, or even using a "cut up" of others' works on both his blog and at* The Sync Whole *blog, which he also contributes to. From his philosophy of shared sync, Will has had many conversations over the Internet with an increasing amount of "Sync Heads," which he records and produces through the* Sounds of Sherwood *podcast. Will plans to put out many more podcasts as well as videos in the near future. Will borrows from conspiracy theory, alchemy, Kabbalah, occult history, and Fortean topics in general.*

afewshotstoshaman.blogspot.com
g8ors.blogspot.com

Confessions of a Sync Head

We fool ourselves.

We fool ourselves into thinking that we may get the upper hand in our own being. But consciousness is a fleeting animal.

Had an art teacher once who laughed at my frustration. . . . I just couldn't draw what was in my head.

"Will," she said, "that's because what's in your head keeps moving."

What would we call what's in our heads but *us*? But that can't be true. Because your thoughts never stand still. Ideas leave, memories fade. If we are our thoughts, then we have nothing, because our thoughts are like the sky . . . Always moving, always changing. But, like the sky, always perfect.

Uranus. The sky. No way to it but Heaven, really. And every night, Heaven would come down and cover the Earth. From their union the great beast that Heaven hated was spawned. And yet he kept coming. And coming. Until Earth made a sickle to harvest his tenders and put it in the hands of her son Kronos.

Chronos is time . . . That which kills Heaven's ability to love the Earth. Heaven and Earth bring forth time. And from time we have everything we know. Everything . . . Every thought.

I wish my older self could go back and discuss the matter to a young me. Organize the little me's . . . I mean adolescent me's dreams.

"You won't always want to animate for Disney," I'd tell him . . . "Well, you might want to, but sooner or later you'll realize there's no time."

But I can't, can I? Because, of course, time has me.

I sat myself down not so many years back and said, "Fuck it. What do I want to do?" I listed three things:

1. Make a book. Not a book to make money, but a good book.
2. Make a comic book. Some roll their eyes I'm sure. But there is magic in a comic that literature can't give you.
3. Make a musical album.

I'm not saying that I have an aptitude for any of those things. But, damn it, that's what I wanted to do. I decided that I'd merge the comic and the book into one. Sorta like Alan Moore's *Watchmen*, but on a grander scale that had never been done.

And if I just forced myself to make music week after week . . . Not really going back to make it perfect, but just keep moving forward, then I'd have something. . . . In time, of course. I'd have something.

But houses burn down. And fire consumes everything, not really caring if you never buy yourself a new guitar or not. Computers malfunction. And girlfriends get pregnant. On a long enough timeline, these things are inevitable.

One then finds one's self doing things for necessity. Day after day driving yourself to clock hours, to pull levers or hit switches, to just keep waiting for your ship to come in no matter how late it seems off schedule.

Never keep lists. After a while you just have lists of lists. Lists explaining where you put this list to mark off another thing you were supposed to do last week.

But, now I find myself doing some kind of inexplicable art. Some sort of poetic interpretation. And, as vain as it may sound, somehow I'm supposed to do it.

I used to come out of movies and internally replay it in my head. Go through each chunk of drama in my head. Split it into sections of scenes so I could recap it. My mom hated it. If I saw a film and she asked me about it, I would replay the entire thing vocally. She just stopped asking me, after a while, which kind of sucked, really, because I always envied her storytelling abilities.

But, if it weren't for these idiosyncrasies, this slight tinge of OCD, then I would never have understood sync.

I have an above average head for symbols as well. And my brothers used to caution me about finding meaning in everything.

When drugs came, which they inevitably did, it got worse. One morning, hung from an Ecstasy binge, I roll over to see a painting in a *Smithsonian* magazine by Jean Léone Gérôme called *The Snake Charmer*, and I stared at that bitch for what must have been an hour. I picked it apart but every time I tried to tell someone what I was seeing their eyes glazed over.

And then my parents got divorced and a family that had been close for nearly two decades was split. I say "close" because it was my mom and stepdad and there were two kids to each side. That's four boys in total. The boys remained fairly close afterwards. . . . But, of course, sooner or later someone does crack and fucks the whole gig up. Before that happened however, I find myself in a little Ford Escort, in the very back hatch, on the way back from seeing *The Fellowship of the Ring*. I, as I said, was in the back, knees to chest while my mom is analyzing the symbolism of "The Fellowship."

"The Fellowship is a family," she says. And all of a sudden I'm mad at her. All she was doing in my eyes was wishful thinking that she and her four broken boys in the car were important.

We weren't important. We were done. Our power and rareness sapped out by "time." Cause on a long enough time-line everything dissolves. Everything.

"You know, Mom," I said, speaking out of turn, "if you keep finding meaning in everything you're gonna drive yourself nuts."

The car got quiet. My oldest brother, Kevin, the one with who I share actual sibling blood, instead of some bloody secret finger slit by a pocketknife, broke the silence with . . . "Look who's talking." Breaking the ice and giving everyone a laugh.

Years later, still being obsessed with the work of Tolkien, I find a prize in the local library. Tucked away in a corner is an interview with the great JRR. And I checked that bitch out . . . I mean, what nerd wouldn't? I sat, getting ready to go and pull levers and hit switches one morning, and watched the video. And then I hear him in the most charming of English verbalizations . . . *"Well, I always thought of The Fellowship as a family."* I sat motionless for a while. . . . Then called my mom and apologized. . . . She had no idea what I was talking about.

After that, how can I not take Sync as special? It is an accumulation of my Time spent here on Earth. Everything I love wrapped into one.

And yet I have tainted the fuck out of it, leaving my stench everywhere. Setting lists and mental plans that Time will never allow.

You know Time raised his Sickle to my modest family on New Year's Eve 2010? Isn't that poetic? The day that we see Kronos (or Saturn) with little Baby New Year, and my brother Kevin has his unborn baby twins harvested. . . . What cruel pathetic words I use! What a heartless idea! They were stillborn and luckily my mom was visiting him for the holidays. She saw him through it.

They were not really expected to make it; I mean the doctors had warned us. But, you're never really prepared. How can you be? See, the embryonic sack didn't split. They could have both made it, but they shouldn't have even been boys, really. Usually that kind of pregnancy bears females. And of course one could overpower the other. Or they could even get wrapped in each other's cords, not being in separate sacks. . . . Which is what happened.

I don't know why I started writing this. Maybe because . . . Because it was about time I got it out of my system. Maybe because I'm just sick of watching relationships ruined in "time" over stupid shit. Maybe I'm just a fucked up Sync Head who saw *The Time Traveler's Wife* tonight and can't get over the fact that the main character was named after one of my brother's boys . . . Henry. I didn't "really" realize that until I wrote it, just now. See Henry in the movie can't have kids because they keep time-jumping out of the womb. . . . The other was named William, of course. My brother's other son I mean. William and Henry. He named them. He told me (sorry Kevin) that they looked like creatures. But, he named them.

My mom saw *Avatar* at the beginning of the year, sometime shortly after New Year's. And, God forgive me, I got angry because she found relevance in that movie too. Found relevance in the fact that the twins become one. My brother's twins were one kid, decided to split, and then thought that maybe that wasn't such a good idea. The sack therefore didn't separate and then, after a Time, they died. They now rest in an urn, both their ashes together as one. Just like our blue star on the silver screen becoming one with his dead brother. And every time I see Jake Sully's deformed legs I see what my mom meant. And I hear my brother's word . . . "Creatures."

How fucked up has sync made us? That we find pleasure in the numbers on license plates. That we find poetry beyond explanation in the headline of a newspaper. I live in a fantasy world, do I? Well, so what? I'm happier than you, if you live without the poetry of meaning in your life. After all these broken and forgotten thoughts, everything I see makes me happy.

I can't remember, in all my explorations of the unsolvable, anything that has given me more insight. Reality as a singular noun makes absolutely no sense to me now.

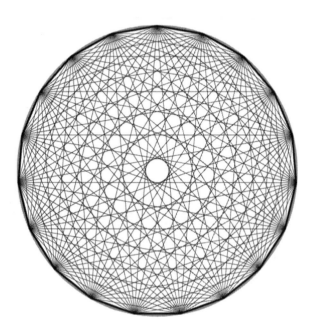

Rammer Martínez Sánchez
Smoky Mirrors

Rammer Martínez Sánchez makes comicbooks, graphic designs, draws, scrawls sci-fi & fantastic weirdums, and dabs poetry, spoken or otherwise. He turned his name into an ambigram, which is in nifty logo books. He, with Alan Abbadessa-Green, had their first publishing venture, The Mind's Overflow Vol. 1 *paperback anthology, as part of an exhibition in the Baltimore Museum of Art. He has been in various comicbook anthologies (like in* Comicbook Artists Guild *anthologies), online publications (like in* Short, Fast, and Deadly.com*), prints (like in* The Manhattan Times*), and/or performed in different events (like Z-Day 2011, part of the Zeitgeist Movement)*

smokymirrors.com
Twitter: @Rammerammer

There Stood the Orb

Trapped in a wide web where eight eyes never rest
Reverse reading your readings, without one behest
With much anticipation filling the workplace
Rub the doubt off your eyes, when catching the first glimpse
Urge to a partner! Quick! Relay the news abroad!
Where, with none but silence, there stood the Orb
What is this nature that churns your young flame,
A Black Sun within reflects in black vain?
Which of the stars will struggle behind
From Hydra's net, sheer god of the sky?
Which will glitter to merely adorn?
With none but silence, there stood the Orb
Will the wind tell the sand to evade the foam?
Or be scooped up, eddied, to be felt no more?
Which tidal hand shall delivereth ashore?
Where, with none but silence, there stood the Orb
Everywhere there's everyplace to stand,
                                        is where stood the Orb,
Shadows where light does not dare to blind,
                                        it gleefully absorbs
Isis to the eye, pupil to the mind, long longings to trespass
The sedentary and complacent ones, it leisurely sees pass
But to the ravenous who seek, its sight gallops beside
To be one with whomever prods, spurs, whips, and rides
And slinking and be the centaur to the half-horse
But which nose is measured for tracks that measure worst?
Touch but don't feel. See but don't look. Bare the coming bore.
Stay where you stand, that there stood the Orb.

You are like me

if I was you

I am like you

and so we are

You take

You give

I receive

I lose

But through it all

Together

We could reach afar

Desperate Skin

Written by: Alan Abbadessa

Illustrated and Lettered by: Rammer Martínez Sánchez

Inked by: Peter Palmiotti

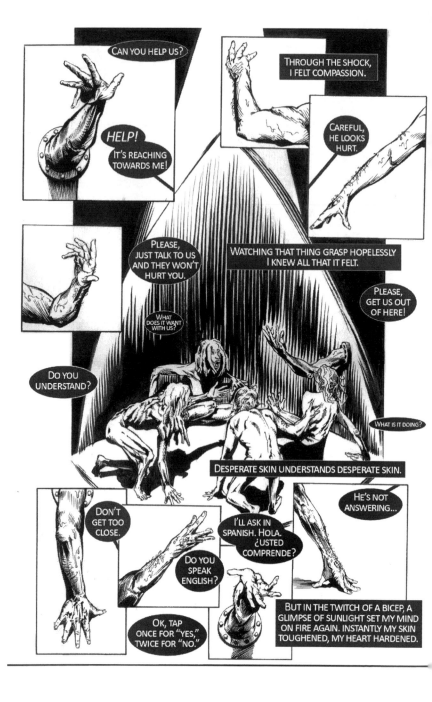

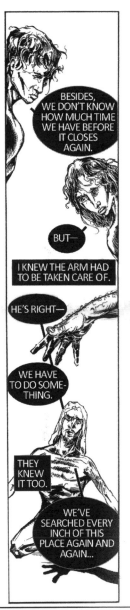

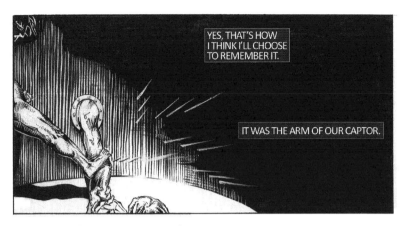
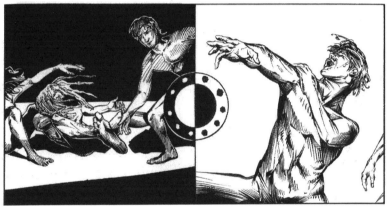

Michael Schacht
Gosporn

Michael Schacht is the author of Gosporn, *a blog that balances uncomfortably between the subjects of conspiracy, apocalypse, synchronicity, science fiction, religious mythology, gay porn and current events. Michael started writing in 2006, when he began seeing evidence for mythical continuity between the Bible, science fiction, and online amateur homoerotic stories, where his examinations were noticed by those who have become known as "synchromystics." He never really intended to become a synchromystic, but apparently that's what he is. "I spend more time than I'd like to admit imagining heaven—it's not what you think." Michael is a guest on* Look at All the Happy Creatures *and also contributes to* The Mask of God. *He lives with his husband in Seattle—the "Emerald City."*

gosporn.blogspot.com
themaskofgod.blogspot.com

Porn Star Jesus

> *A woman, hurls the fire that maddens men for women;*
> *but Eros himself sways the passion for males.*
> —Meleager of Gadara

I've always found it amusing how beauty queens tend to cast themselves into the role of defender of orthodox sexual values, while being all tarted up like the original Ho' of Babylon. Miss California Carrie Prejean is the latest example, but I'll never forget Anita Bryant, the Miss America orange juice queen who became the voice of the emerging Evangelical Right. Maybe they feel threatened by homoerotic attraction? Kind of leaves them out of the running.

The masculine equivalent of the beauty pageant is a bodybuilding contest, and in the old days we had Mr. America and Mr. Universe, inviting some obvious comparisons. While female pageants are undeniably hetero affairs, the male side has always had a strong homosexual sub-current, as much as Joe Weider always tried to sweep it under the carpet. Dare I say it, but perhaps it is that homosexual sub-current that draws in the fans and pays the bills? Apparently homoerotic is fine, as long as it avoids the label. In this respect, erotic male love is STILL "the love that dare not say its name."

Eros is his name, and for the last 2000 years Eros has been "our little secret"—something men do behind closed doors but never, ever discuss in public. Until now, when suddenly Eros is on all the talk shows.

In Puritan founded America, sensual desire was considered to be the domain of the dark side. The Saints abstain from sex, while the devil is always sexy, most likely a perv. We've come a long way from the days of *The Scarlet Letter*, but Puritan ideas about sex still haunt our subconscious. It is perhaps no wonder that peeling away the Christian devil costume we might find Eros smirking back at us.

Every archetype needs expression, and perhaps the reason that homosexuality finds itself in the crosshairs of religion and politics today is that Eros is demanding to be heard. If an archetype is denied conscious expression, then it will seek subconscious expression. What if the natural desire of a man for another man was cut off, through social and religious control? Perhaps it would seek covert expression—"perverting" other archetypes in order to express itself.

Naturally drawn to venues where men congregate, it would find subliminal expression there. Gyms and locker rooms, monasteries, soldier's barracks—all fertile ground for Eros. But still, an existence in the subconscious margins of a straight world isn't exactly living. So Eros infiltrates and perverts, and all the other archetypes hate on him for it, but maybe . . . all Eros really wants is a place to call his own. What if Eros has grown weary of all the sneakin' around, and like the prodigal son, he just wants to come home?

The internal battles of the subconscious play out in our real world, in politics, culture wars, the arts, and comic books. Especially comics. Apparently, the lower the brow, the nearer the subconscious. If Superman is our Solar Hero—the illumination of consciousness, then Batman is our Hades, the lord of the underworld—the subconscious. Metropolis is bright and sunny, Gotham is dark and gloomy, and yet they are both the exact same city—the two sides of our collective Self.

Bruce Wayne is a millionaire playboy who lives in a very close relationship with a handsome youth—teenage Dick Grayson. Any ancient Greek would know exactly what kind of relationship this actually was, but Americans only figured out the subtext after homosexuality became a topic that could be discussed more openly. After the snickering got loud enough, DC and Hollywood made sure to present Bruce Wayne as resolutely straight with plenty of feminine love interests—but the truth is, upper-class straight guys don't live like that, don't create lives for themselves like that. However, ancient Greeks did:

Athenian pederasty entailed a formal bond between an adult man and an adolescent boy outside his immediate family, consisting of loving and often sexual relations. As an erotic and educational custom it was initially employed by the upper class as a means of teaching the young and conveying to them important cultural values, such as bravery and restraint.
—Wikipedia

Did Bob Kane and Bill Finger set out to create a classic Athenian pederast relationship when they introduced the Batman in a 1939 issue of *Detective Comics*? I'd say almost certainly not. The appearance of Batman and Robin was simply an early example of the Eros archetype "sneakin' around" in the cultural subconscious.

Freud would say that Batman and Robin are in denial about their relationship. They're a couple of guys who are madly in love with each other but can't admit their "bromance" goes a bit deeper. The villains they fight are really manifestations of their own—still hidden—subconscious erotic desire. Batman is called "The World's Greatest Detective," which means that eventually he'll figure it out, and so will we. His/our Bat Signal will sweep the dark clouds of our hidden subconscious away, and bring light to Gotham.

The "power of the dark side" is given that power by our fear—our fear makes it powerful. There are many Christians who fear that the "demon of homosexuality" is very powerful indeed, capable of corrupting the church all the way to the very top. Both Catholic and Protestant churches have been rocked by case after case of shocking pedophilia and sensational homosexual scandals, the bizarre story of George Alan Rekers being typical: A founding member of the Family Research Council with James Dobson and outspoken anti-gay activist, Rekers was caught returning home from a European vacation in mid-April 2010 with a young man he had hired from rentboy.com (a site that caters to male escorts and their clients).

The fear of dogmatic, homophobic religion may in fact be well placed—Eros is at war, and he's not afraid to use sex as a weapon!

The modern internal disconnect between the erotic and the spirit runs very deep. Even so-called "Gay Christians" tend to think of their sexual nature as a challenge to their faith and a cross to bear. I've discovered few who will embrace the idea of a homoerotic Jesus—a Savior who isn't ashamed of his sexuality, on the contrary is actually proud of it! The Christ who embraces his inner boner.

> *And they come into Bethany. And a certain woman whose brother had died was there. And, coming, she prostrated herself before Jesus and says to him, 'Son of David, have mercy on me.' But the disciples rebuked her. And Jesus, being angered, went off with her into the garden where the tomb was, and straightway a great cry was heard from the tomb. And going near, Jesus rolled away the stone from the door of the tomb. And straightway, going in where the youth was, he stretched forth his hand and raised him, seizing his hand. But the youth, looking upon him, loved him and began to beseech him that he might be with him. And going out of the tomb, they came into the house of the youth, for he was rich. And after six days Jesus told him what to do, and in the evening the youth comes to him, wearing a linen cloth over his naked body. And he remained with him that night, for Jesus taught him the mystery of the Kingdom of God. And thence, arising, he returned to the other side of the Jordan.*
> —The Secret Gospel of Mark, *trans. Morton Smith*

Rather than wait for this more fully integrated Savior archetype to manifest out of the decrepit edifice of the Christian Church, I began looking elsewhere. You can find remnants of a sexual God in old Pagan religions: Pan, Dionysus, even back to the ithyphallic Gods of ancient Egypt. Even old St. Peter's in Rome features plenty of phallic symbols if you know where to look, but those are all dead religions, and I was looking for something with a bit more life.

How curious that I would find what I'm looking for, not in the hoary books of ancient occult tradition, but in my own backyard. That "backyard" being the drawings, stories and films of homoerotic artists. It's remarkable how the inclusion of Eros into even the dullest and time-worn story can give it new energy, new possibilities, new life. Their work is filled to overflowing with a kind of energy, freedom, love and joy that is singing a different tune, a "new song" as it were. I'm in awe how they can take the old archetypes, from ancient hero to super villain, from ancient herder to the modern cowboy, and make them "born again." If alchemy is turning lead into gold, then these artists are magicians of a high degree, but "shhhh," don't tell them, at least, not too much. If we told them they were busy creating the next great religion—more than that—the next way for consciousness to see and experience reality, our collective Self—well . . . let's just say that writer's block is not what we need right now. We need to keep writing!

To the heads of derelict religions and politics, Eros is Apollyon, the Destroyer, and he seems to delight in bringing them down. But to us . . .

> *To the angel of the church in Philadelphia write: These are the words of him who is holy and true, who holds the key of David. What he opens no one can shut, and what he shuts no one can open. I know your deeds. See, I have placed before you an open door that no one can shut. I know that you have little strength, yet you have kept my word and have not denied my name.*
> *—Revelation 3:7-8*

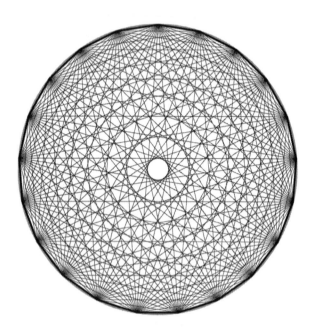

Jake Kotze
Seallion

Jacob Pieter Kotze was born in sunny Johannesburg. At a young age he experienced many peculiar synchronicities, putting him on a lifelong quest to poke at it with a stick. On the Internet the subject has been explored and documented, under the heading "Synchromysticism," through numerous blogs, short videos and Twitter. Home for the past 7 years has been less-sunny Winnipeg.

Twitter: @seallion
g8ors.blogspot.com

Sync

Generally speaking, when one seemingly significant thing or event echoes another, in a way that can't be understood causally, some call the phenomena synchronicity. As the connection between these thing-events[1] and what makes them significant, is up to the interpretation of the individual, this kind of sync is relative. The decision that the relationship between one thing and another is entirely understood (being then normal cause and effect), or not (being then sync), also rests with personal interpretation. It is then an opinion to say "this" is connected to "that," or not.

The word coincidence is generally associated with thing-events that echo one another through chance.[2] The decision that something is chance or more mysterious also lies in the murky phantom world of opinion. Synchronicity and coincidence are the same thing, only the individual bias over whether the relationship is meaningful or arbitrary changes. Two people will witness the same events and one will call it coincidence and the other sync. This is an issue of individual temperament—and does not change whether the thing-event took place or not.

All is sync or nothing is sync

Everything is connected to everything else,[3] sync being the cases when our current perspective allows us to see these thing-events as related (or as not divided). Often the seemingly random and meaningless will later be understood as perfectly "in sync," when the perspective shifts appropriately. In this view of sync, we now move away from seeing synchronicity as the connections deemed special and move into a knowing of that property which makes one connection meaningful or not—a property that is always present, because it is ourselves. Syncs offer endless insight into the world, but their most essential quality is in vivifying what and who really allows for them.

If we reflect on one of those amazing animations where we zoom in (or out) infinitely on a fractal Mandelbrot set, we notice that, at points, the entire shape comes into focus and then recedes into strange and dazzling complexity. This happens repeatedly, regardless of where we travel on the infinite complexity of the fractal, as it always resolves into the same familiar shape eventually.

Our macro/microcosm has the same property. We have all seen films where the camera moves rapidly between vast amounts of space containing familiar forms like atoms, molecules and cells—eventuating into a creature or plant that would be part of our normal experience or magnification. Further "up," we have the same dynamic: the clutter of streets and houses resolving into patterned cities; later becoming the planet; moving through the vastness of empty space; resolving into the solar system . . . much more space and we see the galaxy, etc.

Sync compares, in the fractal example, to the points at which we see a whole familiar shape after lots of complexity, and, in the micro/macro images, to the moments when we recognize a familiar form resolving after much empty space. The sync is always part of the whole, made up of the interconnected infinite thing-events, but stands out as where we—owing to our unique perspective—resolve this complexity into something conceivable and as associated to other parts of our experience.

All understanding is sync, which is simply association, relationship or connections between thing-events. We derive meaning from putting things and events together to tell ourselves a story. Without constantly making associations we would be lost in perplexing noise and chaos, all the information coming at us making no sense at all. What we generally call synchronicity is the fringe of this everyday activity. Creating unusual associations (that eventually become accepted as universal) is how we expand the parameters of the consensus association narrative (our reality), adding depth and texture to the experience of experience itself. The idea that the sun is the center of the local spheres was once an obscene sync, now included in the common story about the reality we all share. The connection between the movement of the earth relative to the sun, causing seasons, are commonly accepted associations between thing-events (or syncs), while the connection between 9/11 and *2001: A Space Odyssey* is a more occult (out of the ordinary) relationship.

On 9/11/2001, the World Trade Center collapsed right beside "The Millennium Hilton Hotel," a building designed to resemble the black Monolith from the film *2001: A Space Odyssey*. The building was practically flush with the towers, being damaged by falling debris and was captured in many of the iconic images from 9/11. Both the real life event and the film associate to the year 2001, as well as sharing the presence of the Monolith. The film depicts key evolutionary phases in mankind's history overseen and influenced by the Monolith. 9/11 can also be viewed as a key evolutionary point in our history, and occurred in the presence of the same object as in the film *2001*. Through sync association, the context of the film—evolution involving Jupiter—becomes applicable to the real-life it reflects. Realizing 911 is also the emergency call service number in America, the vivid synchronicities involved in 9/11 act as an emergency wake-up call into a higher state of consciousness, where we become aware of our inseparability from thing-events. I call this process the "9/11 Mega Ritual."

The boundaries between things and events are collectively and individually agreed upon conventions. We use them in order to make sense of our environment and navigate our everyday lives. The categories we impose on the world are what allow for definition and the creation of all symbols;[4] these are necessary and helpful tools, but not the nature of the actual reality they point towards. The culture[5] of a certain time and place decides the general agreed-upon lines of division we draw between things-events and how we interpret them. Even the divide between "myself" and "other" is a convention or phantom of this process: the labeling of thing-events that creates our understanding of reality. It is conducive to health and well-being to notice these conventions as shadows or phantoms. That way, these playful apparitions will not be frightening or confuse our activities.

Thing-events are not only seamlessly interpenetrating, but are also boundless in their depth and have infinite complexity.

Sync is the experience of the relaxation and dissolution of the boundaries between ourselves and the thing-events of the world.

The more we allow ourselves to notice sync, the less barriers there are and the more our depth of perception will grow, allowing us to penetrate deeper into the world—a world which starts to feel inseparable from what we consider ourselves.

Sync is Sign

People of many indigenous cultures are known for seeing "signs" in their surroundings. Spirits[6] of ancestors and plants communicate through signs in the natural environment with individuals, mystics and shamans sensitive to such matters. These signs help heal and guide the culture.

Sync is the modern equivalent, now recognized, as the false-distinction between *the natural* and *human-created world* exits. All thing-events (whether trees, cars or movies) arise from the great non-local mystery of existence. The entire interrelated process of creation shapes the forest as much as it does the city. Seeing signs in the urban landscape is sync.

I go on regular vision quests or "sync walks" through the concrete jungle with my Ayahuasquero friend,[7] seeing syncs and signs in number plates, T-shirts, billboards and trash. Usually a sync walk will end at the movie theatre, the temple of the city where communion with nature reaches its peak amongst the "stars." Just like signs have helped align the healthy smaller cultures of earth with Creator's plan, sync attunes the modern person to the unfathomable will of the Self realizing itSelf.

How do we know we are understanding the messages from these syncs or signs?

Because the ultimate ever-present reality is total perfection,[8] the greater the amount of joy one obtains from their interpretations of sync, the more accurate, successful and aligned the reading of its meaning is.

The universe is created in all places and times non-locally, right here and now, the home of consciousness. Thankfully (and mercifully) the intensity of this gnosis varies, allowing for the daily ebb and flow of life. We view this bizarre happening of creation sequentially, doing our best to make sense of it. Sync is the new level of understanding (a collective allowing) about the nature of the universe, now making its way into everyday consensus awareness. When noticing the non-local hand during a prerecorded movie, the mind-blowing elegance hinted at by the new "in-sync" perspective starts to become tangible.

I will often sit down in a theatre or at home and watch something, noticing how the situations, objects and words align with things I have been meditating on, realizing the movie echoes activities and conversations I've been engaged in recently, with uncanny perfection. On occasion, watching media during moments where the context has already allowed for particularly heightened states of awareness, the reactive mirroring between the screen and myself is immediate. As a teenager, glimpsing this reality with a head full of conspiracies and misperceptions about power and influence, I perceived syncs in movies as hints of a nefarious agenda. Now I realize this entrainment, between my personal experiences and films made independently from me, is the emergent awareness of myself as a non-local organism-environment.[9] I bleed into everything I perceive, my boundary or what I consider as "myself" and the "world" is a flexible convenience, and my perception detaches from the individual focal point. That a prerecorded film is alive and interactive—reacting to my specific context at a given moment—shows that what creates both myself and the film, is ever-present, interrelated and, by implication, non-local. The intensity of holy communion with a film (as with life in general) varies appropriately with our degree of presence. I can enjoy watching TV with my mom, noticing a few light entrainments here and there. Or, I can do Ayahuasca with my friend Jim Sanders, the next day stepping out to the cinema; shaking in my seat with vivid, seemingly impossible boundary loss.

Entrainment hints at a property inherent in sync associations that draw them together. The concepts of sync and entrainment are so interrelated that the words are regularly interchanged.

Often a word will arise in the mind[10] of the organism and, at the same moment, consciousness will notice this word somewhere in the environment—perhaps on a passing T-shirt or in a song playing in the background. Old models try to say: "either the T-shirt was seen first, prompting my mind to issue the same word" or "perhaps my mind thought the word, then, out of all the clutter in my surroundings, was primed to notice the chance occurrence of the same word." Indeed they are coincident (in the sense of happening at the same time) and this is entrainment between myself and environment. Both myself (which thinks the word) and the environment (which contains the T-shirt) share the same source that is primary to both.

These examples of entrainment, those happening at the same instance or perhaps very close to each other, will help us make the leap to the more unusual ultimate reality of sync.

As all is sync (or nothing is sync), regardless of the length of time between events; they are always entrainment as the non-local self is present in any instances, never mind the justification put forward by the inherently-limited mind. All the associations we make are portals opening between ourselves, across the barriers of timespace, organism-environment and thing-event.

The most recognized of such portals is love. When we meet a future lover, and our upcoming associations are to be moments of intense shared awareness, we might even recognize it from the first glance.

The sensation that things are specifically being orchestrated for (or even by) yourself, is a normal result of the emerging sync consciousness. Depending on the temperament and makeup of the specific belief system, the interpretation of sync can be nefarious or benign. If concepts of influence over what happens in spacetime are associated to pyramid-type hierarchies, the syncs can form a reality of peculiar control networks, manipulating the texture of the moment.[11] To satisfy the ever-increasing depth of the experience, the limited self (ego) needs increasingly powerful and subtle top-down organizations able to manipulate the environment, sometimes extending "them" beyond the physical (into the spiritual, inter-dimensional and godlike spheres). If the external control concepts are replaced by the personal and internal, the individual experiencing sync can start thinking him or herself God. Many undergoing this particular process (awakening as a united organism-environment field via synchronicity) will have a hodge-podge of these symptoms.

The faulty idea that the universe is a hierarchy of power and influence, introduced at a young age, is responsible for these phantom menaces.

This is not to undermine the models of external higher power and internal personal divinity, but to help put them in the most helpful context we can imagine. The nature of reality clearly corresponds in some areas to the two seemingly opposing ideas. This vivifies the continued joke being played on us as we try and impose concepts and symbols over the (thankfully) indefinable transcendent nature of what ultimately *Is*. If we could fit the nature of our Selves and God into a conceptual map or box, it would imply that *It* is finite, and not bottomless eternal perfection.

Imagine a ladder extending infinitely up and down, that all possible beings are climbing. The ladder represents our progress and success as entities in the universal enterprise. As this ladder extends eternally higher and lower, regardless how far apart Gods are from humans, or humans are from ants, we are all still in the center. Only relatively speaking are there higher and lower beings. All are in the center from which consciousness emanates.

From a profile view, power represents the top of the pyramid. When we continue up a dimension, and see the pyramid from the overhead perspective, we notice the tip is the center and balanced point. Real power comes from being in harmony with the totality and filled with a joy ultimately free from concept.

If the ultimate controlling and manipulating force were not inside of us right now (and in everything else) it would not be ever-present, and not the true eternal Master.

Investigating sync leads one, not only to relaxing the boundaries between things and events, but also to letting go of the rigid classifications of these thing-events. In order to notice that one thing-event (situation, object or symbol) has an affinity to another, often means being "loose" with our associations. In a sense, to see and understand sync we must become fools—free from the limitations, but not the benefits, of mind.

For example, a few years ago I was struggling with actress Robin Tunney climbing K2 (the mountain) in the film *Vertical Limit* and also passing signs reading "2K" (in reference to the year 2000 Millennium) in another film, *End of Days*. K2 is obviously 2K backwards, but my mind was resistant to accept this as a clear association, which it now plainly recognizes. The old model of perception was concerned with the simple relaxation of associating something backwards (letting the box that fits K2, now also accept 2K). This shows how we can be confronted with sync and miss it— owing to how we discriminate between *what associates* and *what we think is not associated*.

Sync is realizing all associations are agreed upon conventions, and we are free to re-appropriate the process. The symbol representative of the planet Jupiter[12] clearly looks like an amalgamation of 2 and 4. In synchromysticism[13] it has come to symbolize "42." 42 is "The Answer to Life, the Universe, and Everything" in the popular book series and major motion picture *The Hitchhiker's Guide to the Galaxy*. 42 is also the angle at which light refracts, becoming the colors of the rainbow.

Now when I see the number 42, concepts like "Jupiter" and "rainbow" are evoked, perfectly reasonable given the above context. In the same fashion, any symbols or words or concepts are up for re-association, unlocking their infinite potential. We saw Jupiter associating to the sync-starting "9/11 Mega Ritual" and here it is freeing our symbols. Jupiter is the source of words like "jovial" and "joy"—and we know that the ultimate reality is perfect Joy. The evolutionary jump we are undergoing, assisted by sync, is overseen by Jupiter.

Sync is time travel

The one unambiguous ever-present factor in any and all synchronicity is the witness or consciousness.[14] Consciousness itself is the ultimate sync, present in all sync. All syncs point towards consciousness and arise from it. Like water is to the fish, consciousness is so central and ubiquitous to sync (and all else) that we tend to miss it.

Consciousness is present whenever you see a 42 or any other sync. The next time you witness a 42, there will be a non-local bridge between the past and present self. This is part of the exciting charge of seeing syncs. The past, present and future selves, all created now, witnessing resonant events and becoming aware of each other beyond time. It is also why significant events (like 9/11) are encoded heavily in the sync architecture of the present.

Syncs are signs of our potently aware non-local selves bearing witness to thing-events.

Often syncs are interpreted—including 2012 phenomena—as pointing towards an imminent massive collective spiritual experience. This event—collective consciousness realization—does, by its very nature, singularly stand out in the fabric of all we perceive. The great perceiver, perceiving itself through us on the largest planetary scale in known history.

Individuals are becoming aware of themselves across space-time. At the same moment, many different individuals, who are noticing the same syncs, start perceiving their shared transpersonal essence. Real-time synchronicity sharing (what all communication/association essentially boils down to) across the internet and on networks like Twitter, are the result of this emergent process (of the collective awaking into a unified greater Self), as well as facilitating in its increased realization.

The ultimate sync is consciousness in this moment, and we have it already. This does not remove from the delight of processes and play in the world around us. Knowing you are the Self makes you the best player you can possibly be.

Movie stars are "as below" resonators of the skies above

Even though our current general associations are agreed upon conventions (and we are free to make new ones), they still arise from the ultimate mind that orchestrates all thing-events and are not arbitrary. The map is not the territory, but is part of the territory, and both share the same fountainhead.

A wonderful example is how we use the word "star" for celebrities. Our oldest myths and stories are associated to the heavenly spheres. They have been personified, deified and their movements become elaborate dramas. Kings, Queens and other big players in our cultures have been connected to these bodies and vice versa. The stories about the stars and humankind are inseparably intertwined and are reflections of each other. Our cinema is a recent incarnation of this dynamic, the obvious giveaway being the word "star."

The mystery and beauty of the stars (that would pull man deeper into the void), had to be increasingly turned away from at the onset of "mind." Playing right into Creator's hands, as he/she had put them into the silver screen to keep telling us stories, and continue our process of becoming stars ourselves.

Astrology studies the relationships between us and the heavenly spheres. Synchromysticism realizes the same dynamic exists between our world and celebrity stars. Meditating on the film strip ladder—passing at 24 frames a second—we climb the stairway to heaven.

Film and pop culture offer a rich and immediate portal into the collective awakening psyche when treated as creative flux emanating from the heart of all Being. The artist is acknowledged as shaping his/her medium, yet channeling the energy to create, directly from the greater Self. The ever-changing patterns and themes surrounding us (via our omnidirectionally mediated and increasingly mercurial environments) are taken as the externalized collective Body. We can investigate this dynamic entity—disguised as the forms and context of the environment (that we ourselves comprise)—by treating all that arises in our awareness as sacred and ready to be re-contextualized—with joy as our guide and the sky as the limit.

The mainstream culture, no longer a toxic river, is the major artery from which all other strange subcultures branch and receive nourishment.

The original collective context of our media and forms are not lost, but celebrated and elaborated upon. The world remains cohesive and integrated (and its individuals sane), yet open-ended for infinite exploration, as depth and meaning penetrate everything continually.

The pool of pop and meaning we collectively swim in anchors our experience and supplies a shared framework from which we can launch our experimental, far out and freaky, sync depth charges. Which of these will explode . . . ? New connections that are caught up and pulled in by the gravity of others' interests, only to eventually go "pop" themselves and enrich the sync whole.

Notes:

(1) Using "thing-events" helps highlight how things and events are not ultimately separable or essentially different. I could say, "the tree I am looking at right now is . . ." a thing, or an event, if I realize all the infinite processes that are involved in there being a tree. "Tree" as a "thing" is a convenient label for all the processes that comprise the limitless mysterious reality of the object I am seeing. Syncs are values of mundane versus profound we place upon one thing-event associated to another.

(2) Chance is a label for the occurrences between the initiation and outcome of thing-events *far too subtle* for current perspective to understand. Chance happenings (coincidences) versus meaningful synchronicity, are different models mapping the same phenomena beyond the scope of both. All models are inherently beyond the reach of our labels of the unlimited thing-events. If a map had all the detail of the area it represented it would be identical to it, and useless as a representation.

(3) Reality isn't ultimately connected or not connected (one or many), it is something beyond understandable categories. The ultimate nature of sync goes to the indefinable core of all that exists, and our words about it will always only be *relatively* true. The words can guide towards transcendental understanding of sync, as they (and the reader) arise from the same source.

(4) To "symbolize" is to give a finite shape and definition to a thing-event (ultimately indefinable) for the purpose of creating associations, which in turn create our perception of the world. The letters and words you are now reading are part of just such a system, symbols creating associations and giving rise to this story of sync.

Symbols are in flux, new interpretations are constantly being associated to them, and new symbols are being added to our collection; the story of reality.

A collection of symbols, like "letters," can make up another symbol, such as a "word." Our entire perception of reality is a big symbol for the indefinable mystery it represents.

(5) CULTure is the reigning collection of sync associations that make up the current reality of entities (ranging in size from the entire planet down to a single individual). Large cultures are the familiar ones, like countries or regions. Smaller groups, like synchromystics, share many associations with symbols only agreed upon by the group itself. Cults of only one person exist and they are often labeled eccentrics or mad men/women. Smaller cults are the breeding grounds for associations that could go viral and become accepted by the bigger groups of association networks (a.k.a. realities). The more joy and harmony emanating from your cult—whether a large or small group—the more it resonates with the ultimate purpose of the totality.

(6) The essences of things are infinite and boundless. When we draw a perimeter around a thing, by the necessity of conceptualization, we place a border we can recognize around part of it. The parts not contained, yet still perceived by those sensitive to such matters, are often called spirit. Other spirits are things so subtle that no model has yet been created to contain it. The spirit world is the realm of thing-events beyond the event horizon of human conceptualization. There is a continual process of evolution where the human nervous system grows to acknowledge new facets of this realm and include it in the consensus. What was once spiritual is now science. What is now sync will soon be regular association.

(7) In the forests of South America, certain Shamans have cultivated a profound relationship of feedback between themselves and the environment. They have a partnership with a conscious plant brew, Ayahuasca. The feedback between the individual and the environment (through the plant) is a singularly powerful portal for what-creates-both to come into this world. The practice has spread to new cultures all over the earth as the living biosphere self-organizes for the next dramatic evolutionary leap. In my home of Winnipeg, I have been fortunate enough (clearly sync entrainment) to stumble upon just such a movement, headed by Shaman and man of sync, Jim Sanders.

(8) The more sensitive and free from imperfection the film stock, the more clarity and depth we can capture in the picture. Considering the infinite nature up and down every point of the macro-

and microcosmic spacetime manifold, we realize the most ultimate and perfect substrate allows for it. That we can never grasp *It* is even clearer proof of *Its* existence, for to be graspable, *It* must be containable, thus finite. This perfection and the joy that is every moment is beyond the understanding of the limited mind, from which it itself is born. Often the mind is perplexed at how the events of our lives and societies reflect this ultimate of realities.

The total eternal and ever-present perfection, regardless of context, is self-evident to the ultimate Self.

(9) Using "organism-environment" helps highlight how *the perceiving entity* and *what is being experienced* are interrelated and ultimately united (or not divided). Both the organism and its environment are thing-events that arise in primary consciousness. When I notice myself (organism) and what I am seeing (environment), the real I is the witness of both.

In any spacetime dynamic there is an organism-environment-thing-event.

(10) The mind is a localized collection of symbols, forming a map or model through which the ultimate consciousness perceives the world. As a collection of limitations, the mind and all it generates (including the persona) are never to be taken primarily for the realities it perceives. Again, the mind is not the territory, but it is part of the territory, and both share the same fountainhead.

(11) My reality tunnel at this stage resembled *The Truman Show*, *The Matrix*, *The Illuminatus Trilogy!* and *1984,* all put in a blender.

(12) The Jupiter symbol as 42, and its association to rainbows, was explained to me by Jim Sanders.

(13) Synchromysticism is a name I started using to describe thoughts about synchronicity in 2006. "The art of realizing meaningful coincidence in the seemingly mundane with mystical or esoteric significance." I used this summary on an old blog site to try and encapsulate synchromysticism. I still see it used on new websites today. Nothing is essentially wrong with it. Perhaps too slippery on the brain and open for misinterpretations. This is likely also its strength as a catchphrase. I hope this current document clarifies, or at least confuses in the right direction, the continuing

process of creating a better understanding of the phenomena of synchronicity.

On the Internet, an ever-changing community of people have come and gone associating themselves, willing or otherwise, with the word.

(14) Consciousness is the mysterious property, always out of reach, that knows. Consciousness can refer to this essence in individuals or groups, depending on the context it is being used in. There is an ultimate consciousness underlying everything, directly connected and primary to all other levels of consciousness.

The unknowable I that knows it knows.

JUSTIN GRAY MORGAN

Justin Gray Morgan is an Artist, Designer and Writer, living in the Bay Area. He has a background in the study of design, symbols, myth and shamanism. He is currently working on a series of illustrations and paintings on Tarot, Kabbalah, Alchemy, Sacred Geometry and Gnosticism. "As fate would have it, I came into contact with Alan (the editor of this book) through a series of interesting synchronistic events and ended up doing the cover design and tarot illustrations for this book." He works as a freelance Artist, Designer and Illustrator and can be contacted through his site at justingraymorgan.com.

justingraymorgan.com
themaskofgod.blogspot.com

Awakening at the Center of the Mandala

The Temple

It's January 10th. Over the past week I have been working on a Mandala. Less of an art project, the Mandala is a way to organize my thoughts as a form of meditation. A way to map physical and spiritual reality. On the bottom half of the piece is a man sitting in Lotus Position, his body forming a temple pyramid. The temple has seven layers, one for each of the chakras.

The first level is the Root, an Eden like garden, the literal roots from which all life arises. Next is the Sacral, the center of sexual energy. Like the Khajuraho temples in India, bodies intertwine, coming together at the center with statues of Adam and Eve. Above that, the Solar Plexus, the source of will power. The thousand arms of Guanyin reaching out in an expression of supreme will. The next level is home to the Heart. A giant drum, vibrating with each beat, keeping harmony with all that is. At the Throat are sculptures of the many teachers, the Buddhas of all ages.

At the center of the piece is the Third Eye. Within the head is a star, a man within the man, a self within the self. The Crown Chakra lies at the top of the head, the gateway to higher realities. Through it comes an understanding of higher worlds.

Above that things begin to get murky. I want to maintain symmetry and mirror the bottom half in keeping with the old adage "As above, so below," but it feels like I'm forcing the design, rather than it being an honest representation of what is above. I play with overlaying the Tree of Life, Jacob's Ladder and a few other old alchemical maps of the cosmos, but none seem to be a true fit.

I'm determined to figure it out based on my own experience. While the books I have been reading are helpful guides, nothing can substitute for actual experience. I'm no stranger to the subconscious, shamanic realms, but most of my previous explorations could be equated to jumping into the deep-end head first. As I've matured, I have found more methodical approaches based on readings from texts on psychology, meditation, alchemy, Tarot, Kabbalah and the occult. Using these as a guide, I feel more comfortable approaching these subconscious realms.

The Elements

I begin to meditate. The technique I'm using is based on a five-pointed star, the pentagram. The human body is a star. Two legs, two arms and a head make five. From each of these points five extends again. Five fingers, five toes, five senses. Five is the way through which we know the outer world. It can also be a way to know the world within. In symbolism, the pentagram represents the harmonization of the four elements, bringing a fifth into existence. Each element corresponds to a point on the star. Each a vibrational aspect of the inner and outer world.

Earth. Body. Disks. Rather than trying to transcend the physical I go deeper into it. Bringing my awareness from my head to my toes and back up again. Increasing speed with each pass, I reach a point of equilibrium feeling my entire body pulsing with energy. These dense vibrations establish a stable foundation, allowing me to channel in higher energies.

Water. Heart. Cups. In this realm, consciousness is like a boat, floating on a vast sea of emotions and feelings. The water washes over the edge at times, threatening to drown us in its depths. Too often we identify with these waters rather than letting the feelings wash away after they have run their course. Even beneath still waters strong currents may flow, waiting for a chance to break the surface. Aware of these depths, I let them calmly wash away. As the waters grow still they begin to reflect what is above. The silent surface becomes a mirror.

Air. Intellect. Swords. The winds of thought, invisible, but full of power. Blowing to and fro, it is easy to get caught in their movement. Mixing with the waters of emotion, clouds form, a storm develops. The strong winds disturb the surface of the ocean below. Huge waves come crashing down. In the midst of the clouds and rain you can barely see at all. During the storm you get lost in the violent movement. Eventually the storm passes. The winds quiet, clouds part, and the air becomes clear. In this invisible world you can see forever.

Fire. Will. Wands. The sun shines brightly above, embodying the fiery spirit of creation. If the fire burns too bright it will quickly burn itself out, consuming all that it touches. If too dim, one freezes to death in the coldness of the world. When the flames are properly stoked they remain in balance, giving off just the right amount of warmth, allowing the light to shine through.

Spirit. Archetypes. Trumps. As the other elements are brought into harmony a fifth element is activated. The Bright shining light of Spirit, the highest vibration in our reality. Descending from above, transforming all beneath it. The fifth point is activated. The star is complete.

I am now entering into the realm of archetypes. Reflecting upward as a white fiery star of light, into the realms of the subconscious. As I ascend I see her again. A black inverted star is descending, swallowing everything in its path. Full of darkness, Kali the Black Goddess threatens to destroy all that she touches. If I get any closer I fear she will tear me apart, teeth gnashing, claws digging into my flesh. I try to get past her to deeper realms, but she blocks my every move.

Then I realize something—she is mirroring me. I have been treating her as a gatekeeper I needed to slip by. Kali is not the gatekeeper, she is the gate. A demonic form of the Anima and Shadow revealing itself as a monster, I had been treating her as something foreign, so she had become a demon. As soon as I realize this, she transforms from a terrible demon to a beautiful goddess. What I perceived as darkness is infinite unfolding space. As I look deeper into her I see a million stars shining inside. I go into her, merging, forming a ten-pointed gray star. The gatekeeper has become gate, the demon an ally. Kali has become my guide to deeper levels.

The next day, 1/11/11, I'm telling my friend Al about my experiences the night before, when a young woman stops by my house. She smiles as I greet her. Her name is Mali.

Into the Headlands

We hang out again a week later. After going out with some friends, we all decide to go for a walk at Land's End, a park on the northwest corner of the San Francisco Peninsula.

The night is clear and a full moon is in the sky. The trail leads along steep cliffs through groves of Eucalyptus and Redwood trees. The moon is shining through the trees and reflects off the waves as they crash against the rocks, hundreds of feet below. We stop on a cliff looking out at the Golden Gate Bridge and the Marin Headlands. I tell Mali that I spend a lot of time walking around in the Headlands. I like the name because it reminds me, as I walk, that what I perceive as the outside world is actually within my head.

We exist as a point of consciousness. Consciousness itself is like a void, creating a vacuum for the experiences of life to flow into. When we walk through the world we are in a constant process of creating what we perceive to be the outer world—forgetting at times that what we are experiencing is actually aspects of ourselves. This is not to say the outer world does not exist, just that the there is a larger reality that exists outside of the five senses. I enjoy walking in natural areas like the Headland because it reminds me of this. I become a point of consciousness/awareness experiencing the outside world within myself, realizing they are one in the same.

Although we are now aware of the larger movements of the solar system, there is some truth in the old alchemical geocentric models of the universe. Each point of consciousness is at the center of its own universe, within a series of concentric circles, forming a Cosmic Mandala.

The first layer is body and who we are outwardly. The persona or the character we play in the world. This reflects inwardly as the ego. Out from there is our environment corresponding to the conscious mind, the outer and inner world we are conscious of. Our bodies exist in the Earth's environment, our ego exists as the environment of our mind.

Next is the sphere of the Sun and Moon. Although the Sun is roughly 400 times larger than the Moon, and interestingly also around 400 times further away, they appear almost exactly the same size in the sky. Day and Night, Male and Female, they represent the polarities. Again this pattern is reflected inward. Even the brain itself is divided in 2. The left or masculine side of the brain dealing with analysis, the right feminine side home to creative thought. As these polarities cross the threshold from inner to outer, they reverse, with the left-brain controlling the right hand and the right-brain controlling the left. The outer is a mirror of the inner. This polarity is furthered by the activities done either under the ruling influence of the Sun or Moon. By day we work, traveling out into the world, affecting it largely through analytical thought. By night we dream, traveling deep into the creative realms of the subconscious.

Next are the spheres of the planets, each corresponding to inward archetypal forces and phases of human development. The 7 days of the week were named based on the 7 bodies in the sky visible with the naked eye. From the penetrating light of the Sun, the Father, we enter the mother Monday (Moon-day). At this first stage, we only know our mother. Her body is our world before, and for a time after, birth. As we begin to develop, we become aware of our physical body. In Tuesday from the Germanic *dyeu*— "to shine" we become a mini sun or son. Tuesday is also *Martes*, connecting to Mars, the god of war. March, the third month, is the month of Mars. Containing the vernal equinox, it is the time of spring, the period when growth begins. In the warrior cultures this is when they began venturing into the outer world.

The next stage of development is language. From the Norse Wodin we get Wednesday—from the Roman Mercury, *Miercoles*. Wodin and Mercury are the gods of language, the messenger gods. Mercury, also a god of trade, represents learning to make one's way in the world during this phase. Thor and Jupiter rule Thursday. The father or parental gods, both wielding hammers and lightning bolts. This is a time of work and action. Jupiter or Zeus, known for his many conquests, leads nicely into Venus and Freya for Friday. After developing and becoming an individual, we are lured by the power of the opposite polarity. Freya or Venus, the goddess of love, calls us back to unite and become one again.

Saturday = Saturn's day. The dark god of time, holding a sickle in his hand—he reminds us of our mortality. The father of the Pantheon and eater of his own children, Saturn is a reminder that death is the father of all.

With Sunday the cycle repeats. From the darkness of Saturn comes the light of the Sun. With each new birth the process begins anew.

Inwardly these forces operate on archetypal levels. Father, Mother, childhood, growth, language, work, love, time and death are all universal to the human experience. As much a part of the inner world as the outer, they shape the landscape of the psyche in ways we do not always understand. Operating out of this deeper unknown realm, the spheres of the planets leads us out to the stars.

On a clear night like tonight, one cannot help but be overcome by the beauty of the stars and the vastness of space. Few things capture the human imagination in such a way. The constellations on the zodiacal belt also mirror the stages of human development, taking on the characteristics of the time of year they come into view. From birth to growth to harvest to death, the cycle repeats each year, again representative of Archetypal forces within. The universe reflecting within as the cycles of the human experience. The universal human experience reflected outward in the naming of the stars.

From here we venture into the unknown. The vast expansiveness of outer space mirrored by the vast inner space of the subconscious. Through outward use of the masculine technologies, we find what seems to be empty space is actually full of countless galaxies. Through the inward use of feminine methods, such as meditation or psychedelics, we find the vast seemingly-empty inward space is home to an infinite number of galaxies as well.

I can't help but feel that, if I could reach up and peel back the outer layer of stars, I would find myself peeking out from the inside of my skull onto the outside world, as it exists outside of the limited perceptions of our five senses.

I think about this as we are walking through the woods. The silver moonlight. The sound of the waves. The smell of the eucalyptus trees. All part of myself. All hinting at some greater reality.

Into the Labyrinth

We walk down a winding staircase through a dark grove of trees. The path continues along a cliff's edge. As we get out into the open, the sound of the ocean grows louder than before. It is high tide and the waves come crashing in. As we walk the narrow path, I assure them that we are almost there. We walk around the edge on an outcropping and we see our destination. A large circle of stones 40 feet wide with smaller circles inside it. It is a labyrinth. Mali looks amazed at what she sees and exclaims that her mother gave her a book about labyrinths earlier that week.

The book is *Walking a Sacred Path: Rediscovering the Labyrinth as a Spiritual Tool,* by Dr. Lauren Artess. On the cover is a labyrinth, the same as the one we are walking through. Artess works at Grace Cathedral in San Francisco, a beautiful building at the top of Nob Hill, on California Street. There are two large labyrinths at the cathedral, one on the inside, the other outside. If you follow California Street west across the city, it dead-ends at a grand staircase that leads into Land's End.

In the book it details the history of the labyrinth as being based on one from Chartres cathedral. The design is based on a thirteen-pointed star for the 13 moons of the year. Around the edge there are 112 lunations, half circles. This part of the design is based on four sets of 28, encoding the twenty-eight days of the lunar cycle and the four quadrants of the year. Through encoding these large cosmic patterns into a symbol, the labyrinth acts as a meditative tool, synchronizing the walker with these larger cosmic patterns.

Mali, our friend Henry and I walk into the labyrinth. As we make our way in, we pass each other on adjacent paths, handing a bottle back and forth as we go. We make our way into the center. The full moon shines brightly above us. Below it to the west is Saturn, the only other planet visible at the time. Mali, a definite embodiment of the Moon, has a big black pit-bull named Kronos. I joke, "That's you and Kronos in the sky above."

As we walk back along the cliffs and up the winding staircase, I can't help but feel we haven't left the labyrinth. Though no longer in the stone circles, it feels like we are walking on a winding path, laid out in some sort of cosmic pattern, based on some larger unknown geometry.

That night my dreams start out in the usual way. A moving collage of daily events, environments shifting as I try to complete some task from my waking life. At some point during this I realize I'm dreaming. I begin floating upward, looking out on the dreamscape below. As I continue to drift out, I begin to see beyond my dreamscape—there are others dreaming. Friends, family and those from waking life share the closest proximity. The landscapes of their dreams spill over the borders as the environments change. I keep floating out. Hundreds then thousands of dreamers are visible. Eventually I begin to see the edges of this huge continent. Below millions are dreaming. A large pulsing body, its skin made of constantly changing landscapes. As I look at it, it begins to writhe around, tossing and turning. The giant dreaming creature begins to wake up. Millions of eyes begin to open. When the last one opens I wake up.

As I lay in my bed I'm reminded of the myth of Daedalus, the creator of the labyrinth. After creating the labyrinth, Daedalus and his son, Icarus, are cast into it. This echoes the story of Brahman—the dreaming Hindu god, or even ties in to the Luciferic myth of a fallen angel cast out of heaven because he wished to create his own world. What I find fascinating about all these myths is the common theme of a God entering into its own creation. Dreaming a world and then wakening within it. This is even an unspoken theme in modern science. The Universe, as some sort of cosmic event, explodes into existence through the big bang. Stars and planets form. Life evolves and eventually becomes conscious. The Universe is waking up inside itself.

The Stargate

A few nights later I decide to do another meditation using a different technique. Barefoot, I face north, take a deep breath and begin to spin. Slowly at first, I begin to build speed. I spin faster and faster with each turn, counting as I go. Spinning counterclockwise, like the spin of the Earth. Counterclockwise, like the Earth around the Sun. Counterclockwise, like the Solar System around the Galactic core.

105, 106, 107, I stop counting at 108. It no longer feels like I'm spinning. The whirling images of my surroundings have formed a seamless panoramic. I begin to reduce speed. If I tried to stop immediately I would crash to the ground like a ton of bricks. Gradually, I go slower and slower until I stop. I lie down on my back and close my eyes.

I begin to spin my consciousness in the opposite direction. Clockwise, like the void of space that all unfolds into. I spin back through the events of the day. Back through the events of the week. Back through the years. As the speed builds, time begins to collapse. Through my childhood, toward my parents, my mother out of her mother, out of her mother—rapidly enfolding like Russian dolls. Layer upon layer builds until I reach the origin, the original void from which all emanates.

As I stare into the darkness, I begin to see a tiny point of light. As I look at it, it begins to grow in size. A bright shining golden disk, it appears to be made out of light. Concentric circles pulsate. Opening and closing, spitting out smaller disks that go back in as another opens.

I open my eyes and I'm shocked to see the disk floating directly above me. I stare into it dumbstruck by what I am seeing. I suddenly panic. "What the hell is this thing?" As soon as I think this, it disappears. I sit up and look around. Again I think to myself, "what was that?" Then I think back to my Kali meditations. Perhaps this thing too is some sort of gate. Not something foreign, but another aspect of myself. With this in mind, I lie back down and look up into the sky.

No sooner have I done this than the gold disk reappears. Breathing deeply, I stare into it and it descends. As it touches me, Space seems to collapse around me. Folding like an accordion it bends the space between objects, but it feels like I'm flying towards the Sun. The Sun folds on top of me, blinding me for a moment as it hits. I'm now heading towards another star, this one larger and brighter then the Sun. As this star hits there is another flash of light. When I can see again I'm almost at the next star. As I pass through each star, it layers on top of the previous, forming concentric spheres of light around my body.

As the folding of space begins to slow, I realize it's taking me toward the center of the Galaxy. I am overcome with the brilliance of the light emanating from the Central Sun. As I look at it, I become aware of some sort of beings or energy moving around inside the light. Swirling around, it pulsates, sending light out through the stars in the outer limbs of the galaxy. The light doesn't travel between stars; it seems to simultaneously come out of the center of each. The beings almost seem to be working. As they make something they like, they send it through.

Looking around, I see the same thing happening in adjacent galaxies. Flashing like lightning during a thunderstorm, the Central Suns are pulsing, lighting up the outer limbs like millions of tiny fireflies.

As I near the center, I come to a wall of light. Shining like a liquid mirror, it appears to be an event horizon. I can feel a tremendous pull from behind it. I can also feel the beings on the other side almost ushering me through ready to catch me. I'm afraid to take the plunge, but I slowly move into it. As I cross, I am sucked through with tremendous force.

As I pass through, I see what would best be described as a giant tree of light. The tree seems to be a higher dimensional object that penetrates space-time at different points. In the same way you could poke a pencil through a sheet of paper in several places by folding it, this tree pokes through our reality. Revealing itself as separate stars, all are actually branches in the tree, coming off of the trunk that is the Central Sun, the earth and planets growing from its limbs like fruit. To get an idea of what this looks like, imagine a galaxy stacked on top of itself several times then connect the dots.

I'm pulled into the center of the trunk, speeding down towards the roots, drawn through by a singularity collapsing into itself. As I reach the bottom, I go through into another, larger trunk—revealing the trunk of our core as just a limb on a still larger tree. This process continues at an exponential rate. The diameter of the trunk increasing in size as the singularity becomes infinitely small. As I reach the Omega point, I become one with everything that ever was, is and ever could be, simultaneously becoming nothing at all.

Gradually I begin to see things. Through this state of infinite being and nonbeing my eyes come into focus. I find that I am looking back out through my own eyes, into the blue sky above.

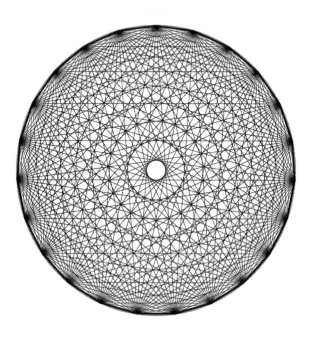

Steve Willner

Labyrinth of the Psychonaut

Steven Willner is a symbologist and psychedelic video-editor who posts videos up on his "Soundlessdawn" YouTube channel that are centered around symbolism, mysticism, astrology, entheogens, the underlying meaning of religious doctrine, how music affects consciousness, secret societies, extraterrestrials, and the occult in modern day Western Society. Much of his research is geared towards uncovering the mysteries that are hidden in plain sight, often stating that the universe is a holographic coding system that shows undeniable signs of intelligent design, purpose, and therefore destiny—and that every single human thought is a new creation in it of itself, which is then immediately combined into the infinite collective of eternity.

He is the creator of the Labyrinth of the Psychonaut website.

He has been a guest on Red Ice Creations *on numerous occasions—and has appeared on* The Freeman Perspective *and* The Occult of Personality *as well.*

labyrinthofthepsychonaut.blogspot.com

HACKING SOURCE CODE CIPHERS
*Cosmic Keys to the
Original Fragmentation of Consciousness*

The original language of source was not a complicated one. It was the root structure of a self-similar budding lotus, a singularity of increasing intrinsic definition and compression moving towards some strange kinetic hyper drive oscillation. Corridors of mirrored cosmic synapses fired into a spontaneous knowing, dreamscapes of ultimate truth arose in velvet plasma hive mind elite. This formless sentience nebulously drifted in the throne room of role play and imagination. Stellar masters before materialization sat 'uncreated' as ultimate perfection, in absolute silence. Then sound, the great germination which birthed structure as we understand it, erupted as self-adapting spider web geometries of infinite potentialities in unwavering balance. The music of the spheres, the birth of self-realization came with this ancient vibratory rainbow, an ethereal programming language with unimaginable depth and malleability. Enter, grow, evolve, duplicate, communicate, improve function, and return. Create rules, bend rules, destroy rules, repeat. The soundless sound 'I' began to pulse and interpolate until settling upon wrapping in on itself, forming a fractal torus made of flame. The spoken word is creation, the kinetic movement of micro bodies working together in a larger host where communication occurs on every possible level and dimension.

Symbols were birthed in this torus of flame as interpretive pillars or aesthetic markers pointing towards some distant ultimate truth arriving in the mind's eye as hovering monolithic visual adjectives for cosmos. Their purpose is to energetically imprint and link themselves to the collective psyche of all self-aware beings that have splintered from the original vibratory essence, thereby creating an ongoing game of telephone with our ancestors. A sentience with amnesia of the macro body it is attached to uses the symbol instinctively as breadcrumbs in the darkness, to be brought closer together with the ultimate goal of becoming reabsorbed into the source code it splintered from via self-surrender and contemplation over the ultimate mystery of mysteries. To Sync is to analyze these breadcrumbs, develop a sharable theory of everything, apply a structured language for interconnecting thought forms which attempt to explain unification with the all, and to experience the joy and humor embedded inside living algorithmic patterns/spirals/worker elves that make up the entirety of our holographic environment.

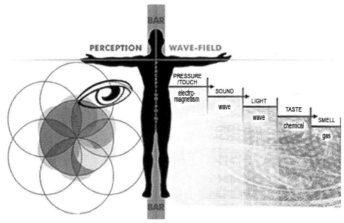

Within the loose parameters of Kotzian Synchromysticism and inspired free association, these algorithms manifest themselves as coincidence 2.0; a reality tunnel in which artists, code breakers, linguists, circus midgets, Psychonauts, and 'normal' folk alike focus intently on a plane of interaction that is geared towards conceptualizing a larger network matrix which may potentially hold a space for the whole of humanity; Big Daddy Sapien. Big Daddy leaves a footprint wherever he walks in the cosmic sands of universal experience. Sync bloggers playfully analyze the more subtle characteristics of this 'larger' being's movement

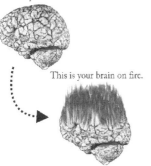

through the celestial seasons, attaching an evolving definition to the force that connects the heavens and the Earth. We are snakes weaving rhythmically back and forth, like sea grass rippling under the sea. We are snakes until we see that we are the mitochondria in a much larger being, creating its RNA template with every exhalation. Bridging the gap between a lost state and a found state of being allows for escapism and transcendence beyond our perceived collective reality. No secret of the universe is held for certain or for very long, however the afterglow of experiencing a divine truth even temporarily reminds us that we are alive, uninterrupted, and complete. Divine truths need not be heavy or heady; they can be light and absurd, jester-like in their orientation. Syncs are transformative heart anchored coordinates living on the map of creation. In their levity and humor they tumble and trip over themselves while still managing to point in the general direction we must travel to return back to center, to return home. In the presence of these moments we don't just *feel*, but actually experience a subtle *knowing* that an oversoul nexus is warmly communicating and joking with us all the time.

Numerologically, the first book of the Old Testament GENESIS totals 260, the same numerals as the count of letters in the alphabet. 26 articles of creation, designed out of the void, out of the darkness of the unconscious. GENESIS is the only Old Testament book spelt with capitals, in the index of the authorized King James Bible. The first book of the New Testament is Matthew, written MATTHEW in the index and totaling 272, a palindrome (cyclical) number which is 12 more than 260—or a solar cycle more. When Matthew is written, and its numerological values concentrated, it also totals 26 = 8 or infinity.

The alphabet is designed according to the ancient scheme of 22 letters and 7 basic shapes which match the magical formula for Pi (22/7) an infinite and mysterious cycle. The seven shapes are all variations on the serpent and the circle: | / \ o _ c ●. The Tarot deck is assigned to the alphabet construct, from A to V (= 22 being the master number). All letters are ideograms, pictorial representations suggesting an idea. As with all written symbols, they are constructed from the egg (the dot) and the serpent (the line).

$$| \ / \ \backslash \ o \ \_ \ c \ \bullet$$

HACKING SOURCE CODE CIPHERS

Image courtesy of **Jean Beauchard**

Every little aspect of language and numbers has an impact and causes a reaction in some way. Letters are crafted symbols designed to trigger memory and evoke a specific response. They are probably the most invasive system ever devised and have been used as a tool to control the way that humans think. Every word uttered or written will enforce the programming of whoever is exposed to it. It is true that the sounds of letters and words work very well as consciously recognizable signs and symbols of elemental sounds, but what do they say in secret, to our unconscious?

Those who do not fully understand language and numbers tend to flounder like fish out of water crawling upon the surface world without the appropriate appendages. They're forced to drink from the cup of illusory duality and separation, constantly being bombarded by symbolic & linguistic sorcery that enters through their neural pathways but remains outside of their full awareness. One of the major secrets to this illusion is that it is rooted in Rep-Tile energy, patterns that are all based on one thing; AWAKENING. The checkered floor is a repeating pattern of black and white tiles. It is representative of the clever reptile, coiled seven times, containing the intertwined Kundalini serpents traveling from the base of the spine upward towards release, culminating in coronation;

corona, sun, enlightenment. The board of opposites is our gauntlet here on 3D Earth; it is the chrysalis, bridge, and vehicle we must fully understand if we are to enter the abyss and take our collective leap of faith into another dimension of being.

While not fully conscious of the entire spectrum or prismatic light show of indigestible stimuli that is sigil casting and alchemical advertising in the modern world, we are still subject to an astonishing amount of aesthetic bombardment. Still pulled and manipulated as marionettes, and we are exhausted. Magical manipulation of source code can be used to create a closed system universe, a trap system. Those with total understanding of the construct *create* the game, those living in ignorance of its rules *play* the game, and those with an understanding of the rules and parameters can *choose* not to play the game at all. That was the troublesome variable in the *Matrix* films, choice. Luckily the ciphers, legends, and keys to break these seemingly hostile magical forms into the sum of their parts are easily accessible and hidden in plain sight.

Every letter in every word, including their intonation and phrasing, evokes a fleeting memory, building a subconscious picture of something that the speaker or writer may or may not have intended. This causes a reaction and produces an opinion. The potentials of this are enormous—and very well known by those who seek to rein or chain consciousness. What is a sentence but a coherent string of words, a condemnation, a punishment or a term of imprisonment? The capital letters are CA—PI —T AL PUN—ISH—MENTAL.

a b c d e f g h i j k l m n o p q r s t u v w x y z
ABCDEFGHIJKLMNOPQRSTUVWXYZ

Image courtesy of **Will 777 The Great Work**

Each capital letter is seeking power—knowledge. They are the lord Gods of their circle. They use the other letters in the name, sentence, paragraph, chapter, book, library to gain that knowledge.

To do this, it instructs the subsequent letters in turn to collect information from the letters that follow it. Each letter has a different viewpoint. Once the last letter in each domain is attained, the details are recycled back to the lord of that domain—the capital letter that will pass them on to its governor, until the original capital letter, symbolic of God, is infused with the details of every experience its subjects have met and felt.

At the same time that the information is being passed along the chain, the exploratory letters continue their forward mission, and report back in the same way. Each word is a pause, allowing assimilation of the collected information before moving on to other experiences.

All spoken word is the mystical dance of the Tarot; all written words conceal a broader etymology or association of meaning pertaining to the original essence of that character, shape, or symbol.

Simple sync connections and free associative language cracking highlight this phenomenon.

1. You're not in Kansas anymore. Kansas spelled backwards forms the word snakes. Kan or Cain is Mars = Aries the Greek God of War = Hurry Cain = KAN (EYE) = 9—WEST or CAIN 9 WEST. K9 = 11-9 = 9/11 = Mars Energy = March = Ram = Memory = Kundalini, Snake City Misery for some, Kansas City Missouri for others.
2. Jupiter aka Zeus = Thunderbolts = Bolt = Dog/God Star = Jupiter (24 42) Rules Friday = Fri = Fir = Fire = Dr. S(Z)ues(s) = Cat in the Hat = Fire and Sekhmet = Freya. Freya is the Girl FRIDAY or FREEDAY AKA PAY DAY = Green $$$ Eggs and Ham, Bilderbergers—Build a Burger.
3. We look in the Mountain DEW and see the WED-ing of polarities, through reflections. When we don't C reflection, we fall through the looking glass. "Do you take her to be your lawfully wedded wife?" EYE DEW. Obey the Law—waL—or be imprisoned behind walls—WalMart. WED = SUNDAY = The Wedding of the Sun Day, the "joining of the two halves." Isis is WED to Osiris and Osiris is said to have been killed by Seth. Brides marry Grooms. If we reverse the word GROOM, we arrive at the MOORG—a place where the dead (Osiris) is awakened and raised.
4. LINE = NILE = LOTUS. Achieving balance in the middle, not on either side of the river BANKS, as in Money. Return to the Source = $$$ Isis = Is-ness.
5. Spine = spin = 360 degrees = 33 vertebrae or 11 11 11 or KKK.
6. The letter Q is 17, and the tonQue has 17 muscles. The tonQue is the flame or phallic symbol in the mQuth. Q corresponds to the Hebrew YO-d (Sunny D Touch-Down), which is the first emanation from the void. So Yod is a code for boy. Yoda = Soda = The light of Truth = The darkness that lies. Coca-Cola—333—Choronzon—C Horizon—Event Horizon—Starg8.
7. TIN MAN = Ten Man Jupiter—Jew-puter—Tiger Woods—The Alpha/Omega = 10 = The Tin Man who has No Heart—AKA Heavy Metal, with an AXE to Grind—Axel Rose—AU-S-10-POWERS = The Power of Gold (AU), the Phallic Gold Member.

8. The Michael JAK = 22 SUN, 11th card in a deck of cards = All Seeing Eye—Horus—Set—Odin—Thor—Rainbow Bridge—Heart Chakra = Jak-Sun died of Cardiac Arrest = Apple Jacks = Pythagoras—11:11—K2—Y2K ARCH—Angel Michael ruler of the 4th Heaven (Heart Chakra) and the Sun. His zodiac sign—Leo—ruler of Sunday. Lion—Zion—Oz—NY (the big Apple Jack)—2012.

9. Last Supper—Bilderbergers—Build a burger—Menu = Mn(3.14) U—Meat = Taurus = Season = Spring—Meat cooked in grease, Bilder(ham)burgers meet in Greece—Cook county = Chi cago—Fry = Friday—Heinz 57 = foot long HEINZ = H=8 N=14 877=22—Hein Zight = Hind sight = the left thigh of Taurus = Pleiades—Zero point and the Eye of the storm. In the land of the blind the one eyed man is king. C'ing into the future.

10. ScorpioNorth
    AquariusEast
    LeoWest
    TaurusSouth → The SALT of the Earth & the cardinal points; The N.E.W.S. lulls you to sleep.

"The stroke of the *whip* maketh marks in the flesh, but the stroke of the *tongue* breaketh the bone." The pyramids are an architectural depiction of the Superman. I've never read that in any book, I just know it. The mortal man is made of bone; the immortal man is made of stone. Hive mind internet consciousness lubricates and expedites one's ability to see future potentialities as well as review the ripples of the past. Synchromysticism is a word jumble, a heady and artistic exercise in establishing the assemblage point for the coming dawn. It acts as a window to dreams not yet formed with ultra-low latency ancestral recall as an added bonus. There is no ceiling or limitation attached to this form of expression, that's the point. This kinetic firewire effect is cumulative and building and truly only in its infancy. We are approaching an electric zero point horizon in which we will become a type 1 civilization, fully telepathic and in control of the power of the sun. Sync will eventually evolve to a point of immediate understanding, speed of thought transfer rates, instantaneous understanding of complex emotional and dream states, synchronal orchestras performing representations of the harmonic balance and imbalance created when entire solar systems collide and/or orbit each other; it will be a time outside of time, illusions will be shattered.

Sometimes words are simply inadequate to describe the perfection of cosmos. We can take it a step further and utilize visual representations of how syncs connect, collide, and disconnect in our mind's eye. Take for instance these images below:

The Ibis bird dips his beak in the water like a writer dips his pen in the ink. He stares at his reflection in the water and the abyss below, waiting patiently for a fish to swim by so he can pass beyond the mercurial waters and temporarily enter into a new Aquarian world. In this moment of passing through the water door he realizes the nature of the game, the nature of the illusion. Ordinarily, the veil of thoughts and the five senses draw the mind outside, to the external world. This obscures our awareness of consciousness that is beyond the mind, that which exists into the infinite labyrinthine, the stellar hallways of always. When we touch that energy we touch a higher octave of our essence of being; a unique vibratory signature that can not only 'think' outside the box, but has absolutely no need for the box. To sync is to remember that aspect of ourselves, to remember what it feels like to create as we create in our dreams. You can let your environment inform you of its intentions and genuineness, know when men seek to persuade, disrupt, or entrap, know when a voice is speaking to you that is not your own, know how you are not yourself.

A question I get asked often when people examine my work is if some of the patterns and coincidences I highlight are put there intentionally by men, aliens, or gods with some elaborate nefarious goal in mind. We are an overly paranoid species. There is no conspiracy in the way most of us view it. Look at the word itself. The center of the word is Pi. Piracy is concealing Pi, light and shadow, knowledge and ignorance. Both are necessary for growth. Con = "with," Spire = "breath." Conspire means breathing together, the breath of interaction between the hemispheres of the brain, between the polarities. Many get tripped up by the expression of a dualistic world, red tie, blue tie, us against them. It's simply never been the case. We are exerting large quantities of energy unnecessarily. This personal identity we feel eternally fused/stuck to is transient, temporal, a rental suit. The ego does not like to acknowledge this, it will make more invisible enemies for you then you can shake a stick at. Things are only hidden if you are unaware of them. There is a process that we evolve through where each level of desire becomes empty, habituated to. Nothing will replace our insatiable desire to reach towards the heavens, to approach the moment of original fragmentation. This is spiritual evolution.

The adept adapt. There is a technique that can be used by anyone, called the law of similarity. You can bring the heavens down to earth by mimicking certain shapes and geometrical designs, imposing your will upon the masses by using the ether to manifest structure through will. The Occultist knows that if he is to control energy, the best way, is to place it in a circle. The circle inside St Peter's square is the soul trapped in the cube of matter. In order to free the soul, the 5th element has to be released up the center spinal column (in the film *The 5th Element*, Love is essential in this process). Esoterically speaking, this area of 33 vertebrae, (also the number for the highest degree one can attain in Freemasonry and the atomic number for arsenic) is known as the key row, Chiro as in Chiropractor, or Cairo Egypt. The Nile is the geographical key row or spinal column that separates the masculine and feminine 'waters' of the universe. When the chi flows from the base of the spine, the left crosses over the right side of the  brain, and the right flows to the left. This is a complimenting of polarities. This is the nature of the torus of flame, of all things experienced in this creation. Mary washing Jesus' feet, and Jesus washing Mary's feet, allegorically speaking. When we find balance in these subtle forces, we flow back to center, back to middle C, back to high noon, where the cowboys meet for final showdown, where we meet the sun.

Through the shadows, shines ever the light. The cosmic keys to unlock knowledge of absolute truth exist in the mathematical correlations of signs and symbols, the original language. Stories of old painted pictures that sparked visions of higher realms forming arcs of vivid thought bridging gaps through the glass ceiling of understanding create radiant holographic images within the darkness of the mind that are able to tune every atom of the body into agreement. In these moments Truth is a lightning bolt traveling down your spine, sublimely simple, honest and balanced. The star-clock of change, 11:11 will knock on your door, it is a paradoxical 'catch 22;' like a combination Hollywood style Phi phenomenon and Beta movement hologram. An astral bridge you will be faced with to make a decision to cross over; slip through the cusp or remain comfortable and distracted with where you're at and experience the destiny of that path. The baby is too scared to come out and too big to stay in the womb. Yet the labor pains have already started, the circumstances of 'fate' (your Higher Self), that guides you along does not seem to advocate stagnation. Your 'past' has many generations of light; eons of 7 daylight cycles orchestrating the evolution of creating/maturing your spectrum, as Truth cannot ring inside of you unless you have memories of experience that will spark perception to light up signs and symbols from along your journey. Pi in the sky is apropos. Within the four quartered steps of a circle or elliptical sequence, a spiral of growth straight-a-way unfolds. It is the sovereignty and frontier of freewill of an inherited birthright that provides freedom of choice within self-awareness—Three Gifts. It is what source prepares us for by using nature as an example, and artifacts and signs and symbols of knowledge, and by providing as many parables, fables, metaphors, tales, and stories of life; life as art and art is life, as can possibly be thought of to try and explain how 'it' all works. But it just can't do it for us, make that decision of how or when to claim our 'Empowerment;' that 'One Thing,' for it is impossible for the masculine-creation to do so and he would if he could, but he can't. Imagine that, something Divine Creation just can't do, but Big Daddy Sapien will always be there with us for as long as it takes. And the longer WE take, the longer the pain and suffering go on. Now is a good time to start, just ask for the Truth and it will be shown to you in the best way possible for you to understand it. The signs are everywhere; dare to set your mind on fire and your spirit free.

Image courtesy of **Simon Haiduk**

Goro Adachi

Etemenanki

Goro Adachi regularly shares his thoughts on his two websites, focusing on synchronicity and future pattern prognostication, as he has continuously done since the mid '90s. He has also written one book, The Time Rivers, *revealing how the world's major rivers are "intelligently" designed—literal "rivers of time"—encoded with historical timelines.*

goroadachi.com
supertorchritual.com

Future Knowledge

You are going to die. You know it. I know it.

This life, this thing you think is you, it's going to end. It's gonna happen. Just a matter of time.

That's one of the very few certainties in life, and that's where we ought to begin. Death. The awareness that we all have only a limited amount of time in this world. Time is indeed of the essence. We need to do what we need and want to do, while we can. Scratch that. Before anything else, we need to *realize* what we want. We are going to die. That's the situation. The question is "What are we supposed to do?"

It haunts us. We all feel the psychological pressure, like gravity from which there is apparently no escape. Being alive, we cannot cover our ears to the sound of inevitability. Like the air we breathe, the question follows us everywhere. The silent countdown is deafening indeed and we habitually resort to distracting ourselves from the deadline the mind fears so much. Before long, the distraction *becomes* life. We are then lost. Another casualty in the cycle of life.

Trapped in time, we live and relive "history." The mind adapts, but the heart remembers. Its desperate whispers echo through time. . . .

What we are is the present standing on the edge of the cliff of the past. There is a black hole in our heart that is the sea of unrealized possibilities we call the "future." In pain and in limited awareness, our heart yearns for completeness, to reconnect with the rest of our whole that is suspended in superposition somewhere between existence and non-existence, between present and future, beyond time and beyond death. It whispers to us, saying we must go beyond who we are, beyond physicality, beyond time . . . beyond death.

FUTURE KNOWLEDGE

Our mission in life is therefore one of trying to gain access to that hidden forgotten part of us *before we die*. We want our "future" back—as natural as rivers seeking the ocean, or children looking for their parents. A grand unification of the past, present and future, that is the endgame and it's about time.

The problem is that the future *is* like the ocean or the heavens above with countless stars.

"My God, it's full of stars!"

Needle in a Haystack

It's overwhelming, the sheer number of possibilities; it's truly cosmic, simply unfathomable by the localized human mind. Our brain is quite simply not equipped to handle "the future" beyond the level we already do, which can fluctuate a bit, but within a fairly small range. The official approach to expanding human knowledge is "science." It's empirical through and through. It's past-driven, like driving a car using only the rear-view mirror. Science, as it exists now, focuses on analyzing experiences (i.e. the past). It's like digging deep into the earth to find treasure, ignoring the stars above shining away in silence. Hindsight-driven science fails to excel at figuring out where to look for treasure away from the *linearly* accumulating pile of empirical knowledge. Limit your field of vision and you end up focusing on things you can already see, and you just end up going there. Unnaturally linear, like an incestuous family tree.

The road to a breakthrough discovery does not have one entry path, it has *many*. There are long ones, twisted ones, dead-end ones—and then there are the *shortcuts*, which can greatly reduce the amount of time required to get there. We are in a race against time. We simply cannot afford to take a detour. If there are shortcuts, *we take them*.

Keep relying on hindsight, the empirical approach, and we are in for a long, frustrating ride—like a cab stuck in Manhattan traffic. Sure, the driver can take you anywhere, but he can't do anything about the traffic. Empirical science knows what it's doing, but it is hardly an *efficient* approach as far as making groundbreaking discoveries. All the countless details in all the countless scientific data have bogged down the process and rendered it nearly dysfunctional, just as a government too big cannot keep functioning properly. Focus and vision get lost.

What we need, I would argue, is a whole new approach to sifting through the sea of unrealized possibilities, the heavens full of stars, that is *efficient*. We must have it ASAP, otherwise we keep drifting through time blindfolded. We are wasting time and wasting our lives away.

What we need is a special "radar" to scan the time horizon ahead so that we can steer our ship *directly* toward discoveries or avoid wandering into dangerous storms. We need to be able to find *shortcuts* or the *shortest paths* to hidden knowledge, new discoveries, and world-changing revelations. The key is figuring out how to "time travel," so to speak.

Easier said than done, obviously.

Such a monumental task. Needle in a haystack? If it were that easy. The simple fact is, it's impossible. It cannot be done. That is, without some "divine intervention."

Turns out, we are not completely abandoned on this planet. Turns out there *is* a system of "divine intervention" in place, ready to assist us through this difficult transition phase—going from a temporal being to an inter-temporal being. We call it "coincidences" or "synchronicity."

Whatever the source behind it, most people would agree the mysterious phenomenon exists. They just don't know what to do with it or what it's for. Give a notebook computer to a dog and it will look at you funny and ask for something it can eat.

Synchronicity, Future & Inter-contextuality

Synchronistic coincidences are in effect "road signs" or a GPS signal.

Once we know where and when to look and what to look for, it's a whole different ball game, a real game changer. Not to sound too dramatic, but this is comparable to Noah being able to hear God's warning about the coming Great Flood or Utnapishtim getting "classified information" from Enki whispering through a wall. The story of Genesis, when men and gods interacted directly. What if they are still around (metaphorically speaking, more or less), whispering to us? "Meaningful coincidences" have that kind of vibe.

"Divine intervention?" Why not. But it's an indirect one. To make it work, we have to meet it halfway. We need to do our own part. It's still our Mission Impossible, but it's definitely not impossible *if* we do it right. It's not for everyone, as there is a built-in filtering mechanism allowing only the "worthy" to climb the ladder into the gate of heaven *à la* Noah and Jacob. "They" don't choose; we do it ourselves. This is done by way of how we manage our "anti-truth" human nature, or how much we can control our own ego. One way to visualize this is to imagine one's ego as a magnet; the bigger the ego, the stronger the magnet. The stronger the magnet, the more it interferes with the compass (GPS). Without a properly functioning compass, it's difficult to see where you are and where you are going. You won't find any "shortcuts." No shortcut, no treasure/discovery. Simple as that.

By "ego," I mean something broader than just overtly self-centered/serving psychology—I mean *anything* that causes deviation from the path of *truth*. Truth often clashes with what evolution has programmed in us, with *survival* on the top of the list. For self-preservation/protection, we gladly sacrifice truth. So much so, it's almost second nature—something we just do. Truth is often not even in the equation when decisions are made. We may know the term and have a rough idea as to what it means, but for many it's like the air, it's just sort of there. We breathe it in constantly, yet unconsciously. Stop breathing and we die. Some things we just take for granted.

Truth is universality. The more universal, the truer the claim. So there are degrees of truth. A higher degree of truth means more consistency or reliability. The more reliable, the more we can build on it (i.e. a more solid foundation upon which new technology and such may be developed which represents the mastering of that particular knowledge or possibility). In other words, the higher the truth, the more in tune with the future it is (i.e. consistency across time, or "timelessness"). The more universal the truth, the less dependent it is on timing or temporal context. So, our quest is one of finding that which does not change through time.

Change is time and time is change. Each moment is a unique framework or context. By definition, truth tends to be contextually independent, as it manages to exist simultaneously across different intersecting contexts. Our brain is not easily capable of thinking in multiple contexts. In fact, for most people, "thinking" is automatically assumed to be synonymous with putting things together within a single self-contained context. Such a linear mode of thinking obviously leads to a very limited form of "truth" that cannot remain true outside of one specific framework. But we can also instinctively feel a higher truth and beauty in a *multi-*contextual perspective. Most of us have that radar within us. Poetry, or any form of art which uses a lot of metaphors and symbolism, is generally from that creative part of our mind. Except "art" stops short of *actively* seeking hidden "future" knowledge/possibilities.

Creativity implies uniqueness. To be unique is to *not* rely on what came before. So it may be said that, to be creative is to access the future. After all, in the river of time there is only the past and the future, and we are the interface. The more we interact with the future, the more in sync we become with the future. More creativity, more future resonance. Now we are touching on something that contributes to the phenomenon of synchronicity. It's no "coincidence" that it is often through works of art—including TV shows and movies—that particularly pronounced synchronicities take place, because of the amount of creativity that went into these things. Quite literally, great (unique) artists get many of their ideas from the future. But it doesn't mean they know what they are doing (in most cases, they don't). Creativity, like truth, is an ethereal idea that we only casually think about, not realizing how superficial our understanding of it is.

Creativity is that which enables us to perceive a wider range of possibilities (i.e. a clearer view of the "future"). That is essentially the opposite of "ego." Ego is the force that tries to artificially manage the range of possibilities so as to make/keep things favorable to the self. The ego is therefore intrinsically "anti-truth." This is how those prone to deviating from the path of truth *block themselves* from becoming a Noah—taking themselves out of the game, out of the divine communication.

FUTURE KNOWLEDGE

Most people have minimal understanding of their own ego or psychology. "Know thyself." Without it, one will be running in circles going nowhere. Sync enthusiasts are for the most part no different, typically just running in circles, amusing themselves by playing what is essentially a real-world version of "Where's Waldo?" and silly obsessions with numbers/numerology that are statistically totally insignificant. Keeping one's ego in check is a full-time job. For humans it *is* that difficult. But we must do our part.

Synchronicity may be noticed by anyone (open invitation goes out to everyone, I guess). However, again, rarely do people know what to do with it. Sync enthusiasts are at least somewhat cognizant of the fact that it represents something akin to road signs. For conspiracy theorists, it's of course all part of a Satanic plan carefully orchestrated from behind the scenes to bring about the New World Order. "Predictive programming! Predictive programming!" they would scream. A very limited range of possibilities exists in their minds. They take themselves out of the game.

The "language of truth" is used in synchronicity. One therefore needs to have a sufficient understanding of the nature of truth (i.e. how it is intertemporal and inter-contextual) to converse with the invisible future intelligence. (The process *is* very interactive.)

It was about 15 years ago (mid '90s) that I started using *inter-contextual coherence* to accomplish just that, in public. This was my "radar," my kung fu. It quickly became an essential ingredient of who I am. It was probably something already in my nature which allowed me to develop it in the first place (no active Sync Heads around back then) and use it to make significant discoveries (for example, the Nile being an intelligently designed, literal "river of time," revealing the entire course of history) and regularly forecast world-event patterns accurately enough by means of projecting inter-contextual patterns forward. Through flexible multi-contextual view points and careful ego control, I was able to demonstrate how we can turn synchronicity into a practical tool to short circuit time, to accomplish what should be "impossible."

While open minded, I am also very result oriented, again driven by my obsession with not wasting time and being efficient. I'm not interested in focusing on things that cannot change the world. I'm not interested in things that don't matter. Truth matters. The future matters. Possibilities matter. Synchronicity was there to facilitate active and interactive interfacing with these things that matter, resulting in opening the door for dramatically improved foresight and access to hidden knowledge, our missing part.

It's really a matter of learning to discern where, when and how to focus our attention. Humans are naturally quite capable of figuring things out if there is an explicit objective. We have that gift. The trick is to not waste this great gift on things that don't matter. Time is limited. We don't need to be a certified specialist/expert to make important discoveries. We only need to know—in addition to a prerequisite adherence to sound understanding of truth, logic and psychology—where to focus our energy and have the right "attitude" to make magic happen.

Pushing Through Psychological Block

The things I discuss on my websites—all things multi-contextual—tend to perplex people. So out of alignment is it with most people's normal mode of thinking that they get disoriented and end up in a state of confusion. Their inner knowing may recognize a higher order of "truth," but the conscious mind needs a lot more convincing and time before it can digest and begin to concede that there is such a thing as "inter-contextual coherence" that underlies reality beyond the threshold of what is normally considered possible.

It's one thing to notice bits and pieces of "meaningful coincidences" in life. It's harmless. Numerology? Cute. Symbolism? Entertaining. Maybe even inspiring. But, when it gets to the point of super inter-contextual coherence, it apparently gets a little discombobulating and even "scary" for many. The ordinary mind tries to find a way to squash it so that order is restored—no need to radically revise one's view of the world. To accept it is to reject a fundamental bedrock of one's practical, but incomplete, understanding of reality. That would be like experiencing a catastrophic earthquake and then having to rebuild a city. It's a tall order. It takes great effort and commitment. Something we don't normally look forward to.

So I understand the psychological effects. It can be an instant crossroads, in that the mind has to make a big decision concerning the nature of reality itself. Consciously or unconsciously, this pressure is felt and it makes many uncomfortable. But such is the nature of truth. Truth, more often than not, is a major inconvenience. You either decide to accept it or deny it. Life is a series of these decisions. You keep denying and it takes its toll. There is you, there is truth, and in between is time.

The more we go against truth, the more trapped we are in time. And it gets heavier and heavier . . . until it collapses like a star into a black hole. We need to short-circuit the process and escape time. For that, finding truth and accepting it must be our priority. It takes a lot of energy and focus because truth hides like a fox, and we must chase it into the rabbit hole where it's dark and you'll need a map to navigate effectively, otherwise you just end up going in circles. This "map" or "radar" is what is signified by this inter-contextual coherence. It's a bit like using a Venn diagram; you go for the most heavily layered area for the most universal "answer." Put another way, it's like a "meta analysis" of synchronicities. A "meaningful coincidence" here, another synchronicity there, and another there. . . . This much people can notice and they try to interpret each such "sign." But they don't think to, or don't know how to, find connections *between* these "coincidences" that *unify* them. The area of such unification—coherence—is the blip on the radar or an arrow pointing to the direction of truth.

How do I know? Because truth necessarily transcends time and that means you'd know you're on the right path when the "map" you're using begins to point to, by way of projecting patterns forward, things/events in the future *that come true*. That's the "Holy Grail" in the search for hidden truth. It's the Stone of Destiny.

It's through the use of this "Holy Grail"—making the hidden nature of reality undeniable via accurate predictions—that the readers' conscious mind can be sufficiently and quickly motivated to start "revising" its model of reality. It becomes a "wake-up call" that facilitates a plunge into the rabbit hole.

I should at least give one example. . . .

One of the recent predictive "hits" was the Royal Engagement & Wedding of Prince William and Catherine Middleton. Their announcement came suddenly in November 2010, catching everyone by surprise. Everyone except yours truly and my readers.

- Oct 20: Prince William secretly proposes to Kate Middleton in Kenya
- Nov 16: Engagement publicly announced

"Coincidentally" the exact day they got engaged in total secret, October 20, 2010, was the day I publicly predicted the same on my websites. I couldn't be more explicit on *Super Torch Ritual Underground* where I wrote:

> Alright guys . . . I think I got it. And it is, as usual, both expected and unexpected. This will probably not make you go 'ah ha!' right away, but you will soon see it and get it. This is pretty special, in a way the **first multicontextual gateway** to the 'next season' . . . **2011/2012**.
>
> What am I talking about? I'm talking about what's at the intertemporal core of the recent and ongoing **Underworld Resurrection** rituals, most notably the Chilean miners rescue which is heavily entangled (via pentagrams) with the upcoming window around Halloween (opening perhaps as early as the 24th).
>
> And we may well see it come to life right there around late October-early November. I wouldn't be surprised at all. It would make perfect sense. I'm talking about. . .
>
> the announcement of the engagement & imminent wedding of...
>
> **Prince William & Kate Middleton**.
>
> Are you scratching your head? That's understandable. But you will get it soon. [. . .] This will open the 'floodgate.' And I'm projecting that, based on the trajectory of the collective pattern I've discerned, the impact could easily arrive during our 'Halloween window' which I would define as **late Oct-early Nov**, anchored by the Venus inferior conjunction on October 29.
>
> The level of the multicontextual coherence is such that I feel quite confident in saying that, even if not *the announcement itself*, the window will *produce unmistakable signals related to this*, what amounts to the **Rebirth of King Arthur**. [. . .]
>
> It's about to kick into a higher gear. It's about to begin. . . .
>
> You heard it here first, and I will be discussing in depth the decoding that led to this line of thinking.

So this is some of what is possible through synchronicity and inter-contextual coherence. (The Wright Brothers were flying successfully for some time before it was officially accepted as fact.) Our future awareness can be greatly enhanced if we learn to do our part—which is basically to seek truth. "Seek *truth* and you shall find." That would be the true form of "praying." Easier said than done. But remember, each breath you take is one breath closer to death. We are here to pull off Mission Impossible, Time is a countdown and we literally have a *dead*-line.

The long and short of it is that we are in an *unnatural* state of existence as temporally half-blind beings. So unless we seek equilibrium—a natural state—there are going to be devastating consequences. Pressure keeps rising like water in a dam (we call it "history") until it finally collapses (i.e. "Great Flood") . . . the end of the world. Truth is water from the future pushing against the wall of the present. Either we start opening the gate to the future in a big way or it *will* surely destroy us and the whole world. That's the fate of anyone who cannot face the truth in time.

As I say, denial *is* a river in Egypt, which shows our time is almost up. We are rapidly reaching the end of the river

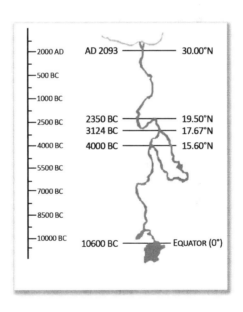

of time. History is set to end this century. This is decision time.

The future awaits. . . .

NEIL KRAMER

Neil Kramer is an English writer, speaker and philosopher in the fields of consciousness, metaphysics, shamanism and ancient mystical disciplines.

For over 20 years, Neil has independently studied philosophy, psychology, shamanism, Zen, ancient indigenous wisdom traditions, inner alchemy, occultism and esoteric world history. He shares his path of inner transformation in writings, interviews and lectures, as well as giving one-to-one teachings.

He is a frequent guest on leading alternative radio and internet shows, enjoying international audiences and enthusiastic support. His work is regularly published on cutting-edge web sites, news portals and popular media networks. Neil has spoken at international conferences on the nature of human consciousness, as well as touring the USA and Canada, speaking in cities such as Los Angeles, San Francisco, Portland and Seattle. His talks have been broadcast on Sky TV *in the UK*.

His acclaimed essays and his audio book the Audio Cleaver *attract large, discerning audiences around the world.*

Neil gives interviews, teachings and live presentations on many fascinating subjects including: Paths to Authentic Being, Sovereign Empowerment, Transcending Systems of Control *and* Dimensional Shifting.

Neil is currently working on a book and film project. He lives in New York, USA.

neilkramer.com

GO YOUR OWN WAY

You have to work on yourself before you can really get anywhere. No one can do it for you. The magical codex and the dimensional escape hatch remain firmly out of reach for now. The flame will burn those who are unable to hold it safely in their hands. The universe insists, most adamantly, that we learn how to do it all by ourselves. Gnosis, spiritual attainment, esoteric wisdom. Whatever you want to call it. No cheating, no looking at your friend's paper, no plagiarizing—you must do your own thing in your own way. Otherwise, we are compelled to repeat the same tests over and over again, through multiple lifetimes, until we finally figure it out. So you have to do the homework. Sharpen your blade. Keep moving. Fortunately, there is no time limit and everyone's ascendant path is custom-built for their own unique growth pattern. In spiritual terms, it's a win-win situation.

To help penetrate the all-pervading mists of the illusion, one must first acknowledge that consciousness is not the accidental and purposeless by-product of the human condition. The perceived world that we appear to be locked inside, like the silver ball in a pinball machine, is wholly a construct of consciousness. The pinball constructs the machine around itself. Whilst a testing notion for even the most elastic of modern philosophical minds, it has been known for aeons by the ancient mystical traditions and experienced directly by the indigenous shamanic cultures of every continent. Now, it is being evoked again as a progressive scientific theory in quantum physics. It is not new information we are bringing to mind, not by any means. It is better described as a remembrance.

Consciousness is a transcendental music with which we can attune, conduct and create. The spiritually synchronized mind instinctively discerns this. Consciousness flows through all things. It follows that consciousness itself does not originate in the brain of the individual. It is at root, a non-local force. The quantum and holographic traces of this have been unfolding for some time now, most intriguingly in the works of Gebser, Bohm, Pribram and Laszlo. The personal experience of consciousness is better conceived of as a tunnel, or an uplink, to the Akashic field (AKA the universal field, vacuum field, noosphere etc.) which is dynamically connected to everything and everywhere. Perhaps the field is composed of the same subspace luminous filaments that Castaneda's mythical figure of Don Juan spoke of so enigmatically; these being the fractal structures of consciousness itself, elaborately extending themselves across the multiverse, articulating every conceivable resolution. Our thoughts, feelings and articulations are unique expressions [configurations] of the field. Our imaginal thoughtforms sculpt its physical and psychic manifestations.

Subspace and Not-Thinking

Consciousness operates in a field which is not bound by the restrictions of third density conditions (time & space). Consequently, it may seamlessly reach into higher dimensions/fractal resolutions and potentially innumerable parallel universes, as indicated in superstring theory and M-theory. This is how telepathy, precognition, clairvoyance and similar extrasensory perception phenomena function, by jumping into the subspace field and observing any point along it, instantly and completely. Travel without movement. The coherence vector or signal quality is the difference between a faint intuition of something (I think my Aunty Barbara might call this evening) and a full-on vision (a 25ft meteorite will land in my back garden tomorrow at 9:45 a.m. and destroy the lawnmower). To maximize signal fidelity, to get the most accurate information, the mind must be trained to quieten the perpetual internal dialogue, the chatter of the brain.

Thinking is brain churn. Knowing is field connection. Whilst deductive reasoning is practical for information processing, it can stand in the way of the coherent field connection necessary to attain wisdom. Many deep mystical experiences encountered in different planes of consciousness are so state specific that they cannot easily be brought back into the third density for adequate expression using the modern linguistic symbol set. Articulation is not always necessary for total comprehension. Standard 'remote viewing' technique (the psychic ability to gather information about a distant or unseen target) teaches the student not to think. The collective consciousness within the field knows everything already. It can communicate any information about anything right into your head at supraluminal speeds. So why are some able to remote view and others not? Impulsive brain chatter obscures the incoming data, like static on a TV screen. We need to learn to step out of the way. Meditation brings insight into the thinking process, helping to smooth it out and sometimes stop it altogether, allowing deeper perceptions to be received. Toltec shamanism teaches the apprentice the procedure of 'stopping the world' as a means of placing false egoic thinking aside in order to perceive the world shamanically, or if you prefer, to establish a stable uplink to the field.

Interfacing with reality is more instructive than purely theorizing about it. We have long since reached the saturation point of the narrow scientific method with its reliance on separation, measurement and reductionism. Such materialist inferences, no matter how scrupulous, are at odds with the holistic multidisciplinary attitude required for actual conscious evolution. They only obstruct efforts to perceive beyond the particulate cloak of Maya. The primacy of felt experience is consistently more edifying and meaningful than the smug abstractions of 'scientism' (the belief that scientific principles are essential to all other disciplines, including philosophical, mystical, spiritual and humanist interpretations of life). The Control System sponsors scientism by overexposing various trenchant physicists, atheists and parapsychologists who all exhibit some form of spiritual devolution. As smart and kooky as some of them are, they lack the psychic integrity and spiritual humility that is so palpable in those who truly walk the path.

Small is Beautiful

Far from being the exotic anthropological oddity it was once depicted as, shamanism is the original spiritual experience of all indigenous peoples. Present in the savannas of Africa, the jungles of the Amazon, the plains of America, the mountains of Asia and the forests of Europe, shamanism was an integral mystical practice of deep esoteric and spiritual importance to both individuals and communities. Thus it remained, organically ascendant, up until a few thousand years ago when the personal, sovereign right to a spiritual connection with the divine was removed from daily life.

This was achieved by hijacking and co-opting all systems of transcendence into the dark canopy of organized religion. The fake priesthood. They took what they liked, pruned the liberating and inspiring bits and threw the rest away. Anyone who sought to practice their own mysticism or dared to resurrect the old ways was executed. Many such religious crusades were prosecuted against ancient spiritual and shamanic practices, campaigns that today would fall under the technical terminology of genocide.

If you trace the origins of the major monotheistic organized religions back far enough, it becomes clear that they were never designed to help the individual grow and develop. They were there to control land, dictate moral and social norms and separate the common man from his divine heritage. Higher consciousness, personal freedom and spiritual communion, far from being the core elements of their basic mystical teachings, were concepts firmly discouraged by the various priest castes. In their place, the disempowering qualities of submission, victimhood, repression and guilt became the preferred tenets of worshipful compliance.

Most who walk the path have long since discarded the unnecessary restraints of organized religion. There are many good people who still operate within the conventions and structures of Christianity in particular, and that is of course, their prerogative. However, it doesn't take much research into alternative history and the ancient indigenous chronicles to discover that the sacred texts that form the backbone of today's megareligions are merely distorted versions of much earlier and authentic methods of spiritual practice. Despite the artful stage-managed resurgence of religious fundamentalism in both the east and west, the crude pious repressions of the Control System are beginning to lose their grip. People are realizing that they can anoint themselves as their own special representative on earth (who else could they be?) and their own personal channel to the holy spirit.

Fractal Dreams

In *The Art of Dreaming*, Carlos Castaneda wrote, "Don Juan contended that our world, which we believe to be unique and absolute, is only one in a cluster of consecutive worlds, arranged like the layers of an onion. He asserted that even though we have been energetically conditioned to perceive solely our world, we still have the capability of entering into those other realms, which are as real, unique, absolute and engulfing as our own world is. Believing that our energetic conditioning is correctable, don Juan stated that sorcerers of ancient times developed a set of practices designed to recondition our energetic capabilities to perceive. They called this set of practices the art of dreaming." When I first read that in 1994, two things sprang to mind. (i) How don Juan was absolutely spot on, and (ii) rather fittingly, how the process of unfolding the onion layers of reality can indeed bring tears to your eyes.

The 'cluster of consecutive worlds' is a fractal model. The essential pattern of creation is encoded into everything, all the way down the line, from galaxies to cauliflowers. It helps to examine fractal formations in nature to properly appreciate their properties.

The geometry and mathematics of fractal forms has been studied since the 17th century (in modern history that is) but their complexity and infinite recursive depth made progress slow. The arrival of computers in the 1970's made things much simpler. Rapid processing, sophisticated graphics and software modelling enabled researchers to explore the depth of fractals to a level never seen before. Researchers categorize fractal generation into three different classes: (1) Escape-time Fractals; Mandelbrot set, Julia set, Nova fractal, (2) Iterated Function Systems; Cantor set, Koch snowflake, Sierpinski carpet and (3) Random Fractals. In random fractals, we see dendritic fractals demonstrate the fundamental natural property of diffusion-limited aggregation (DLA). DLA is best illustrated in the physical manifestations of fern growth, ice crystals, tree branch growth and electrical discharges.

Observing the nautilus shell, we encounter the living embodiment of the Fibonacci sequence of numbers 0 1 1 2 3 5 8 13 21 34 55 89 144 233 377 610 987 1597 2584 4181 6765. So important to sacred geometry, Egyptology and the ancient mystery cults. For those who may have cast off their high school mathematics (understandably in most cases), the Fibonacci sequence establishes the first number as 0 and the second number as 1. Each subsequent number is equal to the sum of the previous two numbers.

The sequence presents itself in nature in the branching of trees, the structure of pineapples, artichoke flowering, uncurling ferns, the arrangement of pine cones and the spiraling florets in the head of a sunflower. Stunningly beautiful.

The recursive, self-iterative nature of fractals, clearly visible in the Mandelbrot and Koch snowflake, begin to speak to the higher consciousness and express some of the underlying structures of reality. The fractal holography of the universe imprints the design of itself into each individual component, each creative Lego brick. All elements are coded with the entire universal design project. The ancient Druidic respect for the oak tree and the acorn were symbols of this core understanding. As then, so now, such meditations lead to a fuller comprehension of the sacred mysteries of creation. Our art is to project into higher and deeper resolutions of the fractal spiral, gathering gnosis and wisdom as spiritual gravitation compels the ascendant homeward journey.

Our life is the journey. We illustrate it with our unique and miraculous stories. Our learning helps to improve the coherence and the elegance of the fractal. Our capacity for consciousness determines how deep we can go. I sense that each lifetime, each self, each frequency of being, emanates fractally from a larger, grander structure, from where our higher self guides us and loves us. Perhaps even these ultra conscious entities are expressions of an even more sublime intelligence. Gazing at the head of the sunflower, it certainly feels that way.

Images courtesy of commons.wikimedia.org

Jason Barrera
Kosmos Idikos

Jason lives in an Erlenmeyer flask at the center of the earth, caressed by magnificent beasts. He occasionally rises to the surface to write online, under the name Eleleth.

kosmosidikos.blogspot.com
themaskofgod.blogspot.com

A Child's Treasury of the Tarot

Think not, o king, upon that lie: That Thou Must Die: verily thou shalt not die, but live. Now let it be understood: If the body of the King dissolve, he shall remain in pure ecstasy for ever.
(Liber AL, II. 21)

It will be seen that our present reality is a holographic construct based around the 22 Major Arcana of the Tarot, wherein the archetypes of regeneration are endlessly played out upon the field of popular culture. Nowhere has this been more overt than in the drama that was enacted after the events of September 11, 2001, when George W. Bush, the great Fool, went on a Quest to immanentize the eschaton and create a New Order within himself.

The Mystic regards the entire phenomenal universe as a grand parable or allegory which is destined one day . . . to give place to a grand reality. In the words of Emerson, the American seer, "The whole world is an omen and a sign." Thus, even in the natural order, the education of humanity is proceeding by type and by symbol; thus, God is the Great Symbolist, who teaches from behind the veil by signs which He writes upon the veil; the stars are secret ciphers with an interior and divine meaning; everything that exists is an outward sign of an inward thought of God . . . .
(Waite, Azoth, p. 36)

---

0. The Fool

God chose the foolish things of the world that he might put to shame those who are wise. (1 Corinthians 1:27)

We do not understand our past, and we cannot perceive our future. We are all born as fools, blind to all that is greater than ourselves; but when we take the first tentative steps on the path, we become the Fool, one who no longer walks in the ways of the

A CHILD'S TREASURY OF THE TAROT

Illustration by Justin Gray Morgan

world but according to his own conscience. The task of the Fool, as being created in the image of the Father, is to create his own Son, which is a perfect realization of his own True Self. No-one else will do this for him; he is consigned to work out his own salvation.

This creation is accomplished through Alchemy, which is the Great Work. As Freud and Jung both recognized, Alchemy is begun by an *introversion of the libido*—and when Nature cannot work by herself, she may be aided by the Alchemist. In the Taoist alchemical text *The Secret of the Golden Flower*, we read:

> Man's heat stands under the fire trigram, Li. . . . When the desires are stirred, it runs downward, is directed outward, and creates children. If . . . it is not allowed to flow outward, but is led back by the energy of thought so that it penetrates the crucible of the Creative, and refreshes heart and body and nourishes them, that also is the backward-flowing method. Therefore it is said, The Way of the Elixir of Life depends entirely on the backward-flowing method. (Wilhelm, Jung and Liu, p. 32)

The three sources I have mainly referred to are Arthur Waite's *Pictorial Key to the Tarot*, Aleister Crowley's *Book of Thoth*, and Paul Foster Case's *The Tarot: A Key to the Wisdom of the Ages*, as they are written by initiates. Case elucidates part of Waite's symbolism:

> [T]he wand and wallet together may be understood to be phallic emblems . . . the awakening of the higher vision symbolized by the eye on the flap of the wallet is brought about by practices which redirect and sublimate the bodily forces related astrologically to the sign Scorpio. (Case, p. 34)

In essence, then, we have a variety of symbols that express the same idea. Actually, all wands, staffs, swords, etc. are phallic emblems, as will become apparent. Sexuality is perceived as worthless foolishness to the world, but it is through this that the Fool will attain the Grail. Those still unconvinced will find that Aleister Crowley's version of this card is much more explicit, showing light streaming from the Fool's genitals and circulating in his aura, but the import is the same. Actually, it's a bit hard to miss. As he states,

The Dove is the bird of Venus, but the dove is also a symbol of the Holy Ghost; that is, of the Phallus in its most sublimated form.
(Crowley, p. 56)

Example: Let it be remembered that Luke Skywalker, the Fool, must enlist the aid of Han[d] Solo, the hotheaded outlaw who always "shoots first," at the beginning of his Hero's Journey. Han and Chewie (the animal libido) pilot the *Millennium Falcon*—the Aeon of Horus.

I. The Magician

The Fool now becomes the Magician, drawing down and at the same time becoming one with the force of Mercury—that is, Air, or Spirit—the one universal substance that forms and animates all things. It will be noted that the symbol of Mercury ☿ is that of Venus ♀, with the lunar crescent of consciousness ☽, showing that the universe is composed of intelligent love. At this point it will perhaps not be surprising to learn that Mercury-Hermes was primarily associated not only with the caduceus, but the phallus as well, represented by the Yods at the end of his wand. Though Waite's card seems to portray the archetypal ideal of the aspirant, it cannot be supposed  that our Fool, at this stage, is entirely conscious of the forces of life at his command; he has not yet mastered the elements before him.

Examples: In Catholic theology, the priest, acting *In Persona Christi*, draws down the Logos, and the Holy Spirit transubstantiates the bread and the wine into the Body and Blood of Christ. Within the events of September 11, 2001 there is concealed a celebration of the Eucharist: the element of Air, represented by American Airlines Flight 77, was crashed into the Pentagon, representing the pentacle on the table of the Magician—the element of Earth now impregnated and consecrated by the Deity. This duplicates the "lightning flash" of the descending Logos on the Tree of Life, represented by the number 777.

II. The High Priestess

Hail! ye twin warriors about the pillars of the world! for your time is nigh at hand.

I am the Lord of the Double Wand of Power; the wand of the Force of Coph Nia—but my left hand is empty, for I have crushed an Universe; & nought remains. (Liber AL, III. 71-72)

At the beginning of his Journey, the Fool encounters the High Priestess between the two pillars of light and darkness. So all-encompassing is the symbol of the High Priestess that a description of her characteristics will be necessarily incomplete, as she is both *the light*, and *that which veils the light*. The *anima*, or feminine soul of the aspirant, has positive and negative aspects. In her light aspect, she is Isis-Sophia, the luminous soul of the Adept that exists as a supreme ideal—but she exists only *in potentia* within each of us. In the darker aspect of her nature, the *veil* that conceals the High Priestess from the profane represents an aggregate of those unconscious forces which must be confronted by the Fool.

The Law of the TORA that she holds is exact and unmerciful—until the Woman is well and truly Clothed with the Sun, she will submit the aspirant who wishes to unveil her to every sort of trial and torment. She is also Binah: in the Kabbalah, Binah is associated both with the left side (which harbors the darker, unconscious thoughtforms—*sinister* indeed!) of the body and the heart itself. The journey up the Tree of Life is a journey to the center of the Unconscious. In Jungian psychology, the Law that she holds would correspond to the Man of Sin, the Shadow Self. But Jung was dangerously incorrect when he stated that the Shadow had only to be "integrated"—the Shadow consists entirely of blocked energy (that which separates one from the True Self) that can never be integrated. Sayeth the Wickedest Man in the World:

Remember all ye that existence is pure joy; that all the sorrows are but as shadows; they pass & are done; but there is that which remains. (Liber AL, II. 9)

Illustration by Justin Gray Morgan

Jung knew that the Shadow had to be brought into *consciousness*, but from there he did not know—or tell, at least—that it has to be purged away by the working of the Secret Fire. But he was not a true Alchemist. The problem, then, is that the Shadows are a form of Restriction (Sin) created by the false ego—the dangerous consequence of being able to create things that are unlike itself. For, if the Self is love, then "love is the law," and anything else is suicide.

The phallic flame has both a light and dark aspect, represented by the twin pillars that flank the High Priestess. By drawing out these flames through his Art, the Fool will create a new synthesis, the Middle Pillar—the *anima* then becomes the very body of God. Her veil of palms and pomegranates shows that it is through passion (as in the "Passion of Christ") that we breach the veil. The key is in the Hermetic maxim, I.N.R.I.: *Igni Natura Renovata Integra*, "nature is wholly restored by fire."

Examples: The purification of the soul by fire is depicted in the Book of Revelation when the Whore of Babylon is destroyed by fire (Rev. 17:16), only to be immediately transformed into the purified New Jerusalem (21:2).

George W. Bush's Quest begins when he encounters the Priestess (the Statue of Liberty, Isis) between the two pillars of the World Trade Center. Though the Twin Towers are perceived to fall at the *beginning* of our Fool's journey, this is but a foreshadowing of what will occur at the end. He then goes in search of the Laden Bin (that is, the Holy Grail) and the Philosopher's Stone, the I-Rock. The I-Rock War was called "Shock and Awe," or *Shekinah*, a Kabbalistic term associated with the High Priestess and referring to the fire of the divine presence.

III. The Empress

For the sun never could show me the true God; but that healthful Word, that is the Sun of the soul, by whom alone, when He arises in the depths of the soul, the eye of the soul itself is irradiated.
(Clement of Alexandria, Exhortation to the Heathen, vi.)

"Heart" and "earth" are anagrams. While it is a popular conceit that one is born with an immortal soul, it is a fundamental tenet of all true esoteric schools that the spiritual soul must be *created*, and a New Birth must be accomplished while one is still living (cf. John 3:3). We are born as merely dust of Mother Earth—but within her bosom there exists a seed of the Logos, and this is the black stone which, "to him that overcometh" (Rev. 2:7), will reveal a brilliant golden interior when it is pierced and awakened into a state of Love. Thus is the Philosopher's Stone attained and the lead of the heart becomes gold.

Endeavor inwardly to find the location of the heart, where all psychic powers reside. At first thou wilt find darkness and inflexible density. When, however, thou perseverest day and night, thou wilt, wonderful to relate, enjoy inexpressible rapture. For then the spirit sees what it never has recognized; it sees the air between the heart and itself radiantly beaming. (Abbot Simeon, quoted by Silberer, p. 317)

Her white garment shows her identification with the alchemical White Queen, the cool, feminine *soma psychikon*, who is to be married to the Red King, the *soma pneumatikon*, depicted below (cf. 1 Corinthians 15:44). The Empress is alchemical Salt, the primordial *ground-of-being* within which the Fool must coagulate the volatile Mercury.

Example: It is for this reason that George W. Bush declares war on *Terra*, or his own material nature. *Al-Qaeda* means "the base" or "the foundation," which may be compared to Jakob Boehme's *Urgrund* (the translation has the same meaning), the primordial darkness and chaos before the World is put into a New Order by the Sun God. When he first sets his hand to the work, the Fool finds the four elements in a state of disarray; Babylon means "confusion" (Joseph. *Ant*. i. 4, § 3) and thus is aptly signified by *Iraq*.

Worship me with fire & blood; worship me with swords & with spears. Let the woman be girt with a sword before me: let blood flow to my name. Trample down the Heathen; be upon them, o warrior, I will give you of their flesh to eat! (Liber AL, III. 11)

IV. The Emperor

In the Emperor Tarot card, the element of alchemical Sulphur is depicted as the Supreme Being himself. Like the Ancient of Days, he is depicted in profile, as one side of his face is unknowable to mortal man.

> *This figure is the alchemical symbol of Sulphur . . . This is the swift creative energy, the initiative of all Being . . . His shield represents . . . the red tincture of the alchemist, of the nature of gold, as the white eagle . . . pertains to his consort, the Empress, and is lunar, of silver. (Crowley, p. 78)*

Now, Arthur Waite had a problem here: alchemical Sulphur is the hot, fiery sexual force that is the basis of all existence. But could he really depict something so uncouth as the Supreme Being himself? Evidently Waite preferred to follow the Golden Dawn version, for he changed this card to a full-frontal view, thereby concealing the stark truth that the Devil is God upside-down. The Alchemist must fix the volatile and marry Mars and Venus (Red King and White Queen). To accomplish this, the fire must be *sublimated*, which is why Waite states,

> *He is the virile power, to which the Empress responds, and in this sense is he who seeks to remove the Veil of Isis; yet she remains virgo intacta.*

The Hebrew letter is *Tzaddi*, the fishhook, which indicates that Sulphur is the method of the Work by which one "master-baits" the Fish-Self of the unconscious. Mark it well! "צ is not the star," sayeth our lady Nuit (*Liber AL*, I. 57)—nor could it be, since it is *that-which-is-to-be-hooked* by the fishhook. But Sulphur also represents the *Rubedo*, the final stage of the Philosopher's Stone; and thus the paradoxical fact that the Stone creates itself. It is in this way that the "Stone the builders rejected" is both the cornerstone (KJV) and capstone (NIV). It is in this final stage that the heart (the phoenix) becomes a burning flame. The Stone is:

> *Father and Mother of itself . . . of itself is the son, by itself it is dissolved, by itself is killed, and to itself it gives new life. The "unique thing that contains in itself the four elements and rules over them," the "matter of the Wise," also called their "Stone," contains in itself whatever we may need. It kills itself and then brings*

itself back to life. It weds itself, impregnates itself and dissolves in its own blood." It is its own root—radix ipsius. *(Evola, p. 22)*

Example: In our narrative, Condoleezza Rice, whose last name refers to grain, embodies the Empress archetype as the fertile mother. As Secretary of State, she is quite literally the ruler of the eartH. Donald Rumsfeld meanwhile embodies the fiery, phallic principle of the Emperor as Aries, the god of war. The Secretary of Defense was, until 1947, known much more honestly as the Secretary of War.

V. The Hierophant

He seems to be enjoying a very secret joke at somebody's expense. (Crowley, p. 79)

The voice of exoteric religion indicates the way of the Work: with his phallic staff surmounted by the three bars of Salt, Sulphur, and Mercury, he points upwards. On Waite's card, the face of the Hierophant is that of a lamb, which, coupled with his red garment, shows that he has been purified through the blood of the animal. The Mysteries are ever the same:

> *And habitually there stand in the temple of the Samothracians two images of naked men, having both hands stretched aloft towards heaven, and their pudenda erecta, as with the statue of Mercury on Mount Cyllene. And the aforesaid images are figures of the primal man, and of that spiritual one that is born again, in every respect of the same substance with that man.*
> *(Hippolytus,* Philosophumena, v. 3)

On a higher level, this is Jupiter, the Father, who acts as the initiator of the Self. It is really our own idea of God which holds us back or drives us on. There is also a "sadistic aspect to this card," as Crowley states, as the priest serves the function of creating a barrier between God and Man. The role of exoteric religion, as it is with the ego, is to say "thou shalt"—which is why "if you meet the Buddha on the road, kill him!" (Or, if you meet Tyler Durden.)

VI. The Lovers

All weddings are elaborate alchemical rituals where a black Osiris and white Isis are bound with a golden ring and copulate to create a *homunculus*. The priest (or angel, in Waite's deck) himself is the Alchemist, performing the Great Work under the auspices of the Great Architect of the Universe. The alchemical *coniunctio* is a sort of mysterious "love-death" in which the elements "die" at the same time they are reborn into a new being.

In truth, the Alchemist can be identified with God himself, as he has aligned himself with the part of consciousness that is one with the Universal Will and strives to exalt spirit over matter. Hence the familiar anthropomorphic image of the bearded God in his heavenly workshop is really nothing more than a depiction of the Alchemist brooding over his crucible. Thus is Christ the Son of Man.

We may further refer to the familiar images of the hexagram ✡ and Masonic square and compass as depictions of the Hermetic Marriage that takes place in the heart—the union of Male and Female. In the *Sepher Yetzirah* (Westcott, p. 15), we read:

Ten is the number of the ineffable Sephiroth, ten and not nine, ten and not eleven. Understand this wisdom, and be wise by the perception. Search out concerning it, restore the Word to its creator, and replace Him who formed it upon his throne.

The downward-pointing triangle is alchemical water, the feminine Grail. The upward-pointing triangle is alchemical fire, or phallic energy, which must be raised by the strong grip of the Master Mason. This is the restoration of the Lost Word, which is the Logos.

Examples: In Wolfram von Eschenbach's *Parzival*, Islam represents the dark, lunar forces of the subconscious that must be integrated by the Christian Fool. Thus, we have the two conflicting forces of male and female, *eros* and *agape*, fire and water, conscious and subconscious, Christianity and Islam, that our Fool seeks to harmonize. These are the Lovers, whose *coniunctio oppositorum* of Thesis and Antithesis will produce a new Synthesis.

VII. The Chariot

The Chariot is one of the most interesting cards—and also one of the most misinterpreted. Waite's version depicts the Wounded Grail King. The lingam/yoni in the center shows that this is a depiction of the sexual act, and one in which he is still bound to egoic illusions, as shown by the stone in which his genitals are encased. It is here that we receive our first taste of ecstasy from the Grail; but we have not asked the Question and answered the Riddle of the Sphinx. Astral determinism still rules his destiny. (The Alchemist is said to rule the stars; but we are not yet Alchemists.) The white square does not signify that his heart is pure—it is empty. As the ego, his rule is purely imaginary; the two sphinxes of good and evil are calling the shots. Bizarrely, Manly P. Hall claims that the Chariot card symbolizes the mastery of the Adept over all things. But as Waite makes absolutely clear,

It is to be understood . . . (a) that the question of the sphinx is concerned with a Mystery of Nature and not of the world of Grace, to which the charioteer could offer no answer; (b) that the planes of his conquest are manifest or external and not within himself; (c) that the liberation which he effects may leave himself in the bondage of the logical understanding; (d) that the tests of initiation through which he has passed in triumph are to be understood physically or rationally; and (e) that if he came to the pillars of that Temple between which the High Priestess is seated, he could not open the scroll called Tora, nor if she questioned him could he answer. He is not hereditary royalty and he is not priesthood.

(Waite, Tarot)

Examples: In the famous "Mission Accomplished" speech of May 1, 2003, George W. Bush became the spitting image of the Charioteer, showing that the Work was still incomplete. It was a temporary victory—insurgents from the depths of the subconscious still lurked, waiting for the time to strike.

[O]ur prince assumes the role of both Punch and Judy in the pocket theatre he chooses to call his life . . . the two faces embedded in the shoulders . . . are the standard masks for tragedy and comedy, identifying his reign as a drama of his own composition . . . The

> *curtained canopy cuts him off from the wider world . . .*
> (Hederman, p. 125)

This ephemeral triumph is the Lesser Mystery depicted in *Star Wars: A New Hope*. The destruction of the first Death Star is equivalent to Luke going out, banging a girl, and thinking that he's king of the world. Though Leia is satisfied for a time (see "Justice" below), Luke has not truly conquered himself, and the Empire inevitably strikes back. The medal ceremony is nothing more than a re-enactment of Nazi propaganda. Chewbacca has not been given the golden medal (transmuted). To accomplish the Greater Mystery, he will have to impregnate and give birth to himself.

And the same occurs to Wolfram's Parsifal. He weds Blanchefleur, but as soon as the marriage is consummated, he is whisked away to the desolate Grail Kingdom where he sees the King with the grievous wound in his genitals. We read of a mysterious event in the Grail castle:

For a squire sprang swift thro' the doorway,
and a lance in his hand he bore,
(And thus did he wake their weeping)
from the point did the blood run fast
Adown to the hand of the holder till 'twas lost in his sleeve at last.
And then thro' the lofty palace was weeping and wailing sore.
The folk of thirty kingdoms could scarce
have bemoaned them more.
And thus to each of the four walls
with the lance in his hand he drew,
Till he reached once again the doorway,
and passed him the portal thro'. (Weston, vol. I, p. 33)

The bleeding lance, of course, is symbolically the maimed phallus of the Grail King that subjects him to unendurable torment, and this contact with the four walls of the room symbolizes that the phallus is still tied to the sensory world of the four elements and has not been drawn from the stone. He will wander in the Wasteland until he reclaims the lance; only then can he truly be reunited with his wife. The spear still bleeds, and we have not been healed. And this, I believe, is the true significance of the stone in which the Charioteer is encased, like Han Solo in carbonite—at least as far as Waite intended it.

A CHILD'S TREASURY OF THE TAROT

Illustration by Justin Gray Morgan

VIII. Justice

Nature rejoices in nature, nature subdues nature, nature rules over nature. (Democritus)

As Papus puts it, this is "Nature performing the function of Eve" (p. 141). Her red garment shows her identification with the Em-

press; she is Nature now fecundated by the creative fire. The sword and scales are phallus and testes (cf. Giles, p. 98; Crowley, p. 87); every sexual act is a "test." The great Law of Nature is that she abhors a vacuum and desires to be filled; the Fool must both follow and overcome this law in the process of self-impregnation. Yet Nature is also just, and she responds to the one universal law, which is love. Thus, as Crowley notes, she is the female counterpart of the Fool—"the Woman satisfied."

IX. The Hermit

The Hebrew letter is *Yod*, the point of the "INDIVISIBLE ONE, the Supreme SELF" at the center of the heart (Case, p. 111). The Her-

mit is a depiction of the Self—or God, if it will be allowed—as it dwells, hidden and *in potentia*. If we are to take these in a narrative significance, it is "the general doctrine that the climax of the Descent into Matter is the signal for the reintegration by Spirit" (Crowley, p. 89). Within the unregenerate individual, his divinity is limited to his seminal energy, and a small, almost inconsequential spark in the heart, which the Hermit bears within the Black Iron Prison of his lantern.  Waite has rendered him on the peak of the Mystic Mountain, yet here all is still the Wasteland. A closer look will further reveal that the Hermit has his eyes closed—he is asleep. Ice melts at 33 degrees, and he is sub-zero.

As a form of the Logos, he also holds, says Crowley enigmatically, the "Serpent Wand, which is actually growing out of the Abyss, and is the spermatozoon developed as a poison." We will note that his staff, which even seems to have the bulbous head of a phallus, is the same as that carried by the Fool. And concealed is a further bit of Yogic arcana:

Through the practice of Yoga, the seminal energy—not the gross physical semen—flows upwards and enriches the mind. This has been declared by the sages. You will have to experience it yourself.
(Sivananda)

Example: In our Fool's narrative, it was Saddam Hussein who took on this unlikely role, dwelling as he did both in a spider hole beneath the earth and later behind bars. Saddam Hussein considered himself to be the reincarnation of Saladin, adversary of the Templars, as well as King Nebuchadnezzar. In the Bible, Nebuchadnezzar turns into an animal for seven years, and then back into a King, having thereby learned humility. The secret meaning here is that the King is God Himself, incarnating in the body of an animal, like the lamb slain from the foundation of the world.

X. Wheel of Fortune

Along the rim of the wheel there lies Relative Good and Evil, as dictated by Church and State. In the world of appearances, they are ever-changing: Good is always transformed into Evil and vice versa. At the center, as the unmoved point, lies the heart. We continue to revolve, until we are able to answer the Riddle of the Sphinx: then these become Salt, Sulphur and Mercury, through which we attain Unity. "Every thinking man is an Oedipus called to solve the enigma of the Sphinx or, this failing, to die," says Éliphas Lévi (*History*, p. 121).

Our task is to liberate these animal energies that have been, for most of our lives, caught in an instinctual cycle of repetition. The ludicrous little dictator holds them in thrall . . . its energy is primal; its power is regal. . . . The tarot sphinx presents us with a heroic task, the challenge of human beingness, daring us to find meaning in a system seemingly propelled by mere animal energy . . . the enigmatic sphinx . . . is actually suggesting the humanisation of animality and the total integration of our humanity, without eradicating any of our earthiness. (Hederman, pp. 154-155)

Example: Hurricane Katrina, or the Catherine Wheel, was the Wheel of Fortune.

XI. Strength

Jesus said, "Blessed is the lion which becomes man when consumed by man; and cursed is the man whom the lion consumes, and the lion becomes man." (Gospel of Thomas, Klauck, p. 113)

The Hebrew letter is *Teth*, "'snake,' symbol of what has been known among occultists for ages as the 'serpent-power'" (Case, p. 103). A depiction of the sexual fire, often called Kundalini. The flowers indicate that the alchemical Green Lion rises and is tamed through Love, not brute force. Indeed, this lion is the undying passion which will ultimately unite our King and Queen.

Tamed by this woman's magic, the beast offers honey freely . . . the golden energy of the lion's strength flows through her arms, radiating through her heart. . . . [Through] a woman's loving acceptance of its bestial nature, the animal is both tamed and transformed . . . The hands of the woman are opening the mouth of the lion upwards, allowing him to breathe vertically. The lion is obedient to the force of its own life, to the . . . movement of the serpent . . . Attaching this . . . force to the electrical current of desire produces addictive energy. (Hederman, pp. 159-160)

In Crowley's version ("Lust"), it is Babalon who bears the Grail from out of the waters in a spontaneous act of passion, overflowing with the blood of love and death.

XII. The Hanged Man

Fear death by water. (T. S. Eliot, "The Waste Land")

It is here that our search truly begins in earnest, as we come in contact with the secret God hidden beneath appearances, both in the world and ourselves. Humanity's great trauma, shared yet unspoken, has been the primordial death of Love. For the soul (not the illusory human ego, but the primordial *Anthropos*, the Logos), say the mystics, is made of Love; and as a result of its calamitous union with Matter, "such a soul . . . might be said to die, as far as it is possible for a soul to die" (Taylor, p. 35). Indeed, it is this very abyss of darkness that is first encountered when one looks within—one encounters the remnants of an event so horrendous that it can be properly called the crucifixion of God.

The Kabalists say that the true name of Satan is that of Jehovah placed upside down, for "Satan is not a black god but the negation of the white deity," or the light of Truth. (Blavatsky, vol. II, p. 510)

In the *Acts of Peter*, it is explicitly revealed that Adam is the Platonic World-Soul, crucified in space at the foundation of the world. Peter, being crucified upside-down, states:

Learn ye the mystery of all nature, and the beginning of all things, what it was. For the first man, whose race I bear in mine appearance (or, of the race of whom I bear the likeness), fell (was borne) head downwards, and showed forth a manner of birth such as was not heretofore: for it was dead, having no motion. He, then, being pulled down—who also cast his first state down upon the earth— established this whole disposition of all things, being hanged up an image of the creation wherein he made the things of the right hand into left hand and the left hand into right hand, and changed about all the marks of their nature, so that he thought those things that were not fair to be fair, and those that were in truth evil, to be good. Concerning which the Lord saith in a mystery: Unless ye make the things of the right hand as those of the left, and those of the left as those of the right, and those that are above as those below, and those that are behind as those that are before, ye shall not have knowledge of the kingdom . . . the figure wherein ye now see me hanging is the representation of that man that first came unto birth. (James, pp. 334-335)

And says *The Apocalypse Unsealed* by James Morgan Pryse (p. 91),

This figure of the Sun . . . is a symbol of the incarnated Self, the Second Logos; and, . . . is the inverted reflection of the First: the celestial man is, as it were, upside-down when incarnated in the material world.

It is the great cataclysm of the universe, and yet in His death there was life.

Illustration by Justin Gray Morgan

Thou hearest that I suffered, yet did I not suffer; that I suffered not, yet did I suffer; that I was pierced, yet I was not smitten; hanged, and I was not hanged; that blood flowed from me, and it flowed not; and, in a word, what they say of me, that befell me not, but what they say not, that did I suffer. Now what those things are I signify unto thee, for I know that thou wilt understand. Perceive thou therefore in me the praising (al. slaying al. rest) of the (or a) Word (Logos), the piercing of the Word, the blood of the Word, the wound of the Word, the hanging up of the Word, the suffering of the Word, the nailing (fixing) of the Word, the death of the Word. (The Acts of John, James, p. 256)

This is the subject that we have encountered so many times before: it is the True Self (which is one with the universal Logos, represented by the golden halo of the sun) submerged in the waters of the the Abyss (represented by the blue shirt). The position is meant to evoke the symbol of the Hermetic Order of the Golden Dawn. Arthur Waite says,

the figure, as a whole, suggests life in suspension, but life and not death. It is a card of profound significance, but all the significance is veiled. . . . He who can understand that the story of his higher nature is imbedded in this symbolism will receive intimations concerning a great awakening that is possible, and will know that after the sacred Mystery of Death there is a glorious Mystery of Resurrection.

And Joseph Campbell concurs,

Christ [as] the Logos, Triumphant (as True God), crucified yet without anguish, head erect, eyes open, outward gazing at the world of light, the nails there, but no sign of blood, . . . is the image of that immanent "radiance" (claritas), "thus come," which hangs everywhere, as the world's joy-to-be-known, behind its battered face of torment. In his being . . . there is ambrosia. He too descended into Hell . . . he is still there—as Satan.
(Creative Mythology, p. 425)

But we will notice here a constant dichotomy between the Logos as the point in the heart (2 Peter) and the serpent that must be lifted up (John 3:14). To find God, we must search for Him within the most primordial recesses of our nature; within sexuality and the unconscious. I will let Waite have the last word:

> *God is immanent in creation . . . He is concealed in the abyss of material things—a* Latens Deitas *in Nature as there is a* Latens Deitas *in the Eucharist.* (Freemasonry, vol. II, p. 316)

Example: It is the inward state of the Hermit, and for this reason we collectively experienced the Hanged Man on December 30, 2006, with the execution of Saddam Hussein. Shortly afterward, we entered the *Nigredo* phase, represented by the *coniunctio oppositorum* Barack Hussein Obama—the Other now becomes the King—

> *We have only to follow the thread of the hero path, and where we had thought to find an abomination, we shall find a god; where we had thought to slay another, we shall slay ourselves. . . .*
> (Campbell, Hero, p. 18)

NIGREDO

The cards we have previously encountered are the tools that we have at our disposal; it is now that we come to what is properly called the Great Work. Now, many traditions state that the path of enlightenment is very easy: one merely has to realize that they are already enlightened. But what is it that prevents us from experiencing this enlightened state? It is the *Shadow*, and until we first *integrate* it, and then *overcome* it, it will continue to entice us back into the world of illusion and separation. As the Fool becomes more energetically aware, he comes to realize that the Shadow itself has a tangible quality to it—it is an energy, but a dark, restrictive energy that opposes his Will. It is then that we know that we have reached what may properly be called the first phase of the alchemical work, the *Nigredo*.

XIII. Death

Osiris in the waters of Amennti. (Crowley, p. 100)

We have arrived at the Dark (K)night of the Soul. For the materialists and devotees of exoteric religion, this is the end of the line. It is death, literally and spiritually, though they did not ever live at all. For the Fool, however, this is the time during which the old things in life become meaningless. During the long encounter with the Shadow, the Fool will be led astray with wild ideas and theories that lead nowhere and leave him feeling confused and helpless. Choronzon (333, the ignorant dispersions of the ego asserting itself) seems to appear everywhere, baffling the aspirant with hallucinations.

We have gazed in the Abyss, and now the Abyss seems to gaze back and wrap its icy fingers around us—but who is doing the gazing? It is Osiris, the Lord of the Dead, and he holds the mystic rose. In the distance, we see the Secret Sun of the Self rising out of the abyss. And yet Osiris is man himself in his natural state, a being of half-flame and half-darkness. Thus there is joy in death, for we have come to understand the Hidden God, the dark primordial source of all things within ourselves. And we know that a new life will emerge from it. Light is always found within darkness.

To speak more literally, during the blackening stage, one's heart seems to harden into a small, impenetrable ball of pain and anguish—the *caput mortuum*. Saturn, the Black Sun, is a god of melancholy. But the heart is also where the Secret Self dwells, which, as Crowley indicates, is the real secret creative power which continually projects the fractal bubbles of reality. "Love under Will" is the law of magick—and everything else. As one's Personal Unconscious is connected to the Collective Unconscious, it is seen how this alchemical process takes on a certain dimension of universal redemption.

Examples: The meaning of the Death card is *Change*, the campaign slogan of Barack Obama. The connection with Barack Obama and the Pharaohs is now so well-known as to be somewhat tiresome, but this merely underscores its importance—Obama is *the* returning King, the Black God Osiris. This is why something about his presidency *feels* right, even if Obama the man has really done little to deserve the title—the archetypes are bigger than he is. It must be emphasized that Obama does not represent the Shadow, but the Fool's confrontation and integration of the Shadow into a new totality.

In the *Star Wars* trilogy, this is the moment of anguish when the Man of Sin, Darth Vader (Osiris Ani), reveals that he is Luke's father. It is here, too, that Luke Skywalker sacrifices his right hand (the primary instrument of the Work) and is then given the choice between joining the Empire and taking the great leap into the Abyss.

Jason Barrera: Kosmos Idikos

Illustration by Justin Gray Morgan

XIV. Temperance

Hereof is some part of the Secret of Eternal Life, as it is possible to man in his incarnation. (Waite, Tarot*)*

At this point, the Fool can go no further without wholly dedicating himself to the Great Work and becoming a true Alchemist. The angel with the red wings of sublimation is a depiction of the Fool-Alchemist—the two cups are the Lovers seen above, and the secret seems to be that she is pouring upwards. The road that runs between the two mountains on Waite's card is the Middle Pillar and a visual reference to "Perceval," whose name can be interpreted as "pierce through the valley." This is the path of *Samekh* on the Tree of Life, leading from Yesod (the genitals) to Tiphareth (the heart). In the distance, the crown of the nascent Self rises from the depths. It is thus a complete illustration of the Alchemist at work.

All of this becomes much more explicit on Crowley's card, one of the most striking depictions of the entirety of the Work, so that very few people could mistake its transparent symbolism. The Alchemist draws upwards the fiery energy while grasping "her" Holy Spear, piercing the heart and fulfilling the maxim of V.I.T.R.I.O.L.: *Visita Interiora Terrae Rectificando Invenies Occultum Lapidem*, "visit the interior of the earth, rectify, and find the hidden stone." The two principles of fire and water, which are really only expressions of the One Element, have so completely intermingled as to switch places: the lion is white, and the eagle is red.

Examples: This transmutation and integration was depicted in the primary fight between Barack Obama and Hillary Clinton.

In *The Wizard of Oz*, Dorothy dons the Ruby Slippers of sexual passion (Yesod is associated with sandals) and follows the Yellow Brick Road of the Middle Pillar over the rainbow to the Emerald City in Tiphareth. It is at this point that the Cowardly Green Lion (see "Strength") must be crowned in the Emerald City. Some versions of this card feature a rainbow; Waite has employed irises (Iris is the goddess of the rainbow) instead. Red slippers are used in the Hermetic Order of the Golden Dawn as an alchemical reference to burning away the dross as one "walks" through the order.

XV. The Devil

How 'bout a little fire, Scarecrow?

The Devil is the final confrontation with the "Dweller on the Threshold." Here is the Crossing of the Abyss. On Waite's card, the Devil's right hand shows the sigil of Saturn, ♄, meaning that this is another depiction of the hidden creative force that is half-fire and half-darkness. The Devil's mockery consists in his insistence that the realm of matter is all there is. And yes, the downward pointing torch of the Devil represents the sexual force, indicating that Lust is the demon that must be overcome.

Thus, quite rightly, does Éliphas Lévi say that the fearsome visage of Baphomet represents the "horror of the sinner." The great anguish of Initiation, as we have seen, is the realization that "Osiris is a Black God"—and we are that god. The answer to the Riddle of the Sphinx has always been "Man." It is a full comprehension of the original murder of Love. Beyond this, words are inadequate. Éliphas Lévi equates it to kissing the posterior of a goat during Initiation—here dwells the *anus mundi*—and yet the goat, when the Candidate opened his eyes, had been replaced with a virgin priestess of Isis. The Devil wears a mask.

Examples: This is the stage at which Parsifal, in Wagner's opera, reclaims the Holy Spear from the sorcerer Klingsor. Dorothy must take back the broomstick of the Wicked Witch.

> *When the Wizard says, "Bring me the broomstick of the Wicked Witch of the West," Dorothy and crew are clearly overwhelmed... Reclaiming the broomstick from the Wicked Witch is a metaphor for reclaiming rightful ownership and control over one's own kundalini... one's own source of power. (Kennedy, p. 505)*

Yet there is no force more seemingly intractable and formidable than sheer inertia. It is for this reason that Luke Skywalker must free Leia and Han (the Lovers) from the thrall of the corpulent and immobile Jabba the Hutt. Han Solo must be freed from *carbon*ite, or the rule of matter.

A CHILD'S TREASURY OF THE TAROT

Illustration by Justin Gray Morgan

In *2001: A Space* Odyssey, Dave Bowman must first confront and then deactivate HAL 9000 before he can enter the Stargate. HAL sounds like *Hyle*, the Greek word for matter, making him equivalent to the Devil in its materialistic aspect. The Hebrew letter of the Devil Tarot card is *Ayin*, meaning "eye," and HAL is represented by a single red eye. HAL's last words are "Daisy, Daisy," referring to the Mystic Rose or Lotus, one's innermost Self, which HAL at last releases.

During the George W. Bush presidency, there were sinister forces at work behind the scenes—our Fool was covertly controlled by the Dick Chain (Cheney), the Devil. After integrating his Shadow, the new Fool, Barack Obama, overcomes the Devil Dick in the form of Two-Ball McCain.

ALBEDO

It is necessary, in order to understand the Tarot, to go back . . . to the time when succession was not through the first-born son of the King, but through his daughter. The king was therefore not king by inheritance, but by right of conquest. In the most stable dynasties, the new king was always a stranger, a foreigner; what is more, he had to kill the old king and marry that king's daughter.
(Crowley, p. 54)

After fully integrating the Shadow represented by the eternal Other, a further step is necessary, lest the Fool succumb to madness and dispersion. During the *Albedo* phase, the Fool must kill the King—that is, the ego must be dissolved in its own fire, accomplishing a supreme act of self-immolation.

XVI. The Tower

At this point, the Fire has finally succeeded in breaching what seems like an impenetrable fortress (a product of the *Nigredo* phase) around the heart. Here is the recognition by the ego that there exists a power greater than itself that it must give way to. Exoteric religions suddenly become meaningless, as the aspirant now realizes intuitively that these were little more than symbols of a one, transcendent truth. As Waite indicates, the house of False Doctrine is rent asunder and all things attain their proper perspective. What is revealed? It is the House of God. A close examination will see that the lightning bolt seemingly descending from above is the symbol of Mars, showing that this is the successful application of Sulphur, the Fishhook. Some early cards actually show the Star emerging from the ruined enclosure. The fortress now demolished was a man-made enclosure, a product of all our false and egoic notions that served to sever us from our True Selves.

Crowley's version corroborates this, where we see the dove of the heart and phallic serpent meeting in a flash of illumination. The eye of Horus now emerges from "a spring shut up, a fountain sealed." And now we must take our hands to the Work and purify our hearts in the fire.

Nor let the fools mistake love; for there are love and love. There is the dove, and there is the serpent. Choose ye well! He, my prophet, hath chosen, knowing the law of the fortress, and the great mystery of the House of God. (Liber AL, I. 57)

Examples: This corresponds with the destruction of the Death Star in the *Star Wars* trilogy. The end of the first movie is a prefiguration of the ending of the third. In the first film, Luke is "born" in the desert (the Wasteland)—in the second, he is "born" in the ice, climbing into the body of an animal (the human body) for warmth.

And here we come to the presidential election victory of Barack Obama. "Barack" means "lightning," as well as resonating "Ba-Rock," the Philosopher's Stone. On the Tower are composite figures which we may take as representing the old Fool-Magician, George W. Bush, and the Priestess, Hillary Clinton. After his victory, Obama hired Hilda *Solis* as his Labor secretary, declaring his dedication to the Work of the Sun (*Labor Solis*).

XVII. The Star

We have also a more sure word of prophecy; whereunto ye do well that ye take heed, as unto a light that shineth in a dark place, until

> *the day dawn, and the day star arise in your hearts....*
> *(2 Peter 1:19)*

It is not the end, but a new blossoming of hope that the Work was not in vain. Nature has now unveiled her great secret of parthenogenesis and willingly pours out the spiritual sustenance of the Higher Life. Within the heart has been discovered the most precious substance in the universe, a pure, distilled spark of Love that has invaded our Qlippothic world like a benign infection. The Star will lead the Wise Philosophers to the Christ Child. At this point we are told to throw away our books; if we have made it this far, we can make it to the end. Says Paul Foster Case (pp. 175-180),

> *The activity which lifts the fish up out of the material relations of personal existence, and utilizes the reproductive forces as a regenerative agency, is what is indicated here.... This picture shows the third stage of spiritual unfoldment. It is the calm which follows the storm... The light is dim, like starlight, but these stars are distant suns. Thus it is written: "When you have found the beginning of the way, the star of your soul will show its light."*

The eight-pointed star of Venus (or Sirius, or spirit—all these definitions begin to blur together), the Self, now emerges from the depths of darkness. On Waite's card, the Ibis of Hermes alights on the tree; the ground is newly infused with Sulphur. The four stars on the left refer to the material quaternary of the four elements, while the three stars on the right point to the higher trinity: 4 + 3 = 7, the completion of creation.

Examples: Curiously, some of this same imagery is found on the back of the one dollar bill: the four-sided pyramid shows that the Work begins in the material and is accessible to all, while its capstone is a three-sided triangle—the alchemical symbol for Fire—and ends with God. Who, then, is the capstone of the pyramid of the New World Order? It's *you*—potentially.

The Star is a card of sudden illumination emerging from the depths of darkness, which correspond to many of the news stories in 2010, notably the *Deepwater Horizon* oil spill, WikiLeaks, and the 33 Chilean miners, whose emblem was the Eastern Star.

XVIII. The Moon

The king in the sea swims and cries with a loud voice: Whoever catches and rescues me, to him will I give a great reward.
(Roob, p. 214)

It is the moon, but more properly an eclipse of the sun. We have found the Stone in the waters, and our task now is to whiten it. In many ways, as Crowley indicates, this is Dark Night of the Soul, Part II—which is why the alchemists often say that the great cycle is composed of many smaller cycles of distillation, sublimation, etc.

One is reminded of the mental echo of subconscious realization, of that supreme iniquity which mystics have constantly celebrated in their accounts of the Dark Night of the Soul. But the best men, the true men, do not consider the matter in such terms at all. Whatever horrors may afflict the soul, whatever abominations may excite the loathing of the heart, whatever terrors may assail the mind, the answer is the same at every stage: "How splendid is the Adventure!" (Crowley, p. 113)

Here, the Self emerging from the Abyss is represented by the crayfish—we have not yet "come out of our shells," so to speak. The winding Path leads beyond the Twin Towers of duality, into a place Beyond Good and Evil. It has been trod before—but who has come to the end? In this twilight zone preceding the beatific vision, we are still tormented by the shades of the unconscious—dogs both wild and domestic, unknown and known. We must eliminate everything in our hearts that stands between us and infinite bliss. All we can do is pour on more Yods and hope for the best.

All prejudice, all superstition, dead tradition and ancestral loathing, all combine to darken her face before the eyes of men. It needs unconquerable courage to begin to tread this path. Here is a weird, deceptive life. The fiery sense is baulked. The moon has no air. The knight upon this quest has to rely on the three lower senses: touch, taste and smell. (Crowley, p. 112)

For the magickal adept, the secret of the *Goetia* and other sinister tomes has always been that the "demons" one summons exist only in the realm of one's own subconscious—and they have always been there. These are the *Qlippoth*, or empty shells, which form the bulk of the Shadow—and it is the task of the Fool to replace this dead and diseased energy (or "faeces") with new, living substance (this is the transubstantiation of the Eucharist). To "full-fill the Law," in other words. Here, too, is the stark confirmation of that statement of Valentinus:

> *For the many spirits dwelling in the heart do not allow it to become pure: rather each of them performs its own acts, polluting it in various ways with improper desires. And in my opinion the heart experiences something like what happens in an inn. For the latter is full of holes and dug up and often filled with dung by indecent guests who have no consideration for the place, since it does not belong to them. Just so, a heart too is impure by being the habitation of many demons, until it is cared for. But when the Father, who alone is good, visits the heart, he makes it holy and fills it with light. (Frag. H)*

Examples: Anyone who has undertaken the long, arduous process will fully understand the meaning of the rock pick, slowly whittling away the walls of the Black Iron Prison, in the *Shawshank Redemption*. Even after Andy escaped, he still had to make his way through the sewers—but he emerged spotless. (Thus, also, why the Scarab beetle, rolling its seed in a ball of dung, was an emblem of the resurrection.)

For Crowley, the dogs are not our enemies, but Anubis, our guide through the underworld into daylight. Thus nature and the material is not inherently evil—but it has been placed in the thrall of an evil Shadow. Indeed, it is Toto who finally rends the veil of the Holy of Holies and unveils the Wizard. And Lucas must have had this in mind when he crafted the final Battle of Endor in *Return of the Jedi*, showing the triumph of Nature and the Ewoks over the machinations of the Empire.

RUBEDO

There is no part of us that is not of the gods. We are now reborn in the Grail; there is triumph on every plane. As this phase represents joy, pure and luciform, the descriptions are necessarily brief.

XIX. The Sun

On Waite's card, the white horse is the same one that formerly bore Death; our tormentor Osiris has been transformed into Harpocrates, the Sun of Righteousness. The Berlin Wall separating the flesh and spirit worlds still stands, but it is no longer a hindrance to self-expression. The Work becomes free and easy, and the phallic staff has unfurled the banner of illumination.

Example: Here Obama, as a type of the enlightened Philosopher King, kills Osama Bin Laden, his own Shadow Self as the Sin Laden Obama—in so doing, he harnesses the power of *eros* that was once in the thrall of his lower animal nature, just as Mithra conquers the bull. Once vanquished, the serpent reveals the treasure it had guarded. Says Éliphas Lévi, "the mystery of the Great Work consists in the ruling of fire" (*History*, p. 66). The taking of the "head" of bin Laden, then, refers to a change in consciousness arising from having harnessed this serpent fire—"hence they say it is that the statue of Horus at Coptos grasps in one hand Typhon's *virilia*" (Plutarch, in Mead, vol. I, p. 335).

XX. Judgment

At this point—we are told—the soul is completely liberated from the body. Paul Foster Case explicitly says that it moves into the fourth dimension! The two Lovers whom we have seen on previous cards have now combined to create a third, the Christ Child, Harpocrates.

Examples: The Judgment card depicts the soul being lifted into a higher plane of being, rising perpendicularly to the three-dimensional box. In

2001, Dave Bowman transcends the two-dimensional cinema screen by passing through it, metaphorically going "through the looking glass" into the third dimension. Plato's Cave is illustrated every time you visit a movie theater. In Plato's allegory, the members of the audience (prisoners of the cave) would only see shadows projected onto a wall by figures behind them, temporarily mistaking them for reality (suspension of disbelief). By stepping out of the movie, Bowman is stepping out of the Cave and into the light of illumination. Therefore, there is a profound insight here: Bowman is a character in a movie who at last realizes what he is. Kubrick is deliberately poking at the fourth wall to underscore that *2001* is merely an exoteric rendition of that which must ultimately occur within the individual. This is further emphasized at the end of the film, when the events are again repeated within a different context and narrative, showing that these are universal archetypes.

Harold Camping famously predicted the Rapture to take place on May 21, 2011. According to the alchemists, there are several different *coniunctios* of the King and Queen. Prince Charles wore black on his wedding day, seeming to indicate that Diana would die during the *coniunctio* of the *Nigredo* before being resurrected as Kate Middleton. (This appears to be a separate alchemical cycle, going on concurrently with our post-9/11 cycle.) And while the wedding of Diana and Charles was black, Prince William wore red, as if to proclaim indisputably that the Royal Wedding of Will and Kate represented the final *coniunctio* of the *Rubedo* stage. With focus on his "rebirth certificate" at this time, Barack Obama became the royal *filius philosophorum*, the regenerated King.

XXI. World

And here, the soul reunites with the body, but in a "glorified" form—Mary is assumed into heaven. This figure is actually meant to depict a hermaphrodite, and is a vision of the risen Christ whose nourishing breasts (*mastois*) in the Book of Revelation (1:13) are girt with a golden girdle. She bears the wands of "the radiant spiral force, the active and passive, each possessing its dual polarity" (Crowley, p. 118) and has become one with the stream of Universal Love.

Once the seeker reaches the center, he kills his father (the ego) and marries his (unveiled) mother—the true origin of the Oedipus complex. Then he becomes a conscious, rather than unconscious, creator, "flooding the world with life and beauty."

Example: It is at this point that Dorothy returns to Kansas, or Malkuth. She has become a *Boddisattva*. Our Royal Hermaphrodite can only be Lady Gaga, who is, appropriately, *Born This Way*.

Now you're in on the cosmic joke. The Fool is calling the shots.

Behold the shadows of the infernal sanctuary dissipated! Behold the sphinx of mediaeval terrors unveiled and cast from his throne! Quomodo cedidisti, Lucifer! (Lévi, Transcendental Magic*, p. 309)*

Images from Papus' ***The Tarot of the Bohemians***
Additional images by Justin Gray Morgan

Bibliography

Liber AL vel Legis (The Book of the Law) (2004) [1925]. York Beach: Red Wheel/Weiser, LLC. ISBN 1-57863-308-7.

Blavatsky, H. P. (1888). *The Secret Doctrine*. New York: The Quarterly Book Department.

Campbell, Joseph (1968). *The Masks of God: Creative Mythology*. New York: The Viking Press.

— (2008) [1949]. *The Hero with a Thousand Faces*. Third edition. Novato: New World Library. ISBN 978-1-57731-593-3.

Case, Paul Foster (2006) [1947]. *The Tarot: A Key to the Wisdom of the Ages*. Jeremy P. Tarcher/Penguin. ISBN 1-58542-491-9.

Crowley, Aleister (2004) [1944]. *The Book of Thoth*. York Beach: Red Wheel/Weiser, LLC. ISBN 0-87728-268-4.

Hederman, Mark Patrick. *Tarot: Talisman or Taboo? Reading the World as Symbol*. Currach Pr. ISBN 978-1856079020.

James, M. R. (2004) [1924]. *The New Testament Apocrypha*. Berkeley: Apocryphile Press. ISBN 0-9747623-6-9.

Evola, Julius (1995) [1971]. *The Hermetic Tradition*. Trans. E. E. Rehmus. Rochester: Inner Traditions International. ISBN 0-89281-451-9.

Kennedy, Judy (2004). *Beyond the Rainbow: Renewing the Cosmic Connection*. New York: Infinity Publishing. ISBN 0-7414-2125-9.

Klauck, Hans-Josef (2003). *Apocryphal Gospels: An Introduction*. Continuum International Publishing Group. ISBN 978-0567083906.

Lévi, Éliphas (2001) [1913]. *The History of Magic*. Trans. Arthur Edward Waite. Boston: Red Wheel/Weiser, LLC. ISBN 0-87728-929-8.

— (2001) [1896]. *Transcendental Magic, Its Doctrine and Ritual*. York Beach: Weiser Books. ISBN 0-87728-073-7.

Mead, G.R.S. (1906). *Thrice Greatest Hermes: Studies in Hellenistic Theosophy and Gnosis*. London and Benares: The Theosophical Publishing Society.

Papus (1892). *The Tarot of the Bohemians*. Trans. A. P. Morton. London: Chapman and Hall, Ltd.

Roberts, Alexander and Donaldson, James (eds.) (1886). *The Ante-Nicene Fathers*. Buffalo: The Christian Literature Company.

Roob, Alexander (1997). *Alchemy & Mysticism: The Hermetic Museum*. Taschen. ISBN 382288653X.

Silberer, Herbert (1917). *Problems of Mysticism and its Symbolism*. Trans. Smith Ely Jelliffe. New York: Moffat, Yard and Company.

Sivananda, Sri Swami (1997). *May I answer that?*
<http://www.sivanandadlshq.org/download/may_ianswer.htm>.

Taylor, Thomas (1891) [1791]. *The Eleusinian and Bacchic Mysteries*. New York: J.W. Bouton.

Waite, Arthur Edward (1893). *Azoth; or, The Star in the East*. London: The Theosophical Publishing Society.

— (1911). *The Pictorial Key to the Tarot*. London: W. Rider.

— (1911). *The Secret Tradition in Freemasonry*. London: Rebman Limited.

Westcott, Wm. Wynn (trans.) (1893). *Sepher Yetzirah: the Book of Formation and the Thirty Two Paths of Wisdom*. 2nd ed. London: The Theosophical Publishing Society.

Weston, Jessie Laidlay (trans.); Wolfram von Eschenbach (1894). *Parzifal, a Knightly Epic*. London: David Nutt.

Wilhelm, Richard; Jung, Carl Gustav; Liu, Hug-yang (1962) [1931]. *The Secret of the Golden Flower: A Chinese Book of Life*. Trans. Cary F. Baynes. ISBN 0-15-679980-4.

Suggested Reading

I am of the opinion that, with a proper understanding of synchronicity, the secrets of the universe will reveal themselves in everything. Therefore, every text (be it a dense volume of classic philosophy or the back of a cereal box) is sacred and can potentially lead you to gnosis. That being said, our authors have shared a few of the works that have been helpful to them on their journeys, with the hope that these may do the same for you.

Neil Kramer:

- *Journey to Ixtlan,* Carlos Castaneda
- *Beelzebub's Tales to His Grandson,* G. I. Gurdjieff
- *The Kybalion,* Three Initiates

Sibyl Hunter:

- *Man and His Symbols,* Carl Jung
- *A New Earth,* Eckhart Tolle
- *The Seat of the Soul,* Gary Zukov

Eunus Noe:

- *Parzival,* Wolfram von Eschenbach
- *Moby Dick*, Herman Melville
- *VALIS*, Philip K. Dick
- *The Dark Tower* series, Stephen King
- *The Matrix* trilogy (Film)
- *Lost* (TV)
- *The Inner Reaches of Outer Space*, Joseph Campbell
- *The Mythic Image*, Joseph Campbell
- *Sync: The Emerging Science of Spontaneous Order*, Steven H. Strogatz
- *Point Omega*, Don Delillo
- *The Information: A History, a Theory, a Flood*, James Gleick (This one plays very nice with PKD's idea of "living information" and *VALIS*. This book is incredible.)

SUGGESTED READING

- *All Things Shining: Reading Western Classics to Find Meaning in a Secular Age*, Hubert Dreyfus & Sean Dorrance Kelly
- *The Structure of Scientific Revolutions*, Thomas S. Kuhn (These give one a framework and perspective into which to place "our" movement. Literary theory is also another interesting lens to look through to reach a similar place.)
- *Facing The Dragon: Confronting Personal and Spiritual Grandiosity*, Robert L. Moore (I'm not sure that I agree with this one entirely, but it is worth noting, and contains many valid and insightful observations some similar to Edinger's *Archetype of the Apocalypse*—part of the author's POV undermines much of what we've found to be truth in our esoteric realm . . .)

Michael Schacht:

- *The Book of Enoch*
- *Ishmael*, Daniel Quinn
- *No. 44, the Mysterious Stranger*, Mark Twain
- *The Stars My Destination*, Alfred Bester
- *The League of Extraordinary Gentlemen*, Alan Moore & Kevin O'Neill
- *Harry Potter and the Philosopher's Stone*, J. K. Rowling

Andras Jones:

- *The Dream Poet,* Richard M. Jones
- *The Secret Teachings of All Ages*, Manly P. Hall
- *The Book of Answers*, Carol Bolt
- *Heart of Gold*, Paul Williams
- *2012: Biography of a Time Traveler*, Stephanie South
- *13 Moon Natural Time Calendar,* 13moon.com

Crystal Kanarr:

- *The B∞k*, Alan Watts
- *Practical Training in Thought*, Rudolf Steiner (Lecture)
- *The Holographic Universe*, Michael Talbot
- *The Rabbi's Tarot*, Daphna Moore
- *The Chicken Qabalah*, Lon Milo Duquette

SUGGESTED READING

- *The Esoteric Structure of the Alphabet and Its Hidden Mystical Language*, Alvin Boyd Kuhn
- *Origins and Oracles* DVD series, Michael Tsarion
- *Jungian Synchronicity in Astrological Signs and Ages*, Alice O. Howell
- *Archetypes of the Zodiac*, Kathleen Burt
- *Astrologick*, Antero Alli

Jim Sanders:

- *The Cosmic Serpent: DNA & the Origins of Knowledge*, Jeremy Narby
- *The Jaguar that Roams the Mind*, Robert Tindall
- *The Antipodes of the Mind: Charting the Phenomenology of the Ayahuasca Experience*, Benny Shanon
- *The Corpus Hermeticum*, Brian Copenhaver translation
- *The Nag Hammadi Scriptures*, edited by Marvin Meyer and James Robinson
- *Three Books of Occult Philosophy*, Henry Cornelius Agrippa
- *The Sefer Yetzirah*, Aryeh Kaplan edition
- *The Tabula Smaragdina*, Isaac Newton translation
- *Winnie-the-Pooh*, A. A. Milne

Kevin Halcott:

- *Cosmic Trigger* trilogy, Robert Anton Wilson
- *Man and his Symbols*, Carl Jung
- *The Hero with a Thousand Faces*, Joseph Campbell
- *The Book of Thoth*, Aleister Crowley
- *The Chicken Qabalah*, Lon Milo Duquette
- *DMT the Spirit Molecule*, Rick Straussman
- *Psychomagic*, Alejandro Jodorowsky
- *The Way of the Tarot*, Alejandro Jodorowsky
- *Total Kabbalah*, Maggy Whitehouse
- *The Living Labyrinth*, Jeremy Taylor
- *The Mayan Calendar and the Transformation of Consciousness*, Carl Johan Calleman

SUGGESTED READING

William Morgan:
- *VALIS*, Philip K. Dick
- *Divine Invasion*, Philip K. Dick
- *Secret Teachings of All Ages*, Manly P. Hall
- *The Cosmic Trigger*, Robert Anton Wilson
- *The Dark Tower* series, Stephen King
- *Mysterium Coniunctionis*, Carl Jung
- *The Discoveries*, Daniel J. Boorstin
- *The Mothman Prophecies*, John Keel
- *The Complete Guide to the Kabbalah*, Will Parfitt
- *The Tao Te Ching*, Lao Tzu (pick a translation)
- *The Cosmic Serpent*, Jeremy Narby

Kyle Hunt:
- Did someone already say *VALIS*?

Jeremy:
- WATCH LOTS OF MOVIES & READ A LOT OF BOOKS

Jake Kotze:
- *Cosmic Trigger*, Robert Anton Wilson
- *A New Earth*, Eckhart Tolle
- *Cosmic Serpent*, Jeremy Narby
- Any of many Alan Watts and Terence McKenna audio lectures

Justin Gray Morgan:
- *The Gnostic Jung and the Seven Sermons to the Dead*, Stephan A. Hoeller
- *Man and His Symbols*, Carl Jung
- *The Red Book*, Carl Jung
- *The Secret Teachings of All Ages*, Manly P. Hall
- *The Hero with a Thousand Faces*, Joseph Campbell
- *Quadrivium: The Four Classical Liberal Arts of Number, Geometry, Music, & Cosmology*, Miranda Lundy, Anthony Ashton, Jason Martineau, Daud Sutton, John Martineau

SUGGESTED READING

- *Walking a Sacred Path: Rediscovering the Labyrinth as a Spiritual Tool*, Lauren Artress
- *The Invisibles*, Grant Morrison
   - Audio/Lectures:
     - *The Yogas of the Bhagavad Gita*, Ram Dass
     - *Experiments in Truth*, Ram Dass
     - *The Power of Now*, Eckhart Tolle
     - *Out of Your Mind*, Alan Watts
     - *In the Valley of Novelty*, Terence McKenna

Jason Barrera:

- Jakob Boehme (Cosmogony, cosmology, and eschatology from an alchemical perspective.)
- Franz Hartmann (One of the foremost occultists of the 19th century.)
- Alvin Boyd Kuhn (A profound, if imperfect, writer on the esoteric connections between world religions.)
- *The Mysteries: Papers from the Eranos Yearbooks*, Joseph Campbell (ed.) (The Mysteries of the Aeon, the Serpent, and the Cross.)
- *Philosophumena*, Hippolytus (Absolutely invaluable record of early Gnosticism and the Mysteries from a Christian heresiologist who decided the best way to "refute" heresies was to simply document them in full detail.)
- *Symbols of Transformation* (*The Collected Works of C.G. Jung, Vol. 5*), Carl Jung (Jung here makes the connection between the energies of the libido and the spiritual Self as flowing from the same source.)
- *The Practice of Psychotherapy* (*The Collected Works of C.G. Jung, Vol. 16*), Carl Jung (A somewhat superficial analysis of the *Rosarium Philosophorum* is coupled with a very revealing private letter written to Jane Leade by John Pordage, in which he reveals the secrets of alchemy.)
- Éliphas Lévi (The doctrine of Great Work as magical act, and the ruling of the astral light.)
- *Thrice Greatest Hermes: Studies in Hellenistic Theosophy and Gnosis*, G.R.S. Mead (Mead's *magnum opus* documents the shared milieu of Christianity and early Hermeticism.)

SUGGESTED READING

- *The Nag Hammadi Scriptures*, Marvin Meyer (ed.) (The plasmate. Sync confirms tenets of Gnostic theology. Most films are really Gnostic parables, after the manner of the early *Acts* of literature.)
- *The Catcher in the Rye*, J. D. Salinger (The 20th century Fool's Journey.)
- *Problems of Mysticism and Its Symbolism*, Herbert Silberer (The Hermetic arts are almost fully revealed by a non-initiate who was under no obligation to keep them secret.)
- Thomas Taylor (The mystical Platonist.)
- Arthur Waite (A highly prolific writer on esoteric subjects, and one who had pierced the veil.)

See also:

SyncList.Blogspot.com

Also available from ALLTHEHAPPYCREATURES.COM

Sort of an updated *Animal Farm*,
Set in a Conspiratorial Future,
Intermixed with Psy-Phi, Pop-Culture,
and an Exploration of Consciousness.

Also available from ALLTHEHAPPYCREATURES.COM

Once you begin to connect the dots,
you'll find that everything is touching.

Melissa Green
My beautiful wife
for helping me review these essays,
for supporting me entirely through this process,
and for being the most amazing and loving person I could
imagine. I love you completely and unconditionally.

Justin Gray Morgan
for all your amazing artwork.
I am continually impressed by your talent.
But mostly, thank you for your willingness and eagerness to
assist in making this project all it could be.

Jason Barrera
for laying another set of eyes across these
pages when mine had grown weary and blurry.
You added class and professionalism to this project
with your approach to editing.

Eunus Noe
for helping to coordinate and plan this thing.
Together we have herded cats.

And to everyone who contributed
I couldn't ask for better travel companions
on this long strange trip.

TheSyncBook.com

for information on future publications and live events
as well as updates from our authors
and assorted sync-related goodness

Support independent creators:
If you enjoyed this book, be sure to tell a friend.
We depend on word of mouth.

Peace